THE ALPS

Polity's *Environmental History* series

Introducing Polity's new *Environmental History* series. These accessible books explore the history of human societies and how they have shaped, and been shaped by, the natural world.

Adrian Howkins, *The Polar Regions*
Jon Mathieu, *The Alps*

THE ALPS

AN ENVIRONMENTAL HISTORY

JON MATHIEU

TRANSLATED BY ROSE HADSHAR

polity

First published in German as *Die Alpen. Raum - Kultur - Geschichte*, © Philipp Reclam jun. GmbH & Co. KG, Stuttgart, 2015

This English edition © Polity Press, 2019

The translation of this work was funded by Geisteswissenschaften International – Translation Funding for Humanities and Social Sciences from Germany, a joint initiative of the Fritz Thyssen Foundation, the German Federal Foreign Office, the collecting society VG WORT and the Börsenverein des Deutschen Buchhandels (German Publishers & Booksellers Association).

Polity Press
65 Bridge Street
Cambridge CB2 1UR, UK

Polity Press
101 Station Landing
Suite 300
Medford, MA 02155, USA

ISBN-13: 978-1-5095-2771-7

A catalogue record for this book is available from the British Library.

Library of Congress Cataloging-in-Publication Data

Names: Mathieu, Jon, author.
Title: The Alps : an environmental history / Jon Mathieu.
Description: English edition. | Medford, MA : polity, 2019. | Includes bibliographical references and index.
Identifiers: LCCN 2018027493 (print) | LCCN 2018029306 (ebook) | ISBN 9781509527748 (Epub) | ISBN 9781509527717 (hardback)
Subjects: LCSH: Alps--History. | Alps--Civilization.
Classification: LCC DQ823.5 (ebook) | LCC DQ823.5 .M375 2019 (print) | DDC 949.4/7--dc23
LC record available at https://lccn.loc.gov/2018027493

Typeset in 10.75 on 14 Adobe Janson by
Servis Filmsetting Ltd, Stockport, Cheshire
Printed and bound in Great Britain by CPI Group (UK) Ltd, Croydon

For further information on Polity, visit our website: politybooks.com

Contents

Maps and Figures

Maps

Figures

PREFACE

How many mountains in the world are called 'Matterhorn'? A recent count turned up more than 200. They are found on all continents of this planet and owe their name to a nearly 4,500-metre-high 'Matterhorn' in the European Alps, on the border between Switzerland and Italy. This Matterhorn has a memorable shape, as well as a legendary history. In the nineteenth century, mountain climbers of several nationalities threw themselves into a fierce competition to be the first to stand at the summit. It was not a coincidence that these climbers came from different countries. The Alps are located at the heart of Europe. Today this mountain range is divided between six states. In alphabetical order, they are Austria, France, Germany, Italy, Slovenia and Switzerland. And if you look closely, two small principalities also belong to the list: Lichtenstein and Monaco. It was also not really an accident that the competition over the original Matterhorn took place in the nineteenth century. The summit attempt was precipitated and enabled by the 'discovery' of the Alps by European elites, which had begun more than 100 years before.[1]

We usually connect this discovery with the famous names of the Enlightenment. The most commonly mentioned is Jean-Jacques Rousseau, whose writings moved the reading public deeply in the eighteenth century and called for a reconciliation with nature in general. According to Rousseau, Western civilization was corrupt and must find its way back to nature. 'Nature', this new reference point for moral behaviour, was best exemplified by the Alps. Their higher elevations were only sparsely used for agriculture and so were fairly deserted, and their impressive silhouettes, shaped by mysterious geological forces, could be seen from afar. The Alps were promoted to a *pièce de résistance* of European culture, indeed to an embodiment of nature.[2] And since Europe was on the path of expansion, and for a time struggled in a national competition for world domination, this idea and this example were widely distributed. It is not a great exaggeration to claim that the modern concern for the 'environment' began with the European Alps.

I say the 'European' Alps, because soon they were not the only ones. When the British captain and explorer James Cook saw the mountains of the South Island of New Zealand on his first South Sea expedition in 1770, he wrote the name 'Southern Alps' onto the map. Later came the Australian Alps, the Japanese Alps, the Alps of Sichuan in China, the Canadian Alps and others. Just as the Matterhorn became a pattern for mountains across the world after it was climbed, so the European Alps – thanks to their position in a hegemonic movement of expansion – had already become a model range. This can be seen from the life of Alexander von Humboldt. The German naturalist from Berlin first saw the Alps with his own eyes in 1792, and was enraptured in spite of the poor weather. When he undertook his famous South American voyage in the years around 1800, he referred again and again to these mountains, to bring the public closer to the Andes. How high were particular Andean mountains? About as high as Swiss passes. What was the difference in altitude between two Inca roads? More than that between Mont Cenis and Lake Como.[3]

Examples abound. The Alps played a pioneering role in other fields too, such as Alpinism or particular forms of nature conservation. We should not overstate this role, yet it is not self-evident, and needs to be explained. A first step towards explanation is to engage in earnest with the subject. This book is the product of such an engagement. It is an attempt to write a modern history of the Alps from prehistory to the present day.

Writing a History of the Alps

How does one write a history of the Alps? The historical method has source criticism at its heart, and also requires a justifiable, contextual and possibly theoretical approach. It is clear that an overview of such a vast space over so long a period must be undertaken very selectively. It is a question of working out the broad sweeps and most important connections in the clearest and most plausible manner. I wish to outline the way that this history has been written as follows:

1. The book is historical, which means that it takes as its starting point humans and human societies in their temporal existence and temporal succession. In this respect, it differs from the numerous geographical and also anthropological studies of the Alps, which have their own respective subject perspectives. In spite of these differences, historians can learn from the suggestions and findings of neighbouring disciplines and gain in doing so. In this sense, the book certainly has an interdisciplinary element.

2. The closer we come to the present day, the more space is given to the treatment in this book. This common form of prioritization seeks to take into account both pure historical interest and interest in the past, and the view towards the lived present and possible future. From a spatial point of view, the analysis encompasses the

Alpine range in its totality, as far as possible without the privileging of particular regions. The book takes a transnational approach. To comprehend this vast mountain range, it is often necessary to cast an eye over its surrounding areas in the European south and north. Sometimes it is also enlightening to make comparative reference to other mountain areas.

3. The choice of themes is directed on the one hand towards the supposed demands of an interested academic and also non-academic readership, and on the other towards the opportunity posed by recent historical research. Alongside new insights, this opportunity also comprises new, as yet unanswered, questions. History should ideally be thought and written more broadly by all of us. Only discussion can reveal what we still want to know, and how we could potentially know it.

For our central question, we turn to a proposition from the French historian Fernand Braudel. In his famous history of the Mediterranean in the sixteenth century, he explained why one finds certain 'civilized' achievements in the Alps that are lacking in other mountain ranges: 'but the Alps are after all the Alps, that is an exceptional range of mountains, from the point of view of resources, collective disciplines, the quality of its human population and the number of good roads'.[4] *An exceptional range of mountains, une montagne exceptionnelle* – is that true? In what respects? And why? Various chapters will consider these questions. In chapter 2, I present the biographical background and emergence of this viewpoint, and in chapter 10 we will take stock. There I will argue that the exceptional nature of the Alps has much to do with the exceptionality of their surrounding areas: the Alps were historically closely tied to the surrounding regions, and from a comparative perspective this can absolutely be described as exceptional. In European history, Venice, Lombardy, the area around Lyon, the Upper Rhine and other regions have long belonged to the economic avant-garde.

Braudel was one of the most widely read historians of the twentieth century and a co-founder of modern history, but in particular he was also a pioneer of environmental history. The first part of his *Méditerranée* was explicitly dedicated to the role of the environment. The French historian is therefore referenced in practically every genealogy of modern environmental history, whether eulogistically, critically or with mixed feelings. Examples of this are John McNeill's important essay of 2003 ('Observations on the Nature and Culture of Environmental History') or J. Donald Hughes' introductory volume of 2006 (*What is Environmental History?*, reissued 2015).[5] However, Braudel's long shadow should not dissuade us from illuminating aspects and posing questions about which he had nothing to say. Of these, there is no shortage. At this point, I would like to briefly touch on two points at which the history of the Alps and modern environmental history interact in a special way. We can call them Elinor Ostrom and William Cronon.

Elinor Ostrom engaged in an empirically based, methodologically thought-through and practically oriented way with environmental economics. Later a Nobel Prize-winner, she was especially famous for her work *Governing the Commons: The Evolution of Institutions for Collective Action* (1990). Here she showed how human groups, organized in particular institutions, could function sustainably with limited communal resources, without endangering these resources or the natural ecosystem. According to Ostrom, this did not require either state intervention or the privatization of these 'common-pool resources'. The functions could be taken on by communes and corporations. Ostrom was therefore interested in the Alpine economy with its communally owned summer pastures, which had followed this model for centuries. This long time period was important for her. The first example in *Governing the Commons* came from the commune of Törbel in the Valais, where sources begin in the thirteenth century and become more detailed in the sixteenth. Ostrom's information about Törbel came primarily from a 1981 study by Robert Netting entitled *Balancing on an Alp: Ecological Change and Continuity in a Swiss Mountain Community*. The study also contained a reconstruction of population trends, which tracked available resources and so did not become unbalanced. Chapter 4 in the present volume is concerned with the long-term history of agriculture and Alpine husbandry.[6]

With William Cronon, the key consideration is not the economy, but the power of the imagination. In 1995, this American environmental historian published the controversial but now classic essay 'The Trouble with Wilderness; or, Getting Back to the Wrong Nature'.

Here he emphasized the cultural dimensions of conceptions of nature. These conceptions are characterized by social conventions and world views, and cannot be taken for a one-to-one mapping of an external nature. 'Wilderness' was initially a religious expression, which became widely used in the King James Bible of 1611. It referred to the places at the margins of human society, where one descended all too easily into moral confusion. But in the nineteenth century these became positive, venerable, 'sublime' places, which, according to a saying of Henry David Thoreau, served the preservation of the world. This new viewpoint contributed very significantly to the creation of an institutionalized wilderness in the form of the great national parks of America. The Romantic impulse which enabled this reinterpretation originated in Europe, and not least in the Alps. They were at that time the pinnacle of the 'sublime'. Later, this impulse returned to Europe in a different form. Patrick Kupper has recently shown that the first national park in the Alps was also the result of an intense transatlantic exchange, and today the value of the American-inspired wilderness in the Alps is debated very generally. The present book raises these themes in chapters 7, 9 and 10.[7]

Personal Note and Acknowledgements

One more word on the structure of the book. The first two chapters are concerned with the basic aspects of Alpine history, that is with their place in European history and their investigation in modern times. There then follow several chapters in loose chronological order and with various thematic emphases, covering the prehistoric to medieval periods (chapter 3), the late Middle Ages and the early modern period (chapters 4–6) and the most recent centuries (chapters 7–9). After a summary and perspective on the future (chapter 10), the interested reader will find the most important evidence for my claims in the endnotes, as well as a select bibliography. The book was first published in German in 2015. For the present English edition, I have written a new introduction, and modified – and, where necessary, updated – a few passages.

I first became involved with Alpine history a good forty years ago. I was then working on my dissertation on a series of Engadin villages during the Ancien Régime. I had previously read Jack Goody's *Production and Reproduction: A Comparative Study of the Domestic Domain*, in which he asks how rural economies and familial social structures relate to each other throughout their historical development. Later, I broadened my research to include other mountainous landscapes. The microstudy was followed by a regional study of three Swiss mountain cantons and then a history of the whole Alpine region in a particular period and in relation to selected issues. In a moment of temerity, I then ventured once more into this field, and in 2011 published a book in which I considered mountains on different continents (*The Third Dimension: A Comparative History of Mountains in the Modern Era*). This led me to write essays on the comparison between the Alps and Chinese mountains and, on another occasion, the Andes.

On this mountain path, I have been inspired by many authors who are not necessarily thought of in connection with mountains. When I reflect on it, I would say that the Danish development economist Ester Boserup and the American historian and German specialist David W. Sabean have influenced me the most. I sometimes half-jokingly say that the former represents my macro-side and the latter my micro-side. On this journey, I also had the good fortune, in collaboration with my colleagues, to improve the institutional aspects of Alpine historical research. In 1995, we founded the International Association for Alpine History, which since then has published an annual multi-lingual journal. Later, the Association obtained a research institute at the Università della Svizzera italiana [University of Lugano], which I was able to lead for a number of years. Without these protracted collective efforts, it would not have been possible to write this book. When I moved from the research institute to the Universität Luzern [University of Lucerne], I was able to discuss, try out and develop further these themes with my students. It was they who listened to the present book in lecture form prior to its first publication. I was able to complete that version in a research semester at the Rachel Carson Center for Environment and Society in Munich.

For manifold support in the development of this survey, my thanks therefore go to our Association for Alpine History and to the Rachel Carson Center, especially Luigi Lorenzetti and Luca Mocarelli, Christof Mauch and Helmuth Trischler. Numerous colleagues assisted me with suggestions and comments on earlier versions. I would like to thank Dionigi Albera, Simona Boscani, Franz-Josef Brüggemeier, Andreas Bürgi, Jean-Claude Duclos, This Fetzer, Heinz E. Herzig, Martin Korenjak, Patrick Kupper, Margareth Lanzinger, Jan-Henrik Meyer, Heinz Nauer, Seth Peabody, Felicitas Sprecher Mathieu, Werner E. Stöckli, Simon Teuscher, Manfred Tschaikner, Nelly Valsangiacomo

XVI   PERSONAL NOTE AND ACKNOWLEDGEMENTS

and Ivar Werlen. For this English version, I am ultimately indebted to the translator Rose Hadshar and to the persons responsible for this book series, Pascal Porcheron and Paul Young of Polity Press. They have all ironed out numerous errors, and the remaining ones are on me.

TIMELINE

From 50,000 BC   Sporadic, seasonal visits to the Alpine region by hunters and gatherers.

13,000 BC   Continuous settlement of the Alpine region from the last Ice Age.

5500 BC   Advent of crop cultivation and animal husbandry in the Alps.

5000 BC   The first pile dwellings in the Alpine region.

Around 3200 BC   The 'iceman' (Ötzi) lived in what is now Tyrol.

800–480 BC   Iron Age 'Hallstatt culture', originating from the Salzkammergut.

218 BC   The Carthaginian general Hannibal Barca crosses the Western Alps.

25–13 BC   The most important Roman Alpine campaigns.

7–6 BC   Construction of the 'Tropaeum Alpium' as a sign of the Roman victory over the Alpine tribes.

Around AD 50   Completion of the Via Claudia Augusta from the Adriatic over the Alps to the Danube.

380   Christianity becomes the Roman state religion.

Around 600   Many diocesan towns in the Western Alps; in the east, the consolidation of bishoprics continues into the thirteenth century.

754–1452   The Italian expeditions of the Carolingian and German kings over the Alps.

1336	Francesco Petrarch on Mont Ventoux – perhaps as a literary fiction.
1492	The ascent of Mont Aiguille (or Inaccessible) at the behest of the French king.
Around 1500	Population in the Alpine region (the area of the Convention) around 3.1 m.
1574	*De Alpibus Commentarius* by Josias Simler.
1618	Large landslide in Piuro near Chiavenna.
1713	Peace of Utrecht, with important border shifts in the Western Alps.
1732	*Die Alpen* (didactic poem) by Albrecht von Haller.
1741	Exploration of the glacier at Chamonix by a group of Britons, with William Windham.
1761	*La Nouvelle Heloïse* (Alpine-related epistolary romantic novel) by Jean-Jacques Rousseau.
1786	First ascent of Mont Blanc by Jacques Balmat and Michel-Gabriel Paccard.
1788	General estates of the Dauphiné in Vizille call for reforms – harbinger of the French Revolution.
1800	Napoleon Bonaparte crosses the Great St Bernard Pass with an army.
Around 1800	Population in the Alpine region (the area of the Convention) around 5.8 m.
1809	Uprising in Tyrol against Bavaria and France (Andreas Hofer).
1816	Large climate-related agricultural crisis (the 'year without summer').
1854	The first Alpine railway at Semmering; in 1871 and 1882, Mont Cenis and the Gotthard follow suit.
1857	Establishment of the Alpine Club in London; by 1873, all Alpine states have an Alpinist club.
1860	Italy cedes Savoy and Nice to France.
1871	The first rack railway up Rigi near Lucerne.
1871	*The Playground of Europe* (collection of Alpinist essays) by Leslie Stephen.
1872	Italy creates the first mountain troops with the *alpini*; other states follow.
1880	*Heidis Lehr- und Wanderjahre* [*Heidi: Her Years of Wandering and Learning*] (Alpine-related children's book) by Johanna Spyri.
1898	First crossing of the Alps in a balloon.

Around 1900	Population in the Alpine region (the area of the Convention) around 8.4 m.
1910	First crossing of the Alps in an aeroplane; the pilot crashes shortly before landing.
1914	Swiss national park in Engadin; later many other parks and protected areas follow.
1915–18	Mountain war between the Kingdom of Italy and Austria-Hungary.
1919	Partition of Tyrol at the Brenner; the southern part falls to the Kingdom of Italy.
1921	The Austria section of the Deutscher und Österreichischer Alpenvereins excludes Jewish members.
1924	The first Winter Olympics in Chamonix.
1937	*Der Berg ruft* ('mountain film') by Luis Trenker.
1943–5	Partisan warfare in the Italian and Yugoslavian mountains.
1955	Austria becomes an independent state again after the Second World War.
1963	Disaster at the dam at Vajont near Belluno with many victims.
1972	Arbeitsgemeinschaft Alpenländer [Association of Alpine States]; in 1978 and 1982, working groups emerge in the Eastern and Western Alps.
1980	*Histoire et civilisations des Alpes* (standard work), edited by Paul Guichonnet.
1991	Slovenia secedes from Yugoslavia and becomes an independent state.
1991	Discovery of the 'iceman' (Ötzi) in the Ötztal Alps.
1991	Signing of the framework agreement for the Alpine Convention.
1992	Reintroduction of wolves into the Alpine region.
Around 2000	Population in the Alpine region (the area of the Convention): 13.7 m.

States and regions in the area of the Alpine Convention

Position in Europe

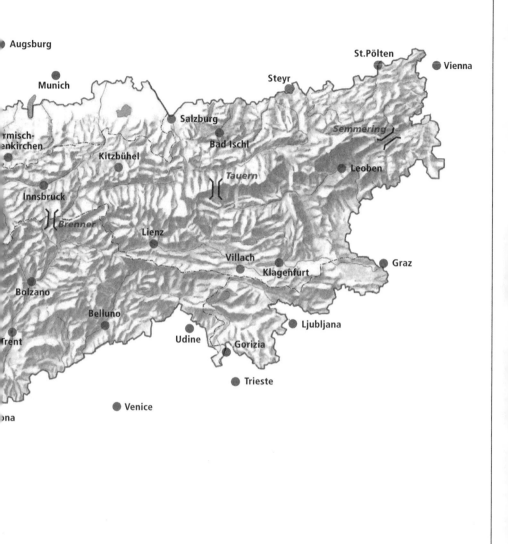

Augsburg

Munich

St.Pölten

Vienna

Steyr

Salzburg

rmisch-
enkirchen

Bad Ischl

Semmering

Kitzbühel

Tauern

Leoben

Innsbruck

Brenner

Lienz

Villach

Graz

Klagenfurt

Bolzano

Belluno

Ljubljana

Trent

Udine

Gorizia

Trieste

Venice

na

100 km   ↑N

Towns and passes in the Alps and
the surrounding area

1

THE ALPS IN EUROPEAN HISTORY

1.1 Borderland, Transit Route, Living Space

The Alps are the highest mountains in central Europe, as Johann Heinrich Zedler wrote in 1732 in his encyclopaedia: 'They are a wall built by nature, so to speak, which separates Italy from France and Germany. They extend very far, from the Ligurian Sea to Nice, Provence, Dauphine, Savoy, the Valais lands, Switzerland, Grisons, Tyrol, Trent, Brixen, Salzburg, Carinthia, Carniola, a part of Milan and the Venetian territories; indeed they seem to stretch even into Serbia.' As early as the fourteenth century, Italian humanists saw the Alps in a similar way – namely, as a barrier or wall which protected Italy from the north. Later, Martin Luther observed in his writings that the mountain wall separated Germany from Italy. This separating function of the European Alps remained an important idea until the Enlightenment. Two centuries after Zedler, it was also emphasized by Denis Diderot in the *Encyclopédie*.[1]

Then, in the nineteenth and above all the twentieth centuries, academics and politicians began increasingly to emphasize the role of the Alps as a space of transit. Now the mountains were described as 'bridges of culture between the Mediterranean and northern Europe', and the wall and border functions were qualified. 'It is not the least paradox of the Alps', so went a study of transport history, 'that this colossal chain of mountains never posed an insurmountable barrier, but rather a link between east and west, south and north, a contact zone, a nodal point for economies, ideas and conventions'.[2] The background to this new perspective was above all the penetration of the mountain range by modern means of transport and the enormous increase in transit traffic compared to the early modern period. Infrastructural development simultaneously promoted Alpine tourism. The Alps thereby acquired an additional role as *The Playground of Europe*, as Leslie Stephen expressed it in a now famous Alpine work of 1871.[3]

With the regionalism of the second half of the twentieth century, a further viewpoint eventually emerged: the Alps as a living space for the local population. Thus, the participants in an international congress on the 'Zukunft der Alpen' [Future of the Alps] in 1974 stated that the Alps must be described as a 'European inheritance' and a 'natural, historical, cultural and social unity of vital importance'. The great currents of civilization had been separated, reshaped and connected by them. 'But in spite of the sometimes difficult relationships and connections between peoples and political systems, an independent Alpine culture developed, and although the Alps have never known political unity, the way of life and activities of their populations demonstrate a striking similarity of character.'[4]

In whatever way this culture and way of life was actually formed (and we shall return repeatedly to this question), it is clear that for a long time the Alps have had a considerable population. If we take the area of the Alpine Convention as a basis, there must have been around 3.1 million people in 1500, growing to 5.8 million in 1800; in 2000 there were already 13.7 million people.[5] Admittedly, the numbers are heavily dependent on the exact delimitation used, and here there are and have been very different takes. Like many naturally defined areas, the Alps cannot be clearly demarcated. The most arbitrary aspect is the demarcation of the lower mountain ranges of the Apennines in Italy and the so-called Dinaric Alps in the Balkans, which had already been remarked upon by Zedler in his reference to Serbia. That the definition also depends on particular interests is shown in the drafting of the international Alpine Convention of 1991, in which a binding territory was agreed. At that time, Bavaria decided to expand its Convention area to the vicinity of Munich, thereby increasing the Bavarian Alps threefold in comparison with earlier classifications. In other countries, on the other hand, some regions were particularly conservative and wanted to avoid integration. This created a politically constituted Alpine region of 191,000 square kilometres in total.

Geographically, this space differs from its surrounding areas in its relief and its altitude. According to chroniclers of mountaineering, there are some 1,350 summits in the Alps. Large parts of the Alpine area lie more than 2,000 metres above sea level, and its highest peak, Mont Blanc, reaches a good 4,800 metres. But the area is also traversed by many low-, and some very low-, lying valleys. Around a third of traditional settlements lie below 500 metres, and only 2 per cent are situated above 1,500 metres.[6] It has often been emphasized that at the higher altitudes there are large stretches of 'unproductive land'. However, no one knows exactly how large or unproductive they are. The differences in the area statistics point to the fact that the precise extent of unproductive land also depends on the measures of value used by the various national administrations. In general, 'nature' and 'culture' are relational, time-bound concepts. From the outside, the Alps seem more like a natural space, and from within more like a cultural and living space.

1.2 Flight and Tunnelling

Today, the fragmented and inaccessible Alps can be observed from the comfort of an aeroplane. Nothing seems easier than to fly over these 3,000- and 4,000-metre-high mountains. But, in the history of flight, the mountain range initially posed a challenge. This was vividly displayed by the first transalpine balloon flight in 1898 and the first plane flight over the main Alpine ridge in 1910.

The idea of a transalpine balloon flight came from the Zurich geology professor and Alpine expert Albert Heim, who wanted one day to see his research subject from above. It was carried out with the help of Flight Captain Eduard Spelterini. In the second half of the nineteenth century, professional balloon flight had established itself in Europe. Spelterini had obtained his aeronautical licence in Paris in 1877 and had since taken paying passengers on his flights. He later made a name

Figure 1   *Aerial photograph of the Matterhorn*
by Eduard Spelterini, 1910

for himself as a pioneer of aerial photographs, which he presented in numerous lectures in the form of coloured slides (see figure 1). A mountain crossing by balloon was for a long time held to be impossible, as there was no means of controlling for fall wind. After detailed aeronautical study, however, Spelterini believed that he could solve the problem with a very high flight of over 5,000 or 6,000 metres. The plan was carried out with the help of numerous scientists and donors. Before a large crowd, the balloon took off on its Alpine flight from the Valais on 3 October 1898. The flight lasted more than five hours and was pulled northwards by the wind currents over the mountains and into France.[7]

The Valais was also the setting of the first Alpine crossing by aeroplane, which, however, was unsuccessful and ended with a crash. The tragic hero was Jorge Chávez, the son of a rich Peruvian who had settled in France. Chávez attended a flight school near Paris and completed his first flight in February 1910. In the following months, he participated in flight competitions across the whole of Europe, repeatedly breaking the existing record for altitude. He then decided to take part in the 'Gran Premio della Traversata delle Alpi' [Grand Prize for the Crossing of the Alps], put on by a committee in Milan. For a flight from the Valais southwards over the main Alpine ridge to Italy, the organizers would pay out a prize of no less than 100,000 lira. On the appointed day, however, three of the five registered pilots had withdrawn without even testing their machines, and a fourth pilot had been unable to reach the necessary flying height of over 2,000 metres in his bi-plane. That left Chávez, who took off on 23 September 1910, to the animated appreciation of the public, spiralled upwards, flew over the Simplon Pass in the Zwischbergen Valley and unfortunately crashed at Domodossola. The death of the young pilot excited much attention: the international airport of Lima in Peru bears his name to this day.[8]

The resistance of the mountains and the endeavours to conquer them are also clearly evident in the history of tunnel construction. In Europe, mining for metal extraction soared from the late Middle Ages. In the Alps there were numerous mines, and the mining technique of tunnel excavation made considerable progress. So, it is understandable that the age of tunnel building began in the fifteenth and sixteenth centuries. For the facilitation of the salt trade between the two sides of the Western Alps, the Marquis of Saluzzo had a summit tunnel of some 75 metres in length excavated in the region of Monte Viso in around 1480. The tunnel was built just tall enough to be traversed by a pack animal and a stooping man, and its time-saving advantages were obviously not insignificant. The facilitation of transalpine commerce was also served by a tunnel created in the second half of the sixteenth century from the Loibl Pass in the Karavanks to the southern border of Carinthia. It was a 150-metre-long passage directly under the ridge. The tunnel was later abandoned because of the imminent threat of collapse and replaced by a ground cutting.[9]

In the seventeenth and eighteenth centuries, road improvements via tunnels were undertaken here and there, but the great period of Alpine tunnelling began in the nineteenth century, as the railway revolutionized the European transport system. The railway was considerably more challenging than earlier modes of transport from the point of view of line management. In the mountains, the costs were all the greater.

Things began in Semmering with the Vienna–Trieste line. The difficult mountain stretch was completed using fourteen tunnels (one of which was 1,430 metres long) in 1854. Then the Mont Cenis tunnel, built between 1854 and 1871, became the first great Alpine tunnel. It crossed the mountains for a distance of 12 kilometres and notably accelerated the traffic between distant capital cities (Paris–Rome via Turin). Slightly longer again at 15 kilometres was the Gotthard tunnel for the Zurich–Milan line. 'The partition which separated the nations has fallen', declared the Swiss federal president at its opening in 1882. 'The countries have moved closer together and opened to world traffic.' As at other opening ceremonies, hundreds of distinguished guests from all countries were present at this occasion. The public was fascinated by the technical feats. However, the dangerous tunnel work and the conditions in makeshift workers' settlements claimed a heavy price in human life.[10]

The twentieth century saw a multiplication of Alpine tunnelling. So many tunnels were built and their standards improved so sharply in the wake of general motorization that public attention now dwindled. From the 1960s, this led to a new generation of Alpine tunnels large and small for individual motor traffic. Overall, a huge amount of energy was invested in transport links. It is thought that today the Alps are the mountain region with the highest density of tunnels in the world.[11]

1.3 How the Mountain Got its Name

Why is a mountain called 'Mont Blanc', 'Jungfrau', 'Zugspitze', 'Grossglockner' or 'Triglav'? Which parts of the Alpine region have older names and which were only named in more recent times? In different periods, how strongly was naming characterized by particular cultural patterns and currents?

The linguistic features of the mountain landscape, as studied by toponymy (the study of place names), reflects the appropriation of space by human actors with their own interests, perceptions and conflicts. However, the terms are often difficult to decipher. There was and is a widespread need to interpret the landscape's proper names and make them comprehensible. The provenance and original meaning of the word 'Alps' was already being discussed in ancient times, and even then the connection with 'white' (Latin *albus*), 'snow-covered', was brought into play. This is still treated as a probable element of the word today. But with the rise of science, traditional and generally associative name interpretations, whether popular or learned, were often rejected as 'folk etymologies'. Modern research placed strict demands on how interpretations were carried out. For example, an interpretation should be supported by thoroughly researched historical documentation. Its uncertainties and limits should also be made clear, and the interpreter may even refrain from any kind of explanation.[12]

For the mountains named above, the following etymologies (word origins) are given in academic literature:

* Mont Blanc (4,810 m, highest Alpine summit, on the French–Italian border): documented from 1598 as 'Montagne Maudite', Damned Mountain, without precise localization; the new name 'Mont Blanc', White Mountain, originates from the naturalists and mountaineers of the eighteenth century.[13]
* Jungfrau (4,160 m, along with the neighbouring Eiger and Mönch the best-known mountain of the Bernese Oberland): documented from 1577; perhaps named after an Alpine pasture 'Jungfrauberg', Virgin Mountain, at the foot of the mountain, which belonged to an Interlaken nunnery founded in 1484; the cloister's ownership is well documented, but that the pasture was thus named has not yet been proved.[14]
* Zugspitze (2,960 m, highest mountain in Germany): described in 1590 as 'Zugspiz'; the name is interpreted as a reference to the avalanche paths below the mountain, which were known as 'Zug'.[15]
* Grossglockner (3,800 m, highest mountain in Austria): documented in 1562 and 1583 as 'Glocknerer' or 'Glogger', later also as 'Glöckelberg', all variants of 'Bell'; the addition 'Gross-', Great, is first found after the initial Glockner expedition in 1799; the reason for the naming is cited as the similarity of the mountain to a bell tower or to a bell; alongside this there are a range of other hypotheses.[16]
* Triglav (2,870 m, highest mountain in Slovenia): documented in 1612 as 'Terglau'; since the nineteenth century, overlaid and replaced with *Triglav*; the name means 'three heads' and is connected with the shape of the mountain or a three-headed deity.[17]

Like Mont Blanc, many mountains first got their names from the exploration of the high mountains of the Alps from the late eighteenth century onwards. Nomenclature really became systematic and permanent with the topographical surveys of the nineteenth century. On the other hand, linguistic usages in farming settlements and in the cultivated field and pasture lands were much older. Here the population had created a vocabulary in earlier times, with which they distinguished, described and valued countless places. Parts of their cultural repertoire were reflected in this vocabulary: alongside people from the local past and present appeared characters from the popular or religious imagination. Descriptions of the land also expressed a decidedly pragmatic approach to the environment. A 'beautiful' region was first and foremost bountiful, easy to work and safe, whereas the 'bad' lands had an unfruitful, inhospitable character. Another manner of speaking related to the difference between low- and high-lying valleys and villages. The 'gentle' areas of the lowlands allowed much more intensive use than the 'Wildnis' or wilderness, where humans depended almost entirely on livestock farming. This 'Wildnis' concept was not particularly socially charged, and as such differed from the American-inspired 'wilderness', which first entered discussion in the late twentieth century.[18]

Little is known about the predecessor of Mont Blanc, the 'Damned Mountain', and as for Triglav, the 'three-headed deity' mentioned was first brought into play at the end of the eighteenth century by a literary man. Sacred topology is better documented in the ancient convention of holy names. They often relate to churches, and their distribution shows a clear polarity: in the centres of settlement, there were and are numerous examples, and in the mountains almost none. Saint-Véran, St Moritz, St Veit an der Glan – all over the Alps, we find communities whose names take the form of Christian saints. In the French department of Savoy, more than a fifth of all communities have a sacred name. Such formations refer much less often, but still regularly, to mountain passes (the Great St Bernard Pass, St Gotthard, San Marco, San Jorio, etc.). On the other hand, Alpine mountain peaks are only exceptionally named after a holy person. The same can be said for the saints' adversaries: there are a few 'Teufelberge' or Devil Mountains, but quantitatively they are of no consequence. Generally, the evidence for their names is also late, so they can be related not just to an older stratum of belief, but also to a modern demand for horror in the Romantic period.[19]

1.4 From Prehistory to Contemporary History

The dimension of time is of central importance to the study of history. For a summary work, it is helpful to give a quick overview of the different periods. In doing so, we should be conscious that periodizations come into being in pragmatic ways and are based not least upon convention. All the same, they help us to develop a feel for earlier and later time periods; their benchmarks make orientation easier. Here I present a conventional schema for the classification of European history and highlight a few dates from the region under study as an aid to memory.[20]

1. *Prehistory* It is thought that the Alps were sporadically and seasonally visited by humans from the end of the middle Palaeolithic period, around 50,000 years ago. Continuous settlement began around the end of the last Ice Age (*c*.13,000 BC) and was consolidated from the Bronze Age (*c*.2200 BC). The glacier mummy found in the Ötztal Alps – known as Ötzi – lived around 3200 BC. At that time, the population had for the most part already transitioned from hunting and gathering to farming with ploughs and animal husbandry. Prehistory is researched using archaeological methods. Initially this changes little with the appearance of the first written sources in subsequent 'early history'.

2. *Antiquity* This epoch refers to the development of advanced civilizations in the Middle East and the Mediterranean, and especially to Greek and Roman history in the long period from around 1000 BC to around AD 500. The Alps were affected by this in diverse ways. This is shown, for example, in the crossing of the Western Alps by the Carthaginian General Hannibal in 218 BC, which was recorded in ancient works of history and has been deeply imprinted into collective memory. In the last century before Christ, the Alps were integrated step by step into the expanding Roman Empire. The erection of the 'Tropaeum Alpium' in the years 7–6 BC signalled the conclusion of this process. The monument in the Maritime

Alps – today in La Turbie above Monaco – commemorated the victory of the Alpine campaigns over a variety of tribes.

3. *The Middle Ages* In Europe, the disintegration of the Roman Empire was followed by the Middle Ages, commonly defined as the time between 500 or 600 and around AD 1500. The focus of political power now lay to the north: first in the Frankish Empire and, after its partition, in the Holy Roman Empire of the German nation and in France. The Carolingian and German rulers, who from the eighth to the fifteenth centuries were crowned Emperor by the Pope in Rome, had to cross the Alps with their entourage for this purpose. The 'early Middle Ages' (500/600–1050) and the 'High Middle Ages' (1050–1250) are text-poor periods. In the 'late Middle Ages' (1250–1500), modern state formation began, and written sources consequently proliferated.

4. *Modern history* The European arrival in the American world, the Reformation and other indicators mark the historiographical beginning of a 'modern' period in the decades around 1500. The Columbus year of 1492 is also symbolic of this change for the Alps: in that year, the French king ordered the daring first ascent of Mont Inaccessible, the 'inaccessible mountain', south of Grenoble (see section 7.1). In the 'early modern period' (1500–1800), the processes of state formation and the intensification of agriculture continued. Industrialization in the 'modern period' proper set the economy and society on a new foundation from the nineteenth century. In the sparsely urbanized Alps, this transition happened in a particular way and was often slower.

5. *Contemporary history* This is the name of our current period, the time which was consciously lived by at least some of those alive today. Generally, 'contemporary' refers to the time since the end of the Second World War, or – for the sake of simplicity – since 1950. The period was marked by rapid modernization in the Alps and elsewhere. Around 1970, however, an 'ecological turn' set in. This change of opinion influenced the Alpine situation particularly and led in 1991 to the Alpine Convention, which was signed by eight states and the European Community (later European Union). The Convention was also an expression of a general internationalization.

In older ethnographic and historical literature, reference was often made to a 'retardation of civilization' in the Alps. The Alps were seen as a museum of the traditional and archaic, which could be valued positively or negatively according to one's standpoint. 'The mountains are as a rule a world apart from civilizations, which are an urban and lowland achievement', wrote Fernand Braudel in the middle of the twentieth century: 'Their history is to have none, to remain almost always on the fringe of the great waves of civilization, even the longest and most persistent.'[21] In recent decades, such expressions have frequently been criticized – among other reasons, because they imply an unacceptably centre-focused conception of history. The notion of a single-track, forward-striving modernity has, generally speaking, dissipated, and a view to the diversity of developments and interpretations has opened up.[22] The question of the relationship between the Alps and modernity therefore needs to be considered in a new and different way. We will explore this further below (see section 8.10).

1.5 Material Culture

The role of the Alps in European history can also be established by means of material and immaterial culture, some of which has disappeared, and some of which is still visible or alive. The buildings and architecture of the general population and the elites are a first example.[23]

The Aosta Valley in Piedmont is especially well researched in this regard. Claudine Remacle, who has engaged thoroughly with the development of rural architecture from the late Middle Ages to the nineteenth century, begins an essay with the clichés of historical house-building: 'Farming poverty, the natural simplicity of mountain dwellers, houses perfectly suited to the difficult terrain and harsh climate, inhabited by people who are simultaneously farmers, pastoralists and expert builders, who work without wages and live without contact with the population of the lowlands and cities'. The author qualifies this conventional romantic image with a wealth of building surveys and written sources. In the Aosta Valley, there is early evidence of more or less specialized and partially very mobile building workers. Rural architecture was closely bound to agriculture, though it changed many times and also varied from valley to valley. For the author, this underlines the significance of cultural factors. In the Aosta Valley and other Western Alpine regions, the seasonal or permanent cohabitation of humans and animals in one barn-*cum*-living-space (heated through this cohabitation) was widespread into the early twentieth century. In the northern and southern areas of the Alps, a structural separation between heated rooms for humans and barns for animals was naturalized much earlier.[24]

While agricultural architecture was embedded in local and regional cultural patterns, religious constructions and the forts and castles of the elites reveal clear references to European style. Population growth and political and religious restructuring since the High and late Middle Ages were generally accompanied by intense building activity. The Alps contained several thousand communities, so the total volume of construction must have been considerable. A meticulous study of ecclesiastical and aristocratic architecture in the Aosta Valley uses conventional stylistic concepts, and names the following general time periods: Romanesque (1000–1200), Gothic (1200–1460), Late Gothic and Renaissance (1460–1520), the transition to the classical Renaissance (1520–1650), Baroque and Rococo (1650–1800), neo-classicism, Gothic Revival and eclecticism (1800–1915). Fénis Castle is famous far beyond the Aosta Valley, and was built in the late Middle Ages before being repeatedly extended. The lords of the castle at that time were high-ranking in politics and the church, and appear to have stimulated an almost conscious transalpine cultural exchange between northern Italy and the Swiss and Savoyard regions.[25]

Castle-building in the Alps also continued after the French Revolution, and reached a high point in the nineteenth century. The 'fairy-tale castle' Neuschwanstein, built by the Bavarian King Ludwig II, was a High Romantic and technically refined throwback to an imagined Middle Ages. At the same time, a new kind of palatial architecture emerged in the form of the Grand Hotel. It was oriented towards aristocratic models and was characterized by an emphasis on image and an elaborate infrastructure. This type of building spread across Europe in the first half of the nineteenth century, at first in larger towns and famous spa resorts. Later, it also conquered various Alpine regions. Upper Engadin and especially St Moritz became famous. In 1850, St Moritz was still a village of 228 souls, but it was more than ten times that size by the outbreak of the First World War. In the meantime, a good thirty hotels had sprung up, including some classical Grand Hotels. Like elite tourism, its architecture also boasted an international character. For example, the Hotel Palace completed in St Moritz in 1896 had pinnacles, turrets and pointed arches in the style of the English Gothic Revival.[26]

If the Grand Hotel was an import to the Alps, the *chalet Suisse* became an export in the same time period. Architects constructed a new traditional form of house using various elements of conventional log construction in the Bernese Oberland and the Waadt. Other countries also had their 'chalets': Austria, for example, had the Tyrolean house; Germany, the Black Forest house. But Switzerland was particularly successful when it came to marketing, because it was seen as the Alpine country *par excellence*. In the second half of the nineteenth century, a real chalet industry therefore emerged. The rapid growth of exhibitions contributed to this. At many national and international exhibitions, 'traditional' and 'exotic' themes were presented alongside the 'modern' achievements of the Western world. The Alps often appeared in this regard in the form of the *village Suisse*, the Swiss village, which was sometimes brought to life by 'natives' in national dress. At the World Fair of 1900 in Paris, the Swiss village was comprised of over 100 buildings in chalet style, nestled in an artificial mountain landscape with a waterfall: 'a miniaturisation of the Swiss Alps, but with all its character', as one observer commented.[27]

In the twentieth century, the chalet lost its national attributes and was considered more and more as a transnational Alpine building. However, the declaration of an 'Alpine architecture' came from another quarter and pointed in another direction entirely. This new concept formed the title of a manifesto published in 1919 by Bruno Taut, a famous exponent of Neues Bauen in Berlin. In sketches and commentaries, he outlined a vast development of the Alps with 'glass architecture' of scintillating beauty, concentrated in the area of the highest peaks around Mont Blanc. He considered his fantastical project as a remedy for the horrors of the First World War; the 'mountain coronation' would release the population from their harsh reality. Taut, who first saw the Alps with his own eyes after this publication, imagined them from a distance as an alternative, utopian space.[28]

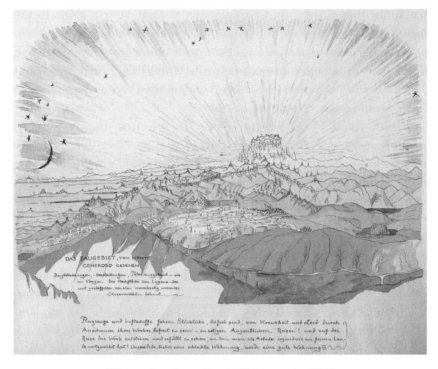

Figure 2   *Bruno Taut's Alpine utopia, 1919*

1.6 Immaterial Culture

Indications of the Alps' position in European history are also given by religious and linguistic developments, which will be briefly treated here and explained in more detail below (chapters 3, 5 and 6).

The appointment of bishops extended over a very long time period in the Alps and demonstrated that Christianization progressed in regionally diverse ways. In the Western Alps – as in their Italian and southern French surroundings – this corresponded with the early and widespread foundation of dioceses (from the fourth century). In the Eastern Alps on the other hand, dioceses consisted of larger areas and were mostly of later date (as late as the thirteenth century).[29] Christian religious practices generally altered from generation to generation, but the change at the beginning of the modern period was particularly drastic, as the Reformation led to deep antagonism between states. The Alps at this time became a border and conflict zone between the Roman church to the south and the Protestant territories to the north. In the Alps themselves, nearly all areas remained Catholic, or were re-Catholicized after a multi-confessional period. An official Reformation was only implemented in the Bernese Oberland and in parts of eastern Switzerland. This religious geography was the result of fierce disputes during the 'confessional age' of the sixteenth and seventeenth centuries.[30]

To counter the spread of Reformed thought and strengthen the papacy, the Roman Curia called the great Council of Trent in 1545. Hosting the Council fell to this Alpine town on the Brenner route, because the Emperor wanted to have the assembly within the Empire, whereas Rome urged a place south of the Alps. The Council met together for several sessions up to 1563. With the clarification and hardening of the positions of both confessions began a long series of conflicts, not least in the Alps. In the French Western Alps (Provence, Dauphiné, Savoy), religious wars raged between the orthodox and the Calvinist Huguenots in the second half of the sixteenth century. The Edict of Nantes in 1598 pacified the area with a compromise, but its overthrow in 1685 brought renewed distress to the Huguenots. Their only choice was between conversion and emigration. A similar fate befell the reformed Waldensians in the Piedmontese valleys to the west of Turin. Later, bitter conflicts flared up here, too.[31]

The religious clash in Valtellina in the early seventeenth century resonated across Europe. The Southern Alpine valley was a subject territory of the mostly reformed Grisons. The pass crossings were of considerable significance for the Spanish Habsburgs, who ruled neighbouring Lombardy, and the ecclesiastical Catholic side wanted to erect a 'bulwark against erroneous beliefs' there. In 1620, the Grisons Protestants in Valtellina were killed in a coup, and the valley seceded from the Grisons. For twenty years, a struggle persisted which involved the great powers and stoked religious tensions far and wide.[32] The last great religiously inspired displacement in Europe took place in the Eastern Alps. Salzburg, a holy principality, had numerous Protestants and hidden Protestants, in spite of previous decrees. Authoritarian repressions were periodically carried out, and were still being carried out even after tolerance had gained ground internationally. In 1731, the conflict between the Archbishop and the open Protestants came to a crisis in the mountain valleys. Thousands were evicted by force from their farms in the middle of winter and banished from the region. In connection with this, there were also further deportations in the Habsburg hereditary lands.[33]

As religion gradually lost power as a source of identity, language became politically charged with the formation of nation states from the eighteenth century. The Alps were (and are) a linguistic contact zone, in which the three great language groups dominating Europe come together: the Romance, the Germanic and the Slavic. Each group experienced general and regional linguistic developments, which led to a richly articulated linguistic geography in this contact zone. Parallel to the Romantic nationalist movements of minorities, in the late nineteenth century linguists began to distinguish the following idioms in the Alpine region: Provençal and Franco-Provençal in the Western Alps; Italo-Romanic in the Lombardian and Venetian Alpine region; Rhaeto-Romanic in parts of the Grisons, in the Dolomites and in Friuli; Alemannic in the Swiss and Voralbergian mountain areas; Bajuwaric in the Bavarian and Austrian Alps; Slovenian as a variety of Slavic in the south-east. According to this classification, there were thus stark linguistic contrasts between north and south in the central and eastern parts of the mountain range, while (Franco-)Provençal linked areas on both sides of the Western Alps.[34]

Alongside internal linguistic facts, external political motives also played a significant role in the classification of languages and dialects. The struggle for the validity of language groups of different sizes was often carried out using historical or geographical arguments. In many places in the Alps, this led to tensions which were partially caused by language. Such tensions acquired broader dimensions from the late nineteenth century with Italian irredentism, which claimed the so-called 'undelivered regions' in the Alps for the 'Fatherland' created in 1861. After the collapse of the Habsburg monarchy in 1919, the land of Tyrol was partitioned at the Brenner. In South Tyrol, which was German-speaking but taken by Italy, this led to a very tense situation. The position in southern Carinthia was also difficult, where the Slovenian-speaking population was caught up in the conflict between the young Yugoslavian kingdom and the land of Carinthia from 1918.[35]

1.7 State Formation and Regionalism

The creation of political space in Europe can be described as a process of concentration: at the start of the modern period, there were around 200 independent states on the continent; shortly before 1900, there were only 30. The increasing scope of state or state-like regions is exemplified by their declining numbers. In the Alps, we can trace this process using dictionaries. Johann Heinrich Zedler enumerated more than a dozen political entities in the Alps in 1732, from Nice and Provence in the west to Carinthia and Carniola in the east. They were a rich array of counties, duchies, provinces and republics (see section 1.1). At the close of the nineteenth century, dictionaries no longer named these smaller entities, but rather superordinate states with Alpine areas, like the Austrian monarchy, the Kingdom of Italy, the French Republic and the Swiss Federation. In spite of – or precisely because of – this reduction, the Alps had now become an area with an above-average density of borders in the political sense, too.[36]

Fundamental to this was the unequal distribution of large towns and centres of power. Since the advent of state formation in the late Middle Ages, the political focus lay for the most part at the edges of, or beyond, the Alps. The flip side of this distance from power was a relatively high degree of regional and local autonomy. Examples of this are found in many parts of the Alpine range, from the west to the east, on the southern slopes and on the northern face. Increasing economic integration, more intensive administration and the rising nationalism of the eighteenth, and above all the nineteenth, centuries had two consequences for mountain areas: the distances to centres of power in the surrounding regions shortened, and Alpine dependence on them simultaneously increased.

This dual process can be vividly grasped from the study of borders. The nationalization of the Alps was, on the one hand, a process of opening, in the course of which local and regional barriers lost their significance. Smaller territories opened themselves to larger state areas. On the other hand, the borders between existing nation states now became barriers of hitherto unknown extent, supported by emotively presented community ideologies and increasing militarization. Following the Treaty of Utrecht in 1713, the border in the Western

Alps between France and Piedmont (later Italy) became a 'militarily armoured zone', as one expert termed it.[37] The international armament of the First World War exemplified this in a most dramatic way, as Italy and Austria-Hungary pursued a deadly Alpine trench war from 1915 to 1918. The front line ran for hundreds of kilometres straight through the mountains, for a considerable distance at altitudes of over 2,000 metres. Conditions on the front were so extreme that many deaths were caused not by enemy action, but by the cold, the snow and the impassable and dangerous terrain.[38]

There were important shifts in borders during this period. In two cases, states in the central Alpine ridge were divided: Savoy-Piedmont and Tyrol. The counts, and later dukes, of Savoy had developed a transalpine state from the late Middle Ages. In 1563, Turin in Piedmont replaced Chambéry on the western side as the capital city. Savoy-Piedmont later became a kingdom and functioned generally as a modern sovereign state. In the nineteenth century, it then became the starting point for the Italian unification movement, but had to cede the Savoyard territories to France in 1860, including Nice. In the case of Tyrol, the expansion came from Italy, as mentioned above. Thanks to the Brenner border drawn up in the Treaty of Saint Germain in 1919, modern-day South Tyrol and Trentino accrued to the Italian kingdom along with other lands in the east. From then on, almost all national borders in the Alps followed the line of the mountains. A noteworthy exception is Switzerland, which, with its territories in Ticino and in the Grisons, retained a transalpine character. This was due in no small part to the localism of the country, which resisted the centralization of the modern period and the separatist tendencies that came with it.[39]

After the Second World War, developments took a different turn. More so than before, the border location of the Alpine regions was now experienced as a problem: Alpine areas were often seen as secondary peripheries neglected by the centres. European integration opened up a certain opportunity to renegotiate the relationship with these centres. The ensuing regionalism emerged particularly strongly in the Alps with its high density of borders. This initially expressed itself in the foundation of transnational working communities at a regional level (Central Alps 1972, Eastern Alps 1978, Western Alps 1982). Shortly afterwards, the International Commission for the Protection of the Alps (CIPRA) initiated a 'convention for the protection of the Alps'. In 1989, the German environment minister invited counterparts from the states with Alpine areas to Berchtesgaden, and, on 7 November 1991, the ministers signed the framework agreement for the 'Alpine Convention', now fully formulated. In this agreement, Germany, France, Italy, Yugoslavia (Slovenia), Lichtenstein, Austria and Switzerland (and later Monaco) committed themselves to implement various environmental and development policies in the Alps, together with the European Community.[40] So, for the first time in its history, this space showed the beginnings of a common political structure.

1.8 Exceptional Mountains?

The Alps in European history – if we want to take initial stock provisionally, we can say that the region was simultaneously a European borderland, transit route and living space. It is not for nothing that these terms come to the fore in different periods; they reflect perspectives and shifts in general discourse. But empirically they cannot be periodized in this simple way. As indicated in the sections above, borders were of a religious, linguistic and political nature and often (but not exclusively) led to problems and conflicts. The significance of transit and communication was illustrated by construction: the transalpine tunnels, in which so much energy was invested, and the circulation of architectural models for public and private buildings. The aspect of the Alps as a living space appears vividly when we think of the endowment of the land with proper names, which reflects the appropriation of space by human actors. The Alps are heavily humanized mountains, and their settlement began long ago: towards the end of the last Ice Age, and sporadically much earlier still. The idea of an Alpine entity and the beginnings of a common political structure are, however, recent. If they are measured by the Alpine Convention, then they date from 1991.

In the following chapters, many of these themes will be considered in more detail. In the process, we shall ask whether modern research can confirm a thesis that Fernand Braudel proposed in the middle of the twentieth century. At that time, he described the Alps as 'an exceptional range of mountains, from the point of view of resources, collective disciplines, the quality of its human population and the number of good roads'.[41] Is this true? And, if so, in which respects and for which periods? What caused it, and what were its effects?

2

MODERN SCHOLARS ON THE ALPS

2.1 'A Natural Laboratory'

Alexander von Humboldt saw the Alps for the first time on 4 October 1792, at Traunstein in Bavaria. The area was 'hyper-interesting', gushed the young aristocratic naturalist. However, he added, his study of mining was currently hindered by poor weather. Nevertheless, 'The country here is divine. Everything here is so other, that I feel as though I had never seen mountains before. Nothing but Alpine mountains, massed pyramid upon pyramid.' In fact, he had visited several mountainous areas before: the Harz Mountains, the Ore mountains and the Bohemian highlands. In 1792, von Humboldt's plan for a mining inspection only kept him on the Bavarian edge of the Alps for a few weeks. Three years later, however, he undertook an extended journey through the mountain range: Tyrol, northern Italy, Switzerland, Savoy, Switzerland again, Bavaria and then back to Berlin. And before he set out on his famous South American voyage, he passed the winter of 1797/8 in Salzburg and its surrounding area, where he improved his skill with scientific instruments.[1]

The Alps were of strategic importance to Humboldt's research in his early career, and he would return to them again and again in his later scientific work over the course of a long and productive life. This was by no means accidental. As a field of knowledge and a 'natural laboratory', the Alps played a large role in the development of the natural sciences in the eighteenth and nineteenth centuries. This was, firstly, thanks to the Alps' geographical location near to the centres of these new developments in the sciences, and, secondly, because the Alps exhibited different environmental conditions from many other areas of the continent. The new flourishing of the sciences was accompanied by a process of professionalization and specialization, which led to a deepening and diversification of knowledge. The publication dates of early standard works in the relevant disciplines give us an idea of this process. The following nineteenth-century dates and subjects are worth mentioning in connection with mountain research and especially the Alps: 1817 plant geography, 1830 geology (the study of rocks), 1854 glaciology (the study of glaciers), 1856 geophysics (the study of the physical processes of the earth), 1862 hydrology (the study of water), 1878 altitude medicine, 1883 climatology, and 1894 geomorphology (the study of the physical features of the surface of the earth).[2]

The degree of specialization was very uneven between individual areas and individual researchers. Geography often possessed a general character with flexible emphases. In Grenoble, Raoul Blanchard founded a geographical institute at the beginning of the twentieth century which dealt specifically with the Alps. From 1913, the institute published the *Revue de Géographie Alpine* [*Journal of Alpine Research*], which really galvanized the topic and remains an important contributor to this day. Blanchard must be seen in the context of the French academic tradition, in which the connection between geography and the humanities remained closer than in Germany. Nevertheless, for Blanchard, the environment represented the decisive factor determining social processes. In his eyes, the Alps had a 'step-motherly nature' (*une nature marâtre*) and were therefore always likely to be disadvantaged: 'For the mountain dweller, the plain is always a land of milk and honey, and the reverse is never true', he declared in 1952.[3]

After the ecological turn in the years around 1970, the political aspect of Alpine geography became even clearer than Blanchard had made it. But the direction changed. It was now no longer primarily a question of getting as much 'progress' as possible out of a dominant nature: instead, nature had to be protected from the consequences of this progress. The most successful publication of this type came from the German geographer Werner Bätzing. It appeared for the first time in 1984 under the title *Die Alpen. Naturbearbeitung und Umweltzerstörung* [*The Alps. The Adaptation of Nature and the Destruction of the Environment*]. After several editions, Bätzing presented a new version bearing the subtitle *Enstehung und Gefährdung einer europäischer Kulturlandschaft* [*The Emergence and Endangering of a European Cultural Landscape*]. Eventually, in 2003 and 2015, respectively, he published a third and fourth edition of the work, which were more than twice as extensive as the original and were called *Geschichte und Zukunft einer europäischer Kulturlandschaft* [*The History and Future of a European Cultural Landscape*]. 'The destruction of the environment' and 'endangering' had made place for the 'future' by then. Sustainable development began to be discussed as a governing social principle in the late twentieth century, and was seen as decisive for this future.

2.2 Historicism

Unlike naturalists and geographers, for a long time historians saw no occasion to consider the Alps as an entity in their own right. The starting point for writing history was, after all, the human community, as seen from the nationalist perspectives of the nineteenth and early twentieth centuries. The rise of history was in large part owing to a close alliance with the nation state. What mattered was therefore political units at the various levels of the political system, and not geographically defined areas. Particularly in the later nineteenth century, national and regional historical societies mushroomed in all Alpine countries, from the 'Historischer Verein für Steiermark' (1850) [Historical association for Steiermark] in the Eastern Alps to the 'Société savoisienne d'histoire et d'archéologie' (1855) [Savoyard society of history and archaeology] and the 'Société d'Études des Hautes-Alpes' (1881) [Society for the study of the Hautes-Alpes] in the Western Alps – to name just a few examples.

A special situation pertained to Switzerland. Here, since the eighteenth century, the Alps had played an almost mythical role in sustaining the nation, so that they were also studied in national histories. For example, much material for discussion was provided by Aloys Schulte's comprehensive work entitled *Geschichte des mittelalterlichen Handels und Verkehrs zwischen Westdeutschland und Italien, mit Ausschluss von Venedig* [*History of the Medieval Trade and Commerce between West Germany and Italy, with the Exclusion of Venice*] (Leipzig, 1900). This work recounted German and Italian economic relations from antiquity to the sixteenth century, and explicitly put the Gotthard Pass at the centre of such interactions as far as the Alps were concerned. In the eyes of this German archivist and, later, professor, commerce over this pass was also the historical reason for the emergence of Switzerland. He therefore treated the unknown builder of the bridge over the Schöllenen gorge as the 'father' of the Swiss nation, and not the 'legendary' William Tell, who had long since claimed this paternal role. This went too far for the patriots, and led to a convoluted debate over whether the Gotthard had made Switzerland, or Switzerland the Gotthard.[4]

Only in the 1960s and 1970s did research move on from this position. For one thing, the formation of the Swiss state was now treated with more distance. For another, the range of sources was being expanded, and it was established from the volume of traffic that, in the Middle Ages, the Gotthard had not been a pass of first-rate importance. Rather than concentrating on a particular crossing, historians now increasingly looked at the whole range of Alpine passes. And criticism began to emerge of the fact that historians had hitherto only treated the Alps in relation to the commerce between the cities to the north and south, and had shown scant interest in the mountain population itself.[5] These new perspectives emerged in no small part thanks to the reception of the work of Fernand Braudel.

2.3 Fernand Braudel between France and Germany

Braudel was part of the innovative current of the French *Annales* School, and in the second half of the twentieth century he became an extremely influential historian. Particularly famous was his *The Mediterranean and the Mediterranean World in the Age of Philip II*, which appeared in 1949 and was later revised and published in many new editions. The first part of the work was concerned with the role of geographical milieus, and greatly inspired research into mountainous regions, as its very first section opened by declaring: 'Tout d'abord les montagnes'

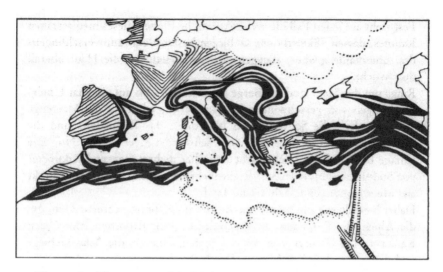

Figure 3   *The contours of the Mediterranean mountain region according to*
Fernand Braudel, 1966

('Mountains come first'). In this vivid, detailed and citation-rich chapter, the mountain ranges around the Mediterranean are described from
various angles. Topics include 'mountain freedom', 'the mountains'
resources', 'mountain dwellers in the town' and other themes usually
associated with mountains.

The origin of the work is also interesting. Before the outbreak of the
Second World War, Braudel had collected a huge quantity of material
and knowledge over many years about the Mediterranean world in the
sixteenth century. In 1940, as a military officer, he became a prisoner
of war in a German camp. In the camp, there was only very limited
access to specialist literature. During this long period of enforced rest,
Braudel developed a three-part historical concept for the presentation of his overflowing material. He broke down history 'into various
planes' and differentiated between 'geographical time, social time, and
individual time'.[6] According to Lutz Raphael, Braudel's geo-historical
project stood 'in close confrontation with the geopolitical and anthropo-
geographical concepts of contemporary German economists, economic
historians and geographers'. This geopolitical style of thinking emphasized the limits to human freedom of action and the interconnectedness
of human societies and their natural environment.[7]

It can be speculated that, in the prisoner-of-war camp, Braudel also read the 1943 Vienna publication by Heinrich Decker on *Barock-Plastik in den Alpenländern* [*Baroque Sculpture in the Alpine Countries*]. The book presented over 300 images of seventeenth- and eighteenth-century ecclesiastical art in Austria. In the foreword, the author praised the scale and beauty of Alpine nature: 'We therefore find in all peoples of the Alps, and especially in the Alpine Germans, an urge for sculpted corporeal forms, the sense of rich emotion and living colours', which, he says, is highly congenial to baroque sculpture.[8]

In his book on the Mediterranean, Braudel uses Decker's illustrated volume as evidence for his thesis of the exceptionality of the Alps, upon which we base the present historical survey. In Braudel's opinion, the mountain peoples of the Mediterranean world withdrew into a space which was too broad and too inaccessible for commerce. Essential goods had to be homemade for the most part, even where environmental conditions were poorly suited to it: 'In the mountains, society, civilization, and economy all bear the mark of backwardness and poverty.' But as the art and culture documented by Decker show, the Alps present an exception to this. Indeed, we are dealing here with a *montagne exceptionnelle*. However, this thesis was not really appreciated. When mountains were discussed in the wake of Braudel, the debate was more often over whether these regions were really as archaic, uncivilized and faceless as Braudel had claimed.[9]

2.4 The Alps as a Historical Subject

In parallel with many other academic reorientations, in the 1970s the Alps began to become an institutionalized topic of historical research. Three factors were especially important in this: international cooperation, interdisciplinary approaches and a certain specialization.

1. *Cooperation* Following an unprecedented period of growth in the post-war period, the idea of international cooperation created a climate that was congenial to Alpine research. For example, with an eye to its own position and the encouragement of such initiatives, the Lombard government organized a large congress in Milan in 1973 on 'The Alps and Europe'. It was a success, and led to the establish-

ment of a special committee for cooperation between the regions in the Alpine range. Twelve years later, the committee organized a further congress in Lugano under the explicit title 'The Alps for Europe: A Political Suggestion'. Similar initiatives emerged from other regions, and there were usually some historians featured on the list of speakers and in the subsequent conference proceedings. At the Milanese conference there had not been many, but at Lugano there was already a much stronger representation of historians.[10]

2. *Interdisciplinarity (the combination of multiple academic disciplines)* Important ideas were brought to the study of history from geography and anthropology. Under the direction of the Savoyard geographer Paul Guichonnet, a two-volume work entitled *Histoire et civilisations des Alpes* [*History and Civilisations of the Alps*] appeared in 1980. It was the first modern publication which treated the history of the whole Alpine region from its prehistorical origins to the present day, alongside other phenomena. Of the twelve authors, nearly half were professional (pre-)historians. At the same time, international anthropology renewed its traditional interest in the Alps, often in the form of local studies. Finally, the Piedmontese anthropologist Pier Paolo Viazzo went far beyond this in his 1989 study *Upland Communities: Environment, Population and Social Structure in the Alps since the Sixteenth Century*. The study was inspired by Robert Netting and his famous investigation of Törbel in the Vallais (*Balancing on an Alp: Ecological Change and Continuity in a Swiss Mountain Community*; see the Introduction above). Viazzo did not limit himself to the local area, but directed his attention to many regions and historical phenomena. Instead of seeing the Alps as a closed space which merely produced emigration as a result of overpopulation, as had earlier been the common view, Viazzo made the case for openness and the complexity of migration processes.[11]

3. *Specialization* Under the direction of the Swiss historian and Braudel scholar Jean-François Bergier, the International Association for Alpine History was founded in 1995. It comprises university historians from all Alpine countries and publishes a trilingual annual journal. The first edition from Bergier, with the programmatic title 'Des Alpes traversées aux Alpes vécues' [From Crossing the Alps to Living in the Alps], emphasized the abandonment of the

transit-related perspective, and the orientation towards the Alps as a living space. The periodic congresses of the society on various themes did have a certain interdisciplinary character, but history was now clearly the main subject. A new development emerged in the 2000s when the Association for Alpine History also began sporadically to embrace global initiatives, and sought to bring together historians of the Andes, the Himalayas and other mountains of the world. In the following years, a new corpus of historical knowledge was established, produced by many researchers from different countries.[12]

Overall, these trends resulted in a considerable broadening of historical reference points and genres since the time of Schulte or Braudel. There were also noteworthy contributions independent of the circumstances already mentioned. For example, a French publishing house, in collaboration with regional cultural institutions, published a large-scale Alpine encyclopaedia, something which had never before been attempted (*Dictionnaire encyclopédique des Alpes*, 2006). With the support of various EU projects, a group of Tyrolian geographers and ecologists developed an *Alpine Atlas*, which collected a rich array of data on the society, economy and environment in the area of the Alpine Convention, presented it cartographically and provided commentary in six languages (*Mapping the Alps: Society–Economy–Environment*, 2008).[13]

Finally, there is the question of the relationship between the writing of Alpine history and environmental history. Here we must first observe that a considerable proportion of historical work on the Alps made reference to the environment long before environmental history had organized and established itself as a specialist area. Even at the time of historicism, when the study of human events was foregrounded, authors were not infrequently disposed to make such references, because they were so obvious and were often mentioned in public discourse. With the gradual establishment of environmental history from around 1970, a debate arose over what precisely belonged to the specialism and what did not. 'Boundary making' is an indispensable undertaking for academic development. In the present case, however, there was a broad consensus that interdisciplinary connections should be preserved and that boundaries should not be too strict. Economic, social, political and cultural phenomena can all bear reference to the environment. Those who seek to shape environmental history should also include these phenomena, because in some cases doing so is the only way to determine what is primarily due to geographical and ecological circumstances and what is due to human influence. Remaining open to other disciplines is therefore a question of analytical potential. This is perhaps even more important in the Alps than elsewhere. In the introduction to this book, I mentioned William Cronon and his essay 'The Trouble with Wilderness' (1995). The essay irritated some environmental activists from the outset, because it gave cultural factors priority instead of ecological ones and invoked self-reflection. Nevertheless, Cronon's essay did not damage the field, but rather contributed to its renewal.[14]

3

IN THE BEGINNING WAS HANNIBAL

This chapter deals with the long periods of prehistory through antiquity to the Middle Ages. These periods were long ago and have left relatively little evidence and written material behind them. However, some figures and events have been especially remembered right up to the modern day. This history of memory forms an interesting historical topic, which also has a self-reflexive value: it provides insight into how historical images form and alter in collective memory. Before we turn to aspects of 'unmediated' history, we will therefore examine the memory of two very different Alpine celebrities.

3.1 Time and Again, the General Crosses the Alps

Towards the end of the year 218 BC, the Carthaginian general Hannibal Barca moved from Spain over the Western Alps to Italy with a huge army, to attack his Roman enemies on their own soil. The Alpine crossing took him some fourteen days. Thousands of horses and mules and around three dozen elephants accompanied the party. That we know of this huge campaign during the Second Punic War is thanks to two authors in particular, and the fact that some of their texts survive. The Greek–Roman author Polybius (*c*. 200–120 BC) wrote a forty-volume history of Rome on the basis of earlier works and his own research. Only one part of this work survived the centuries. Titus Livius (*c.* 59 BC – AD 17) wrote a very much more extensive Roman history, which was likewise passed down only in part. Until the fourth and fifth centuries of our era, the campaign was also discussed by other authors, but, even before this, contradictions between the different versions had invited ironic commentary. On the other hand, Hannibal was endowed with a mythical status early on, for instance through his connection with Hercules.[1]

After the dissolution of the Roman Empire, this story enjoyed a long period of silence. It was first taken up again and re-examined 1,000 years later, when antiquity was consciously re-valorized in the course of the Renaissance. In 1515, Jacques Signot wrote an account of the passes between 'Gaul' and Italy for the French king. In this work, he named Hannibal as the first general to cross the Alps with an army, as King Francis I had done in Signot's own day.[2] The Zurich scholar Josias Simler dealt very thoroughly with the Hannibal crossing in his work *De alpibus commentarius* [*Commentary on the Alps*], which appeared in 1574. His writing is taken as the first specialist tract on the Alps. It is based on a broad knowledge of classical authors and detailed textual comparison (see section 6.4). Of the twenty chapters, which discuss the geography, population, flora and fauna of the mountain range, two are on Hannibal. First there is the question of whether Hercules, Hannibal or another was the first to cross the Alps with an army. Then the tract turns to Hannibal's journey. Natural and military obstacles are at the heart of this discussion, while the question of the chosen route is only raised at the end and left rather open.[3]

In the modern period, visual representations of famous scenes from Hannibal's life also proliferated. The Alpine passage attracted the interest of painters and clients from the middle of the eighteenth century. In 1770, the art academy of Parma announced a competition on the subject 'The victorious Hannibal seeing Italy from the Alps for the first time'. Second prize was won by a then still unknown painter by the name of Francesco Goya, because he had depicted the hero with a warm expression, as an outstanding character. The famous British painter J. M. W. Turner, who engaged with various genres and especially excelled in landscapes, made a painting in 1812 with the title *Snow Storm: Hannibal and his Army Crossing the Alps*. At the heart of the dark picture stands the power of natural forces over the anonymous Carthaginian soldiers, who (as described in the texts) had to fight with the locals.[4]

In the nineteenth century, the Hannibal boom really took off. In 1902, there were already over 300 publications on 'Hannibal and the Alps'; in 2001, this number had reached over 800. Visual representations also proliferated to an extent never seen before, and every time that a new medium established itself in society, it soon turned to the story. From the twentieth century, the Carthaginian army marched over Alps on screen, and later became accessible on the internet on specific websites. While in the early modern period the general had been approached through philology in scholars' chambers, now people also went outside to look for traces of Hannibal on the ground, or reconstructed his Alpine crossing with the help of elephants (see Figure 4). Soon the cult was also reflected among the wider population. In 1950, inhabitants of the Western Alps knew to report that Hannibal had passed right through their village, and their place names expanded to 'Hannibal-wall', 'Hannibal-tower', 'Hannibal-rock' and so on.[5]

Overall, then, the legendary Alpine crossing became ever more

Figure 4   *Hannibal re-enactment – Richard Halliburton with an elephant on the Great St Bernard Pass, 1935*

important over the modern period. In this process, publications on the topic focused more and more on the question of which route Hannibal chose. Little can be gleaned from classical texts on this question. Authors of the early modern period generally preferred the great passes of the Western Alps (Great St Bernard, Montgenèvre, Mont Cenis). Later, smaller passes were also brought into play, so that in the end there was a choice of more than a dozen Hannibal routes. Only from the end of the twentieth century did this – at times, bitterly contested – battle over the choice of route lose momentum. Authors now showed more restraint and more frequently left the decision open, like Simler before them. But hope springs eternal: in the twenty-first century a group of researchers decided upon a particular pass and even managed to publish their hypotheses, backed up by modern methods but still highly speculative, in an international journal.[6]

3.2 'I Was Ötzi'

The reception history of an Alpine celebrity from the prehistoric period has a different origin and trajectory. This is the case of a nameless man who lived at the end of the Stone Age between 3350 and 3100 BC, and reached around 45 years of age. He was found in 1991, astonishingly well preserved, at an altitude of 3,210 metres on the border between Austria and Italy. This 'iceman' was immediately taken up by the modern media machine: after a brief initial phase, news of the sensational find travelled around the world and triggered numerous reactions.[7]

On 21 September 1991, a regional newspaper reported casually that tourists had found a body half-submerged in the ice: 'to judge by the equipment, the dead person is an Alpinist; the accident must have happened decades ago. The dead person has not yet been identified.' A routine criminal investigation was launched into the case. The body had to be retrieved so that the cause of death could be settled forensically. But the prominent mountaineer Reinhold Messner, who was at the scene, realized that this was not a modern glacier body, like the many which had been found that same year. Thanks to Messner's good media contacts, another paper reported that a sensational find had been made in upper Schnalstal: an ancient warrior 'on Messner's path'. At this, several journalists pricked up their ears, and the recovery of the body itself took place on camera. The mummy was flown to Innsbruck by helicopter. On the basis of the media reports, a university professor of early and pre-history also stepped in. On the forensic dissection table, he dated the well-preserved body as at least 4,000 years old from its appearance alone – an extraordinary age.[8]

When, upon more exact investigation, the age was estimated to be even higher, the Alpine mummy made the front pages of the big newspapers and magazines around the world. Driven by the snowball effect of collective communication, every conceivable form of media covered the find. In a short time, journalists had given him hundreds of names, but soon the nickname 'Ötzi' caught on, derived from the site of the find near Ötztal.[9] The mummy could now to some extent shake off its corpse-like aura. In spring 1992, the researchers in Innsbruck decided to establish precise rules for publication and to sell exclusive rights. 'Ötzi' was later entered as a trademarked name. This dynamic spread to the tourist industry: on both sides of the high-altitude site of the find, adventure parks were set up to transport children and adults into the prehistoric world of the mummy. That 'Ötzi' possessed great potential as somebody to identify with was also demonstrated in the confusing multitude of positions surrounding him. Several persons claimed that they were reincarnations of this Stone Age man. A woman from northern Germany conducted a 'recollection' in a systematic way. Her esoteric book entitled *Ich war Ötzi. Die Botschaft aus dem Eis* [*I was Ötzi: The Message from the Ice*] (1994) ran to 300 pages and did not stint on rousing rhetoric: 'In the phenomenon of Ötzi, at last that reality which contains everything that ever was, is and will be becomes directly tangible for us again.'[10]

The interest in Ötzi was not only surprisingly large, but also lasted for a surprisingly long time. Two factors particularly contributed to this. First, the mummy received a lot of attention from the political sphere. As it was found just south of the land border, in 1998 it was transported into Italian South Tyrol and its own museum was established in Bolzano. This was later enlarged with the foundation of a scientific 'Institute for Mummies and the Iceman'. Second, research could repeatedly come up with fresh news stories and stimulate public interest. Particularly exciting was the discovery that Ötzi was killed by an arrow wound, which provided material for mystery stories. And the research also proved itself productive from a scientific point of view. That one could investigate a man in this state of preservation, struck down in the prime of his life and complete with clothing and equipment, enabled surprising insights into Alpine everyday life several thousand years ago. It also encouraged archaeologists to direct their attention to icefields, to expand their methodological repertoire and to cooperate with different sciences.[11]

3.3 From Hunter-Gatherers to Farmers (Stone Age – Bronze Age)

Irrespective of the glacier mummy, archaeology has experienced clear progress in the field of Alpine research in recent decades. If researchers previously limited themselves primarily to the investigation of settlements, now the whole prehistoric landscape came into view with its changing plant and animal worlds. New indicators and dating methods opened unexpected approaches to these unwritten, or sparsely written, epochs. Research also organized itself successfully. For instance, in 2011 UNESCO included more than 100 prehistoric 'pile dwellings' throughout the Alps on its World Heritage List. Dispersed across six states, these settlements in the lakes and wetlands of the Alpine foothills date from the fifth to the first century BC and are of considerable importance. Nonetheless, many questions also remain open at the current state of research.[12]

It is thought that the Alpine region was temporarily used by hunters and gatherers from the end of the middle Palaeolithic period, around 50,000 years ago. These hunter-gatherers were driven out again thousands of years later by a cold period. At its maximum around 22,000 BC, the Alpine valleys were almost completely covered by glaciers and were by and large uninhabitable. Humans returned with subsequent global warming. From around 13,000 BC, the Alpine region has been continuously settled. The hunter-gatherers soon took advantage of really high altitudes of over 2,000 metres, especially on the southern side of the Alps. This is suggested by settlement remains which are considered to be seasonally inhabited hunting sites, on the basis of various indicators. Since around 5500 BC, the foundations of life began to change: crop cultivation and the keeping of domesticated animals replaced the former foraging economy. The origin of this Neolithic 'revolution' lay in the Middle East, and it remains unclear how exactly the change was accomplished in our region – whether through the transfer of technology, the migration and displacement of groups of people, or in a variety of ways. Population growth, which could have contributed to the change, should also be considered in this context. However, this growth and the concomitant densification of settlements first became really tangible in the Bronze Age from around 2200 BC.[13]

Barley, spelt, emmer, millet and pulses were the most important plants of early agriculture in the Alpine region. The animals kept were mainly sheep, goats, cattle and pigs; in general, they were small breeds. Farming settlements seem at first to have been quite mobile. The pile dwellings at the edges of the Alps demonstrate in detail that the houses and villages were abandoned after only a few years or decades and could be relocated. Permanent settlements are first found at the turn of the first millennium BC. The form of animal husbandry is highly contested: do transhumance and Alpine husbandry as we know them today have their origins in prehistoric times? 'Transhumance' is the practice of using pastures both in the lowlands (winter) and in the mountains (summer), and usually requires long migrations. 'Alpine husbandry' takes place in small areas and combines summering on mountain pastures with wintering in farmers' lower-lying barns; it can be described as local transhumance, but unlike true transhumance it includes a period of indoor feeding. The historical age of these forms of animal husbandry has recently become a topic of academic debate.[14]

Generally speaking, the complex modalities of Alpine livestock farming can often only be ascertained in the early modern period or even in the nineteenth century. At that time, the Alpine region contained more than 40,000 Alpine pastures and a range of different practices, sometimes in one and the same place. Using only material evidence, it would be impossible to describe these practices with certainty. A cattle fold or an Alpine building does not tell us where the summer animals came from. Such material remains can be identified in some mountain regions from the Neolithic onwards. Thus, it is probable that in a local context there were certain forms of autonomous summering. However, there is little evidence from the prehistoric period of foddering and stabling, which later became an integral part of Alpine husbandry. It also seems unlikely that the animals were driven long distances for summering. Much evidence suggests that this effort was only exerted once nearby pastures became scarce. Here, archaeobotanical methods provide interesting evidence. Maxence Segard shows for the Western Alps that the landscape had a mosaic appearance: alongside cultivated and pasture land there were many wooded and sparsely used areas. This semi-open landscape represented the norm from the Neolithic through antiquity into the early Middle Ages. Population growth brought a turning point in the twelfth and thirteenth centuries. It made more intensive forms of agriculture necessary.[15]

3.4 Hallstatt (Iron Age)

Hallstatt in the Salzkammergut south-east of Salzburg has long been the most famous archaeological excavation in the Alpine region. Almost 1,500 graves have so far been excavated from this large burial ground in a high valley above Lake Hallstatt. Most of them date from between the eighth and the fifth century BC and are, in comparison to other prehistoric burial grounds, better endowed than usual. This is thanks to the important salt mine above the site and its income. Cremations and burials were roughly evenly matched in the Hallstatt burial ground. In the female graves, a great quantity of brooches, belts and jewellery was found; in the male graves, cloak pins and weapons. Some of the graves contain exceptionally luxurious gifts, particularly items made from valuable materials like gold, amber, glass and ivory. No small number of these originate from distant manufacturing areas, particularly the Mediterranean, and must have come to Hallstatt via economic and other contacts. Taken together, these artistically designed swords, daggers, helmets, glass bowls and precious vessels testify to the impressive possessions that the elites of that epoch must have owned.[16]

The astonishing find and the early scientific work associated with it made Hallstatt a reference site for a whole 'culture'. As early as 1882, an expert stated that the name was now also used in a broader sense: 'The findings in the region of the Austrian salt plant are of so great an importance, that they have lent their name to a whole culture, a whole period in the evolution of central Europe. For the same items which we meet in the graves of Hallstatt are found across a very extensive area between the Alps and to the north of the same.' Later, this extensive area began to be differentiated, and in particular a distinction was made between an eastern and a western Hallstatt zone. Together, these zones stretched from France to Hungary. In the Alpine region, the Eastern Alps and a northern part of the Central Alps belonged to this early Iron Age culture. There were noteworthy excavations of this sort not only in Hallstatt and its surroundings, but also in Styria and in Slovenia.[17]

Hallstatt culture was defined through archaeological findings, but from early on there were attempts to connect it with ethnically or lin-guistically defined peoples. At first Hallstatt was attributed to the Celts, then to the Illyrians, and when the latter fell into academic disrepute, it was the Celts' turn once more. Now only the western Hallstatt zone was counted as a Celtic homeland, and the eastern zone was seen as an area of Celtic expansion. Modern research has problematized older conceptions of early and prehistoric societies in general. Today, most believe that the boundaries between such groups were blurred and changeable, and that the respective images of self and other did not need to correspond. This is particularly clear in the case of the Celts. In early times, this Greek name was only found in a few imprecise texts by classical authors. From the point of view of members of advanced Mediterranean civilizations, the Celts could simply be 'northern bar-barians'. When contacts intensified later on, this foreign appellation was probably known to a portion of the population it described. It is, however, certain that this population was further organized into many small societies and did not form a cultural unity.[18]

The Hallstatt period from the eighth to the fifth century BC, and the subsequent Latène period from the fifth to the first century BC (named after a famous site by the Swiss Lake Neuchâtel), are known to prehistorians as the 'Iron Age', which followed the Stone and Bronze Ages. The increasing influence of advanced Mediterranean civilizations and a strengthened social hierarchy were characteristic of the Iron Age in central Europe and in the Alpine region – and the phenomena are doubtless interconnected. Large-scale transalpine systems of exchange can be traced in even earlier periods – for example, through mussels from the Mediterranean found in northern sites. In the Iron Age, the circulation of goods then intensified considerably.[19] The migration of northern soldiers to developed Mediterranean societies and other contact phenomena contributed to this. The exact extent of elite formation and power concentration is hard to evaluate using purely material remains. However, the almost wasteful use of status symbols found in many sites points with sufficient clarity to the strengthened hierarchy of these groups.[20]

3.5 The Roman Conquest

There are only a few classical texts on the Roman conquest of the Alpine regions in the decades before the turn of the millennium. One originates from the politician and historian Cassius Dio, born in AD 160:

> The Rhaetians, who dwell between Noricum and Gaul, near the Tridentine Alps which adjoin Italy, were overrunning a large part of the neighbouring territory of Gaul and carrying off plunder even from Italy; and they were harassing such of the Romans or their allies as travelled through their country . . . For these reasons, then, Augustus first sent against them Drusus, who speedily routed a detachment of them which came to meet him near the Tridentine mountains, and in consequence received the rank of praetor. Later, when the Rhaetians had been repulsed from Italy, but were still harassing Gaul, Augustus sent out Tiberius also. Both leaders then invaded Rhaetia at many points at the same time, either in person or through their lieutenants, and Tiberius even crossed the lake with ships.

The planned conquest of Germany was then to follow from this meeting of the Roman troops at Lake Constance.[21]

According to the reports of the Romans – we do not know the other side of the story – the 'Rhaetian' groups, who settled in the Adige Valley and parts of the Grisons, repeatedly invaded the Po Valley (Gallia cisalpina) and farther south (Italia). For the expanding Empire with its professional army, this served as grounds to break into the Rhaetians' Alpine settlements and, in doing so, to clear their way to the north. The main attack occurred in the year 15 BC and encountered no united resistance. According to Cassius Dio, only individual groups went into battle. However, the Romans took many prisoners and led a large proportion of the arms-bearing men out of the region, allegedly to prevent a revolt. Traces of this Alpine campaign or of earlier Roman attacks can be found archaeologically in the central Grisons. Among other things, catapult missiles made of lead have been found there, bearing the stamps of the third, tenth and twelfth legions.[22]

The Alpine policy of the Romans was a function of their general policy of expansion. In the time around 220 BC, they had brought northern Italy under their control; in 120 BC, southern France; and by 50 BC, the rest of France (Gallia transalpina). At this point the Western Alps were surrounded by Roman territories, and the passes were also used by military units. The actual seizure of power in the mountain regions happened step by step over a time period of more than a hundred years and in very diverse ways: through alliances with local chiefs and acts of symbolic submission, military campaigns, deportation and enslavement. In the years 25–13 BC, the conquest of the Western Alps was deliberately brought to completion. The Central and Eastern Alps also came under Roman rule in the same period, here against the backdrop of a planned further expansion. Shortly thereafter, a monument of honour was dedicated to the Emperor Augustus at La Turbie above modern-day Monaco – at the strategic junction of the early Roman territories – which celebrated the victory over 'all Alpine peoples from the Adriatic to the Tyrrhenian sea' (see section 1.4).[23]

By the middle of the first century AD, individual Alpine regions seem to have been made into provinces and integrated into the fast-growing administration of the Empire. In keeping with the initial conditions of Roman conquest, the provinces in the Western Alps were small and limited to the actual mountain region: Alpes Maritimae, Alpes Cottiae, Alpes Graiae and Alpes Poenninae (the latter two were soon combined). In contrast, in the Central and Eastern Alpine sections, the provinces were large and reached well into the northern plains which had been conquered afterwards: *Raetia* with its centre at Augsburg, and *Noricum* with its main seat in Carinthia.

3.6 Romanization

Closely linked to incorporation into the Roman Empire was the building of permanent routes in the form of direct, passable roads. A striking example of this is the Via Claudia Augusta, which runs for 500 kilometres from the Adriatic over the Alps to the Danube. It was completed towards the middle of the first century AD and henceforth formed the central artery of the Rhaetian province. In its initial phase, this road only crossed the Reschen Pass and the Fern Pass. In the years before or around 200, the Brenner Pass was also developed for travel with vehicles, which shortened the north–south connection considerably. Construction engineering in the mountains required special efforts, especially in barely passable terrain. There the roads were not made of the customary surface raised with gravel. Instead, galleries, tracks or steps had to be hewn into the rock. If the roads were very steep, lever rods were used to lift up or brake the carts. Road maintenance required great effort. In a peat bog by the Fern Pass, archaeologists were able to prove, using tree-ring analysis, that the Via Claudia Augusta was made there in the year 46 and then had to be heavily repaired in the years 74, 95 and 109. The investigation also showed that road layout was not based on uniform principles, but varied from place to place.[24]

In the first century after Christ, there were around a dozen transalpine Roman roads in total. Of these, the most important were the Via Claudia Augusta in the east and the road over the Great St Bernard (Summus Poeninus) in the west. Building inscriptions and honours to the Emperor on some roads show that they firmly belonged to Roman culture. In peacetime, they could be traversed in relative comfort and safety for long distances. This evoked admiration even in ancient times. From the Renaissance, praise of Rome was revived and often used in mythically exaggerated forms to justify the construction of modern roads. However, almost nothing was known of the actual construction techniques used in ancient times. These were first investigated by modern field research.[25]

Like the road network, the settlement network also changed. Most striking were the towns which emerged in earlier places of settlement or on new sites. They could incorporate a whole array of public institutions and imposing buildings like marketplaces (fora), temples, theatres, bathhouses and water supplies. Admittedly, Roman towns were generally not very big[26] – especially in the Alps. A systematic study of the Western Alps names thirty-nine Roman settlements in the mountain region, and nineteen at the foot of the mountains. Where known, it also lists the areas of the settlements and the type of public amenities. This shows that the settlements in the mountain region were more modest than those at the foot of the Alps. They were more often small and had few or no institutions. The well-provided among them mostly also had political functions. Susa, in the Alpine valley of the same name to the west of Turin, was already settled in the pre-Roman period and quickly expanded, after its peaceful incorporation into the Empire, to a size of 30 hectares (500 x 600 metres). The town lay at the ascent to the important passes of Montgenèvre and Mont Cenis and was the seat of the provincial administration. There was a forum there with a portico, workshops, shops, an amphitheatre and a still-extant triumphal arch in honour of Augustus.[27]

A certain Romanization, that is an alignment with the ascending Roman culture, had been present in the Alps even in the pre-Christian centuries, especially once northern Italy was governed from Rome. After the conquest, this process accelerated significantly. The Roman elites could not eradicate existing practices and power structures overnight, but the influence of the south soon made itself felt in all areas of life. New infrastructure and large-scale integration also promoted innovations in agriculture. These can be evidenced or inferred from the range of plants, the organization of animal husbandry and inventories of equipment. Here the sweet chestnut is noteworthy, which apparently arrived in Italy from the Middle East around the turn of the millennium and then reached the southern foothills of the Alps. Particularly in the eastern part, in Piedmont, sweet chestnuts would later play a large role and become a staple food for the population. The sweet chestnut could be planted in the steepest terrains by means of stepped terracing – although only up to a certain altitude.[28] This is one of the indications that agricultural change in ancient times affected the lower more than the higher altitudes of the Alps, and thereby enhanced the differences in intensiveness between them.

3.7 Christian and Feudal Rulers

Over the course of the fourth century, Christianity in the Roman Empire rose from being an oppositional, and at times persecuted, religion to being the religion of state. An important role was now played by the Christian bishops, who were integrated into the administration of the Empire and carried it out at a regional level, even after the centre lost its earlier significance. The bishop generally lived in a town, and his dominion stretched over a smaller or larger surrounding area.[29] Similarly to the Roman provincial division – and partly because of it – the foundation of bishoprics in the Alpine region progressed unevenly: in the west, many small bishoprics were founded from the fourth century; in the east, the diocesan organization of the territory took a long time, and produced large dioceses as well as small ones.

In 600, there were no fewer than a dozen diocesan towns in the Western Alps, among which there was even an archbishopric at Embrun, later joined by a second at Moûtiers. Some bishops had also established themselves in the Adige Valley and other Southern Alpine valleys. In contrast, from Chur eastward to Vienna, for a distance of 500 kilometres, there were only four bishoprics, and none of them would prove long-lasting. The Christian coverage of the Eastern Alpine region was driven forwards at a later date by two (arch-) bishoprics in the northern Alpine foothills: Salzburg and Freising. With the help of the Frankish king, they made the east their fiefdom and carried out the proselytizing of the Slavic tribes who had settled there. This region only had a consolidated structure of bishoprics from the thirteenth century.[30]

This also shows that cultural continuity from late antiquity was more marked in the west and centre of the Alps than it was in the east, where linguistic and religious change, with or without migration, made for significant alterations. It was long thought that these post-Roman developments played out against a backdrop of steep population decline, particularly in the east. But sceptical voices are multiplying in modern research literature. Thus, Katharina Winckler in her transalpine study of the early Middle Ages pleads for a different perspective:

In the early Middle Ages there are no signs of a population decline for the Western and Central Alps. On the contrary, an increase can occasionally be inferred here. Of the Eastern Alps, because of a lack of artefacts and sources, only a little can be said. Place names and a few archaeological finds point to a thoroughly dense network of settlements, which extended into smaller side valleys.

Increased pollen analysis, which can be used to estimate the extent of forests and cultivated land in source-poor periods, and other methods, will perhaps offer us more certainty on this question in the future.[31]

At the supra-regional level, the early medieval centuries were characterized by changing 'barbarian' kingdoms, which, after the dissolution of the Roman Empire, rivalled one another in its former territories in Gaul, Germania and Italy. Overall, the centres of power shifted unambiguously to the north. With the adoption of Christianity, however, all kingdoms eventually aligned themselves with the late antique tradition. The idea of empire was also very long-lived. After the imperial coronation of Charlemagne in the year 800 by the Pope in Rome, this new form of symbolic assignation of power naturalized itself. From the eighth to the fifteenth century, Carolingian and German kings set out on Italian expeditions more than sixty times. Generally, their armies contained around 20,000 men. They most often crossed the Alps over the Brenner Pass, and also made use of another ten passes. Nearly two dozen of these rulers received the imperial crown in Rome on their Italian expedition. Later, this became unusual. In 1508, the German King Maximilian I had wanted to journey to Rome for this purpose, but the Republic of Venice refused him passage. So he assumed the imperial title in Trent, at least symbolically.[32]

Looking back on this chapter, which has outlined aspects of the long periods from prehistory through antiquity to the Middle Ages, we can ask whether the Alps at this time demonstrated the 'exceptionality' of which Fernand Braudel spoke (see sections 1.8, 2.3). His great Mediterranean work concentrates on the sixteenth century, but has inspired successors who also write on earlier periods. Since the Alps have long been integrated into a Mediterranean empire, the Mediterranean and the bordering mountains can certainly be compared. For this I make use of two methodologically and thematically quite different studies: *The Mountains of the Mediterranean World: An Environmental History* (1992) and *The Corrupting Sea: A Study of Mediterranean History* (2000). The authors of the two books, John R. McNeill, and Peregrine Horden and Nicholas Purcell, respectively, emphasize, among other things, the fragmentation of the landscape and the ecological complexity of small regions, especially in the mountains. There was no uniform human geographical type there. In fact, according to available sources, demographic and socio-economic relationships varied to a very great degree in the Mediterranean mountains during prehistory and antiquity. The Alps in this period make more of an ordinary than an extraordinary impression. Important developments first took place in the Middle East. Only with the shift of power to Italy and the Roman conquest of northern European regions were the Alps directly confronted by an advanced civilization.[33]

4

COPING WITH LIFE – HIGH AND LOW

'Lodare le montagne e stare nelle pianure' ('praise the mountains, but live in the plain') – this ambiguous saying is first documented in thirteenth-century Padua. Wrangling over the evaluation of 'high' and 'low', a sort of contest between locations, seems to have exercised the population in the margins and interior of the Alpine region from an early date. Later, the sources for such value judgements proliferated. For example, in the first half of the eighteenth century, the advantages and disadvantages of different altitudes were weighed up against each other in a description of the Grisons. Under the influence of modern ideas, the author came to the conclusion that the people in the high altitude 'Wildnis', or wilderness, mostly had it better than the people in the low-lying 'tame country' – or at least that the other saying, 'no land is six crowns better than the other', held true.[1]

The present chapter concerns economic developments in the period from the High and late Middle Ages up to the eighteenth and nineteenth centuries. We will give special attention to how altitude-specific environmental conditions in the Alpine region and its surrounding areas affected the population over the long term. This may also provide indications of how best to understand the sayings and proverbs above. The study of urban growth offers a first approach.

4.1 Uneven Urbanization

What is a town? And what is just a small market town or a village? For the Alps, where many ideas meet, it is perhaps even more difficult to give a clear answer to this question than for many other regions. On a journey from Munich to Verona in 1497, a German observer counted twenty towns. But when an Italian travelled the same distance in the opposite direction a few years later, he only counted two places as towns, namely the diocesan towns of Trent and Brixen. In fact, the image of the town in Italy and southern France was more strongly characterized by the church and its late antique tradition than was the case in the north and east, where status in the worldly system of power played a larger role. In the mountains themselves, the Western Alps stood out from the other regions with their many diocesan towns and more urban culture. For comparison, however, it is useful to put these cultural and legal features to one side initially, and to take a demographic definition of the town as a basis – that is, to include all places above a particular population size. Although there were many smaller towns (as the German observer correctly established), we will take 5,000 inhabitants as the minimum size, for pragmatic reasons.[2]

From the eleventh and twelfth centuries, there was a marked increase in town-dwelling in many parts of Europe. Old centres grew, while new ones emerged or were deliberately founded. At the beginning of the early modern period, in the years around 1500, the data allow a reasonably secure quantitative overview of this for the first time. In the regions surrounding the Alps, the distribution of towns at that time was very uneven. In northern Italy, there were numerous towns as well as cities, foremost amongst which were Venice and Milan with around 100,000 inhabitants each, while the regions north of the mountains were less urbanized. Alongside this stark north–south divide, there was also a divide in an east–west direction. The ensuing centuries witnessed a densification and a certain spatial evening-out of the urban population in the areas surrounding the Alps.

In the Alps themselves, the level of urbanization was much lower than in the surrounding regions. This is an essential feature of Alpine history, which can be observed from antiquity right up to the modern day. As demonstrated in the preceding chapter, there were indeed urban sites in the Western Alps during the Roman period, but in a more modest form than in the Alpine foothills (see section 3.6). From the late Middle Ages, various settlements with a minimum size of 5,000 persons then emerged in this region. All of them were already in evidence in ancient times, and with one exception they all presided over a see starting from the fourth to the sixth century.[3] So much for this first phase of urban history. A second phase followed the medieval increase in town-dwelling. The number of population centres now rose gradually in the Alpine region too; the largest among them contained some 6,000–12,000 inhabitants in 1600, and 10,000–20,000 in 1800. But the real thrust of urbanization – which we will call the third phase – happened in the second half of the nineteenth century. If in 1800 there were already nine Alpine towns in the demographic sense, by 1900 there were five times as many, and Grenoble, by far the largest city in this region, now had not 20,000 but nearly 70,000 inhabitants. It is true that the difference between the Alps and their surrounding areas did not become smaller, but in fact grew considerably over the course of this development, as in the lowlands urbanization progressed significantly faster on average. In absolute terms then, the Alps were more urban in the modern period, and in relative terms, more rural.[4]

Socio-political factors were important to the growth of cities in the Alpine region. Grenoble had 2,000 inhabitants in 1500, and later became the largest Alpine settlement, following rapid growth. The nobility and the French king were the driving forces of this growth. From the late Middle Ages, the town established itself as the political centre of a large province, the Dauphiné, and newcomers consequently preferred to settle there. As René Favier emphasized with a view to the Dauphiné, the successive concentration of power in the town gave it its character: 'the development of the administrative functions brought the town an unusual concentration of lawyers and royal office-bearers, and from the beginning of the seventeenth century, the majority of the provincial nobility. Alongside modest little retirement towns, small manufacturing towns and the minority of towns where business elites took the place of lawyers and royal officials, Grenoble was the only town in the Dauphiné which really followed an aristocratic model.'[5] The effectiveness of such forces for urban growth is also demonstrated by the next-largest towns of the Alpine region: Innsbruck was for a time the residence of the Habsburgs, and Klagenfurt formed the centre for the landed nobility of Carinthia.[6]

While urban growth was accelerated by socio-political factors, economic conditions contributed significantly to its delay. The potential for agricultural intensification and therefore urban provision diminished with increasing altitudes. This carried weight even for relatively low-lying settlements, because the environs of the town generally reached into the mountainous zone itself. In fact, in the early modern period, the average Alpine town was found at only 460 metres, whereas almost half the area of the town's environs, which was normally the source of many goods, lay at over 1,000 metres. Altitude became an increasingly important variable for agriculture in this period.[7]

4.2 The Rise of Agriculture and Alpine Husbandry

The rise in towns from the eleventh and twelfth centuries took place against a background of very strong population growth, which continued up to 1300 and changed the Alpine region fundamentally. The change primarily affected agriculture and Alpine husbandry, in which most people were involved. The expansion and intensification of farming stimulated by this demographic change gave the mountains a new face. In earlier periods – from the Bronze Age through antiquity into the early Middle Ages – the landscape seems to have had a mosaic aspect. The centres of settlement and land use were located in the midst of forested and little-used areas. From the High Middle Ages, population growth transformed this semi-open landscape into a cultural landscape. Centres of settlement and land use multiplied and expanded, forest was pushed back extensively, and signs of human presence were now unmistakeable in most places. For the Middle Ages, we can trace this development primarily using qualitative documents. From the beginning of the early modern period, quantitative estimates are also available. In the area of the modern-day Alpine Convention, some 3.1 million people are thought to have lived in 1500. By 1800, their numbers had grown to 5.8 million, and by 1900 to 8.4 million. Although some contemporaries did not tire of emphasizing the sterility of their mountain region (and thus counteracting potential increases in taxation), the population grew almost threefold in this largely agrarian period.[8] How was this possible?

A key means of increasing production was raising the frequency of the harvest in a given area. Instead of cultivating the soil only over long periods of several decades, as with so-called 'slash-and-burn' agriculture, such periods could be considerably shortened: field systems with a fallow period in every second or third year, annual permanent cultivation and multiple cultivation with second crops can all be found in the Alpine region in regionally and temporally specific instances. Alongside old grain types like barley and spelt, peasants now planted oats, and especially rye. However, space-saving forms of land use were generally labour intensive, and yields often did not rise to the same extent as inputs, so that older extensive forms generated higher labour productivity and were maintained as long as land resources allowed. This scissor motion – rising land productivity and declining labour productivity – also meant that new crops were often added rather late to the customary range. Maize and potatoes, the profitable root crop from the New World, were already known in the sixteenth century. But they were only cultivated in earnest from the eighteenth, and especially the nineteenth, centuries as population reached new levels. From one estimate, we know that potatoes required perhaps eight times as much work per hectare as grain.[9]

The harvest frequency of meadow use and hay making was similarly variable. This ranged from the sporadic use of a given area, to annual hay cutting, to several hay cuttings per year. The most important factor limiting agricultural potential in the mountains was the shortened growing season at higher altitudes, and for the meadows the harvest depended proportionally on this factor. According to agronomical estimates, grass yields fall by some 40 per cent with an additional 1,000 metres in altitude. It is noteworthy that altitude and growing season became considerably more important over the long term. In an earlier period, when agriculture in the Alps and their surrounding areas had a relatively extensive character, these factors carried less weight than at later times, when a generally higher level of intensity obtained. The more frequent the land use, the more critical the temporal factor became. In the Lombardian plain and in deep river valleys, cultivators partially switched to four harvests per year in the early modern period

– even to seven or eight in the Po Valley, with cultivated grasslands and green fodder. On the other hand, in particular mountain areas with very short growing seasons, grass growth was so limited that it often only seemed worth cutting once every second or third year. So agricultural intensification in the Alpine region was only a realistic option up to a certain point, after which obstacles abounded. It is therefore unsurprising that its population growth from the eighteenth century fell considerably behind that of the surrounding regions.[10]

The development of Alpine agriculture occurred in various socio-political circumstances and progressed in different economic directions. Socio-politically, there was a particular divide between the regions with many medium and large farms in the east of the Alpine range, and the peasant structures to the centre and west of the range (see section 5.1). Economic differences were expressed through diverse combinations of crop cultivation and animal husbandry. The French geographer Emmanuel de Martonne subdivided the agriculture of the Alpine region for the time around 1900 into several 'agricultural ways of life' (*genres de vie agricoles*). Two of them were strongly characterized by crop cultivation; in two more, animal husbandry had great importance; finally, he described other regions in which both sectors were of similar significance, as in particularly forest-oriented areas. However, a certain unity was demonstrated by the multiple stages of the Alpine way of life. The summering of animals on high-altitude pastures which were not always easily accessible from the settlements was practised nearly everywhere. Whether in the form of Alpine husbandry (with subsequent stabling in mountain areas) or in the form of transhumance (with subsequent pasturage in the plain) – during the summer months, the over 40,000 Alpine pastures swarmed with sheep, cows and other animals.[11]

4.3 The Alpine Cultural Landscape

A pamphlet described Tyrolean peasants in 1677 as 'industrious mountain ants'. A hundred years later, a paper on this large mountain region stated:

> that our countryman does not lack industriousness, we are persuaded by countless proofs. We see him working the most thankless soil with

unwearying diligence; he does not regret the toil of once more drag-
ging up the almost annually descending earth on his back onto the
steep fields in order to obtain the old fertility of the upper part of his
field. He shows no hesitation to extend the fertility of the earth to the
steepest heights of the mountains, although these, since ploughing is
not possible because of the great steepness, must be worked by labori-
ous hewing with the hands alone.[12]

In reality, intensified mountain agriculture did require great efforts.
It is hard to establish in detail, but, overall, farming work must have
increased massively over the long term. This is demonstrated by the
terraced landscapes which can still be seen today in the Alpine region,
in some places only in remnants, half-abandoned, overgrown or built
over, but in other places in astonishingly good condition. The terraces
were generally for crop cultivation (grain, chestnuts, vines). Some of
them were not deliberately made, but emerged as by-products of the
arable cultivation of slopes. The open soil shifted downhill as a result of
this cultivation and had to be carried up again periodically so that the
soil cover in the upper part of the fields did not become too thin – as
described in the aforementioned Tyrolean treatise from the eighteenth
century. Human activity, therefore, aimed at evenness, but with time
terrace-like banks and stepped slopes emerged, which were sometimes
stabilized with walls or bushes. Their appearance differed according to
the technology used (ploughs or mattocks).[13]

On the other hand, some terraces were deliberately erected, to
support steep terrain and protect against the consequences of heavy
rainfall, and also to gain ground. Generally, these terraces were made of
dry walls and additional soil, which first had to be obtained and transported. Because such investments were expensive, the development of
artificial terrace complexes is better documented in the sources – for
example, in early modern Valtellina. The Southern Alpine slopes were
the area of their widest dissemination. The terrain there is often steeper
than in the north, and in many cases the population increased earlier
and to a greater extent. As the few available studies indicate, these
cultural landscapes often reached their maximum extension in the time
around 1900. De Martonne spoke at that time of an 'Insubric' [Western
Lombardian] type of agriculture on the Southern Alpine slopes, and

emphasized its stepped character: 'sometimes the terraces are stacked above one another like actual steps; they bear fruit trees, on which vines trail and under which maize or vegetables thrive'.[14]

A similar chronology to that of terracing applies to irrigation, which served meadow cultivation particularly, rather than crop cultivation. The techniques were known practically everywhere, but the intensity of their application varied considerably. With irrigation, the grass yield of a particular piece of land could rise several-fold. To achieve this, one had to reckon with potentially very high labour costs. In the dry Valais, it was said as early as the sixteenth century that water cost the people more than wine. As some figures show, waterworks could more than double the harvest work on the meadows. The building of supply channels, which directed glacier water from high above into the meadows near to the settlements, was a great collective undertaking, carried out by specialists from early in the process. The dates of many of these channels are known. In the Valais, two great phases of canal building stand out: the fifteenth to sixteenth century and the nineteenth century – not coincidentally, both periods when population rose sharply.[15] In the side valleys, supply channels sometimes ran vertically through the rocks. The creation and maintenance of these passages could be very dangerous. Popular dramatic tales of danger and heroism were seized upon from the nineteenth century by writers and charged with the pathos typical of the age. The novel *An Heiligen Wassern* [*Sacred Waters*] by J. C. Heer was published in 1898, and by the outbreak of the First World War had run to seventy-five editions.[16]

4.4 Pastoralization

An important long-term development was the general shift from sheep- to cattle-rearing. In Slovenia, for example, data from the years 1510 and 1630 show a clear reduction in small domestic animals and a marked increase in cattle. Afterwards, the alteration can be observed on an increasingly widespread basis: from 1630 to the end of the nineteenth century, the number of sheep in the mountain region seems to have fallen by around a half, while cattle showed a further increase. Similar information can be found for many parts of the Alpine region, but everything indicates that the shift progressed differentially. The chronology and extent of the change varied from region to region.[17]

This change was especially early and pronounced on the northern Alpine slopes, in an area stretching from Savoy over Switzerland to the Vorarlberg and into the Allgaeu. For Emmanuel de Martonne in 1900, this was the principal area of the 'developed pastoral type of the Alpine foothills' (*type pastoral évolué des Préalpes*). The whole landscape consisted of a single green carpet of meadows, he explained; there were no fields; the farmers were completely specialized in cattle husbandry. Research into the medieval period has shown that a double shift occurred here from the late Middle Ages. The traditional combination of grain cultivation and animal husbandry was almost completely replaced by animal husbandry, and within this the emphasis shifted from sheep to cattle – in other words, the cow became the new lead animal.[18]

This cattle husbandry and cheese production gave cause for controversy from the fourteenth century and so became a mark of identity for the evolving Swiss confederation. In a table talk from the 1530s, Martin Luther expressed what many in Germany were thinking: 'The Swiss are very strong, but because they live in the Alps, they have no fields, only meadows. Consequently in peacetime the men milk and make cheese.' In the orbit of the Zurich Reformation, the emphasis was usually somewhat different. Instead of bringing up the lack of fields, an admonition to fellow confederates described the Alps and mountains as God's gift, 'upon which your beautiful cows and oxen stand up to their bellies in grass'. The allusion to male cattle-tending by Luther points to the fact that milking and milk processing in Germany and elsewhere were women's work. This Alpine peculiarity could be used polemically. 'They do not shy away from undertaking this women's work with men's hands, to the abominable contempt of the masculine sex and the exclusion of their wives', held one 1451 text against those from Schwyz: 'indeed, which appears even more shameful, they rejoice that they are publicly before all people described as cow milkers'. The author did not accept the objection that the area's wealth in livestock had made animal tending a difficult business. He insinuated, on the contrary, that pastoralists had sexual relations with their animals.[19]

These controversies were encapsulated in the common swearword 'Kuhschweizer' – meaning 'cow-Swiss' – and in the sexual insult

'Kuhghyer'. These insults must be seen against the background of political separation from the Holy Roman Empire and competition on the market for mercenary soldiers. For the Swiss part, this negative foreign stereotype was transformed in the sixteenth and seventeenth centuries into a positive self-image. In the process, the cow was in some sense promoted to a symbol of Swiss virtue.[20] In the eighteenth century, the positive assessment of the pastoral life then found a broad appeal across the continent. *Briefe über ein schweizerisches Hirtenland* [*Letters on a Swiss Pastoral Land*], which were published by an author from Berne in 1781, became a European concept, expressing the new Alpine experience and the aspirations of the Enlightenment. If livestock- and dairy-farming mountain dwellers had to justify themselves now, it was against the charge of idleness. Inspired by literary idylls, many thought that the 'pastoral life' left one little to do, which in the context of modern industriousness seemed particularly reprehensible. This assessment was later taken up by historians, who described pastoralization as merely a process of extensification which freed up labour. On closer inspection, however, specialization in large-animal husbandry generally did not reduce regional labour volumes, but increased them. The development of the 'pastoral land' and the 'developed pastoral type' could also be seen as a form of agricultural intensification.[21]

There was an important regional exception to the advance of cattle: in the French Southern Alps, especially in Provence, sheep rearing was still dominant in 1900. De Martonne described this area in his agricultural typology as 'sheep country' (*pays à mouton*). Many sheep were kept in a system of transhumance. In summer, the animals pastured in the mountains, and in winter, on the plain, which entailed long migrations. This system seems to have developed in the High and late Middle Ages, first in the mountains, where an additional demand for wintering spaces had emerged, and then, in the fourteenth and fifteenth centuries, increasingly in the opposite direction from the plain.[22] One reason for this special development lies in demographic history. Even at its high point in the early nineteenth century, the population density in the French Southern Alps and their surrounding areas was strikingly low. But what united both cow and sheep regions was market orientation. All around the Alps, and especially in northern Italy, there were many towns which created demand for animals and animal products.

Pastoralization in its developed form must be seen against the backdrop of this urban pull.

4.5 Climate, Crises, Catastrophes

In the premodern period we are discussing, the highest permanently inhabited settlements in the Alps lay at over 2,000 metres. Such settlements were especially prevalent in the Central and Western Alps, partly for topographical reasons. In some regions, the average altitude of all parishes was as much as 1,000 metres or more, and land used in Alpine husbandry could reach to well above 3,000 metres. This impressed many external observers, and it is understandable that climatic factors are commonly given a leading role in histories of the Alps.

The historical changeability of the climate is evident from the glaciers and their variable size and length. In the last millennium, there were three great glacial advances. The first reached its high point in the late fourteenth century. The second began around 1570 and experienced its largest push around 1600; afterwards, most glaciers remained in their advanced positions with small fluctuations. In the first half of the nineteenth century, they reached a third and final maximum, and then retreated massively up to the present day. The period of high glacial levels is described in the literature as the 'Little Ice Age'. This usually refers to the period from the fourteenth to the nineteenth centuries. Changes in the glaciers are best understood through their tongues, which could move hundreds of metres, or even kilometres. The traces that they left behind in the terrain, as well as in the archives, can be used to reconstruct these formations. The 'Mer de Glace' ('Sea of Ice') at Mont Blanc and the Lower Grindelwald Glacier in the Bernese Oberland are especially well documented and researched. Both were also early tourist attractions. The annals of glacial history present dramatic moments there and elsewhere: Alpine pastures and huts which were overtaken and destroyed by ice; outbursts from glacial lakes which devastated whole valleys; isolated attempts to surmount these dangers technically with drains or dams; many acts of spiritual defence such as penitential processions, crucifix erections or invocations.[23]

However, this immediate danger affected only a vanishingly small part of the Alpine region. With a view to the whole, glaciers are therefore especially significant as indicators of weather conditions. Using these and other indicators, historical climate research has in recent times produced astonishingly detailed time series for temperature, precipitation and other variables reaching back for many centuries. These findings suggest, for example, that the 'Little Ice Age' was not a constantly cold period, but rather a period of contrasts, in which adverse conditions sometimes prevailed and at other times lapsed for long periods.[24]

Compared to historical weather patterns, very much less is known about their effects on the Alpine population. Linear explanations, which suggest a direct relation between unfavourable weather, crop failures and general shortages of food, are not very helpful, as many factors played a part in crises: the structure of agriculture, commercial opportunities, socio-political conditions – but also other dangers, primarily those of a medical nature. In the years around 1350, the great plague dramatically decimated the population of the Alps, and the 'Black Death' remained a constant threat up until the early eighteenth century. Especially in 1630, it returned to some regions with great severity. Even in extremely inauspicious times, crisis situations were heavily influenced by local conditions. The year 1816 was known as the 'year without summer', as during the summer months it snowed almost every week as far down as the valleys. The cold and wet seemed endless. The (then unknown) cause was a violent volcanic eruption on an Indonesian island, which changed the climate worldwide. In the Alps the harvest was miserable, prices for basic foodstuffs soared, and some sections of the population starved. However, a comparative study shows that the extent of the crisis varied greatly by region, and that the Alps were no worse affected than the surrounding lowlands.[25]

This local character was even more prominent for natural disasters: avalanches, landslides, floods, earthquakes and major fires caused (in part) by the environment. Triggering factors might affect larger areas, but catastrophes befell particular places, and the extent of the damage depended on the situation. For instance, at the beginning of September 1618 there was intense rainy weather in the central Southern Alps. On Monte Conto above Piuro, near Chiavenna, the already destabilized slope lost its purchase, and within a few minutes 3 million cubic metres of rock fell on the large and relatively prosperous settlement. In some places, the rock was piled as high as the church spire. It was thought that more than 900 people met their deaths. The Piuro landslide attracted a great deal of attention. Numerous pamphlets – especially broadsheets with before-and-after pictures – declared the unhappy fate of this place across Europe and interpreted it as a sign of God's wrath. This media reaction was also dependent on time and place: it was the beginning of the Thirty Years' War, and confessional emotions had recently led to an explosive situation in this precise area. But catastrophes in general were often interpreted theologically, into the nineteenth century. 'Oh let us pray, yay ardently, that God assuages his great wrath, and punishes us not according to our deserts', wrote the regional incumbent to his government on the day after the landslide.[26]

4.6 Migration

Mobility and migration in the Middle Ages and the modern period were part of the usual conditions of life, in the Alps as elsewhere. Migrations led in all directions – from the mountains to the lowlands, from the lowlands to the mountains, from one mountain region to another – and followed diverse agendas. Migrants pursued agricultural, commercial or military employment; there were temporary and permanent forms of migration; it could lead away individuals, particular categories of person (for instance, the menfolk), or whole families, sometimes to a neighbouring valley, sometimes to remote destinations, where contact was occasionally maintained with a migrant's place of origin. Among the early forms of migration, the most well-known are those that remain visible in the form of linguistic islands over the centuries: those of the 'Walser', who originated from the Haut-Valais and dispersed in the Central Alps, and the 'Cimbri', who in the high Middle Ages migrated from Bavaria to the Southern Alpine slopes. In Romance Italianate surroundings, the German dialects of these communities stuck out and stimulated research into their heritage, especially under the sign of the linguistic nationalism of the nineteenth and twentieth centuries. We can also consider them here as indicators for other migrations in the late Middle Ages.[27]

In the early modern period, emigration is better represented in the sources. It was often temporary, and created numerous connections between places of origin and destination through the constant back-and-forth of people and goods. Previous researchers saw in this a motion of repulsion: the sparse resources of the mountain areas would quickly have led to overpopulation and compelled emigration for practical reasons. The mountains were a 'fabrique d'homme à l'usage d'autrui' wrote Fernand Braudel – that is, a factory of men produced for other people's use. In recent decades, research has engaged intensely with the topic, and in doing so has come to partially different conclusions. Other factors are now seen as more important than overpopulation: the appeal of urban centres, the pull effects of earlier emigrants in the context of chain migration, and the influence of local elites, who could direct labour from their areas into foreign parts. In the mercenary world, this hierarchical character is at its most obvious: captains often had the military emigrants of their regions at their command. Similar dependencies can also be seen in commercial occupations.[28]

The attractiveness of urban centres for Alpine migration enables us to hypothesize about their regional intensity. As we know, northern Italy and southern France were considerably more urbanized during the transition to modernity than the regions to the north of the Alps. That migration was particularly intense on the southern slopes of the Alps can also be discerned in the literature. For example, in 1679 in the Carnic Alps of Friuli, then part of the Venetian territory, all emigrants were registered. In Vienna, the plague had broken out, and migration was controlled as a means of policing the disease. Most of the emigrants recorded by the enquiry were adult men. They came to 8 per cent of the total population in the destination. Amongst men aged over 15 years, emigrants made up a full 25 per cent, so every fourth man was on the move. Generally they left in winter, following different traditional regional or local commercial links with specific markets. From the Venetian lands over Lombardy into the Piedmont, such male migrations brought about very one-sided gender relations at home. There were actual 'valleys of women', in which agriculture depended heavily on the female population. Occasionally, roles were even reversed in politics due to the lack of men, as in the case of the woman who became the mayor in 1722 in a valley near Como.[29]

With more efficient means of transport and a new economic environment, migration changed considerably during the nineteenth century.

Figure 5   *Women with agricultural tools in Sant'Omobono near Bergamo, 1927*

Emigration overseas now became a more common option in the Alps, too. Although it was characterized again and again as an escape from poverty, there were also many other reasons to do it. This is plainly indicated by the commercial emigration agencies which mushroomed and eagerly advertised their business. In Switzerland, the first agencies were founded in the middle of the century. By 1885, the country already had more than 350 agencies; in the mountain cantons, they were particularly well represented in comparison to the population size. However, the quantitatively dominant form of emigration was still to the cities surrounding the Alpine region, which in the late nineteenth century experienced a massive growth spurt. Here, too, there was often a transition from temporary to permanent migration. In spite of this increased immigration, overall contact between mountain villages and towns possibly became weaker. According to one expert, Milan was an 'Alpine city' in the early modern period thanks to temporary migration. Later, when the migrants became settled, the Lombardian metropole lost this character.[30]

4.7 Mining

The relationship between mountain areas and the centres of economic and political power and the mobility of experts and labour also shaped the history of mining. Gold, silver, copper, iron, quicksilver, salt – the Alpine region contained a wealth of mineral resources. They were found in many places, but not always in the same volumes, and they were not exploited everywhere with the same intensity. Two regions in particular became prominent due to widespread small-scale mining. In the Lombardian Alps, metal extraction and metalwork developed in the late Middle Ages into a regional speciality; thus an early commercial scene emerged in the mountain valleys of Brescia and Bergamo in association with Milan, which was especially famous for its weapon production. During the transition to modernity, the Eastern Alpines then emerged as a leading mining region; here, too, connections to urban centres like Nuremburg and Augsburg were important. From a commercial and political point of view, mining soon played a leading role. It also represented a kind of laboratory for technological development, both in the extraction of ore and in its processing.[31]

The most spectacular boom was experienced in the Tyrol region, where mining fever broke out in the early fifteenth century. At the forefront of this was ore extraction in Schwaz, whose three main regions were numbered among the most important producers of silver and copper in Europe between 1470 and 1535. During this boom time, some 10 tonnes of silver and 800 tonnes of copper were mined there every year. At least 9,000 people were employed in the mines. In Schwaz itself, a whole range of sacred and larger secular buildings emerged, not least the palace of the Augsburg merchants the Fuggers. The increasing

depths of the mines and the concomitant transport and drainage problems became a challenge for the engineers. For example, the famous
'Schwaz waterworks' of 1554 replaced hundreds of labourers, who had
previously hauled the water from a particularly deep gallery by hand
with leather buckets. Shortly afterwards, however, Alpine silver mining
suddenly declined. An important reason for this was the drop in prices
caused by the large supply of silver from the New World.[32]

Business proved more stable for the mining and processing of iron,
concentrated in Styria and Carinthia. True, the iron industry also
had a long crisis in the second half of the sixteenth century, but two
centuries later it reached the level of the earlier boom and thereafter
experienced very considerable growth. In 1750, annual production in
Austria reached some 20,000 tonnes; in 1800, 30,000 tonnes; and in
1850, nearly 95,000 tonnes. But, in relative terms, Alpine iron mining
was quickly losing significance. In the middle of the eighteenth century,
Styria alone seems to have outstripped even England. A hundred years
later, English production had accelerated to such an extent that Styrian
iron only made up a few per cent of the total output. Even so, the iron
industry of the Eastern Alps remained of lasting value for regional and
interregional markets: weapons for the Habsburg armies, scythes for
extensive markets, and many other goods originated from their galleries, furnaces and hammer mills.[33]

4.8 Inter- and Trans-Alpine Traffic Flows

At one point in his famous 1761 novel *La nouvelle Heloïse*, Jean-Jacques
Rousseau describes the particular hospitality of the upper Valais and
explains it through the scarcity of money in the regional economy. The
people of the upper Valais produced enough to live, he wrote, but never
exported, and in the interior of the valley abundance did not tempt
any to luxury consumption or idleness: 'If they ever have more money,
they will infallibly be the poorer. They have the wisdom to sense this,
and there are gold veins in the area which it is not permitted to mine.'
So much for the novel and its anti-market ethics. In reality, there
was indeed an export of agricultural products from the upper Valais,
and the relationship between household and market economies, here
as elsewhere, varied sharply according to class, occupation and time

period. But looking at the Alpine region as a whole, one cannot help but agree with Rousseau to some extent. Even in 1870 (the first year of statistical coverage), a good two-thirds of the whole active population in this area worked in agriculture, considerably more than in the surrounding areas. The high agricultural quota is an indication of its comparatively limited level of specialization and monetization.[34]

Another indication is given by the differences between the Alpine region and its surrounding areas in terms of urbanization, as described at the beginning of this chapter. At the same time, many cities of the plain were also important factors for market formation in the mountains. Their demand promoted the commercialization of livestock farming and specialization in cattle breeding (or, in the southern part of the Western Alps, in sheep transhumance). They were target areas for the temporary and later permanent migration of the mountain population. Without demand in extra-Alpine areas, mining and the subsequent processing of the metal extracted would never have been possible to the same extent. From the twelfth or thirteenth century, all of these commercial areas grew, though not at a steady pace. For instance, in times of crisis, exchange could take on a quite different urgency from that in normal harvest years. The increase in trade and traffic flows can also be seen in the institutionalization of periodic fairs, especially annual fairs. The one at Bolzano was substantial and well known. In the late Middle Ages and in the transition to modernity, annual fairs spread everywhere, and they experienced another proliferation in the eighteenth and nineteenth centuries. Even small settlements aspired to such an event.[35]

The fact that cities with an economy of long-term growth existed on both sides of the mountains also formed a precondition for transalpine trade. In the eyes of Fernand Braudel, 'the number of good roads' in the Alps was a sign of their exceptionality (see section 1.8). Here, he was surely thinking of the paths and roads that led over the watersheds everywhere. Around a dozen of them were over the most important pass crossings. The available estimates of transport volumes show that the Brenner was the most-used pass. It could already be crossed by wagon in the fifteenth century, while the Gotthard Pass, for example, only obtained a vehicle-worthy road in 1831. On the large routes, transport developed into a side-line for local peasants. It was generally organized through stage traffic, where the wares were unloaded and transferred to other local carriers. In principle, the people with a right to transport work were those responsible for the maintenance of the respective roads. But the frequency of traffic should not be overestimated. It was on a completely different level from in the age of the railway and, later, the lorry. At the Brenner, by far the most important pass, the annual volume of transport for 1500 is estimated at 5,000 tonnes, for 1734 at 12–14,000 tonnes, and by 1840 at 100,000 tonnes. When in 1867 the railway over the Brenner was built, some fifty freight wagons would have sufficed to transport the entire load for 1500.[36]

Overall, living conditions at high and low altitudes – the starting point of this chapter – were characterized by numerous differences. Even the performance of everyday life was not the same in the high and often steep 'Wildnis' and the flat and low-lying 'tame country'. At a general level, these differences can be conceptualized as a question of population density. The Italian saying quoted in the introduction advised that the mountains should indeed be praised, but that it was better to choose the plain for a home. This probably alluded to the urban life and comforts enabled by demographic and economic concentration; the mountains played the role of exciting the imagination, and perhaps served temporarily as a refuge, when it was too hot in the plain or when one wanted to escape the crowds. This position was not, however, the only one, and the disparity was not so great that everyone fell on the same side of the argument. Low population density also had its advantages. At any rate, during the early modern period, one could plausibly defend one's home in the mountains and claim that life was about the same everywhere, and didn't come down to the difference of a few crowns.

5

PATHS TO THE NATION STATE

After surveying economic history in the last chapter, we will now turn to social and political history – again in the *longue durée*, from the late Middle Ages to the early twentieth century. From a social and political point of view, the Alps in this period often formed a frontier. Even before, and during, the period of early modem territorial states, differences and borders were discernible between different sides of the mountains. These then became considerably sharper in the period of nation states and nationalism from the late eighteenth century onwards. One reason that frontiers are of scholarly interest is that they enable a comparative perspective over a small area – indeed, directly provoke such an approach. The results may then be relevant to other non-adjacent areas. This is evident, for example, in the case of the household and family, with which we will begin.

5.1 Household and family

The anthropologist Dionigi Albera recently produced a comprehensive study of domestic organization in the Alpine region from the fourteenth to the twentieth century, in which he summarizes the rich historical and anthropological research into the family in this area and expands upon it empirically and conceptually.[1] In doing so, he uses several criteria to distinguish three constellations or ideal types of household and family. They can be briefly characterized as follows:

• *Bauer type* in the Eastern Alps: social relations focused on the farm and its head (*Bauer*, peasant); the community as a collection of clearly delineated, often dispersed, farm units; impartible farm inheritance with social declassification of other family members.
• *Bourgeois type* in parts of the Central Alps: embedding of the family in the communal organization, which often included larger settlements; egalitarian division of inheritance between both sons and daughters; public roles of men bound to local citizenship (bourgeois).
• *Agnatic type* in the Southern and Western Alps: embedding of the family in kinship and neighbourhood networks in small settlements; strong position of the male side (agnatic); egalitarian inheritance portions among sons, daughters compensated with dowries.[2]

These patterns and regions should not be thought of too homogeneously. The ideal types are a useful tool for bringing many sources and studies on household organization into a manageable order. The sharpest distinction is between the *Bauer* type in the Eastern Alps and the other types in the Central and Western Alps. Agricultural statistics in 1900 and many scattered earlier sources show that medium and large farms with a productive area of 10 hectares or more were frequent in the Eastern Alps, while the Central and Western Alps had very small farms. Because of this, the Eastern Alps were also an area with numerous servants. The (extreme) case of a Pinzgau 'peasant king' has become famous: in 1798, he had no fewer than forty-three farmhands and maids in service on his farm. Michael Mitterauer has spoken in this context of 'servant societies'. Rural servants generally could not marry. In the Eastern Alps, there were therefore numerous illegitimate births. In the nineteenth century, these constituted up to two-thirds of all births in some districts.[3]

Historically, forms of household and familial organization emerged parallel to the formation and development of state constitutions. The agnatic type emanated from the strong emphasis on the male side in the city states of northern Italy. As laid out above, northern Italy and southern France were already relatively densely urbanized in the late

Middle Ages (see section 4.1). Urbanization formed the backdrop for the development of literacy and learned 'Roman' law. Through legislation and the notary's office, urban ideals of agnatic family associations also spread to the countryside. The transmission of goods and positions from one generation to the next now occurred with the help of notaries and their new documentary techniques. An important role in the dissemination of agnatic models into the mountains was played by nearby towns, like Udine or Como. In time, notaries also established themselves in small towns in the Southern and Western Alps. The agnatic order reached its high point in the early modern period. In the strictest variants, daughters came not only behind their brothers in the line of inheritance, but also behind their uncles and cousins. Outwardly, the importance of the male side became apparent in the relatively frequent households where married brothers lived together. In the regions of the Central Alps, which had gender-neutral forms of inheritance (bourgeois type), such extended households only rarely appear in surviving population registers.[4]

In the transition to modernity, from the late eighteenth century, male dominance weakened. The trend now passed, on the one hand, to gender-neutrality in the line of inheritance, and, on the other, to the closed inheritance of peasant farms. While the undivided passing on of large farms in the Eastern Alps fell under the control of landlords until the replacement of feudal privileges in the middle of the nineteenth century, modern forms of indivisibility became increasingly economically justified. Farms needed to make an income and be profitable in order to compete. While the dynastic dimensions of family order retreated, alliances gained in importance during this period. In many places, marriage among relatives increased significantly in the eighteenth and nineteenth centuries. In adjustment to the economic and political conditions of modernity, a kind of family 'nationalism' now prevailed. In this, the Alpine region followed a European pattern.[5] In general, the Alpine types of household organization can be classified into a wider framework. The agnatic type, as discussed, emanated from the urban models of northern Italy. Conversely, the *Bauer* type in the Eastern Alps resembled the rural models which stretched from Slovenia and Austria through Germany right up to Denmark. Dionigi Albera is doubtless right when he describes the Alps in this regard as a 'place of transition' and uses the expression 'Alpine Europe'.[6]

5.2 Social Inequality

'It is easy to see that this picture refers to the perfect equality of the Alpine people, where there is no nobility and even no governor, where no possible promotions awaken agitation in the mind and ambition has no name in the vernacular', wrote Albrecht von Haller of his didactic poem about the Alps, which was published in 1732 and afterwards re-issued repeatedly. This antithesis of the critically perceived 'civilization' of the cities and royal courts of the continent was well suited to literary purposes in the century of the Enlightenment. It gave a concrete setting to many civic desires and utopias.[7] However, in reality, inequality in the Alps was widespread, including in the form of nobles and governors – which Haller as a Bernese patrician knew very well (he knew the governors personally and visited them on his Alpine trips to the Oberland, whose population was subject to the city of Berne). Certainly, there were communities and regions in which social hierarchy was relatively undefined, or at least not very visible. In comparison to the surrounding lowlands, these regions could seem egalitarian. In other parts of the Alps, however, even this modest difference may not have been present.[8]

To draw a socio-topographical outline, we can start with the household organization types presented in the preceding section. For the *Bauer* type in the Eastern Alps, differentiated and formalized hierarchies were the norm. Here, peasant farmers on the medium and large farms formed a particular status group, which contrasted starkly with the lower class of smallholders and servants. Since the nobility in this region exercised comprehensive economic and political power over the population up to the middle of the nineteenth century, rural society also had clear external contours: noble landlords – peasant farmers – servants and other members of the lower class. It was different in the smallholding areas of the Central and Western Alps. Here, there was no middle-status group; properties were gradually split up, and the '*Bauer*' or 'peasant farmer' was no special honorary or legal title. Depending on region and period, the nobility also held a less formalized position than in the east. This does not mean that wealth inequalities were necessarily smaller. But elites had to depend more on the flexible mechanisms of patronage in order to exercise political power.[9]

Other dimensions of social inequality, such as gender hierarchy and the relationship between generations, also mapped on to both general history and different patterns of household organization. For example, the dominance of men was more striking under the agnatic type than under the bourgeois type, which had a largely gender-neutral line of inheritance. But in other household issues, and especially in the public sphere, the supremacy of men could not be overlooked, even in the bourgeois model. The practice of the gendered division of labour varied according to the size of farms. In the smallholding conditions of the Central and Western Alps, general norms of labour allocation could often not be implemented because too few hands were available. Men therefore took on some 'women's work', and in particular women engaged time and again in 'men's work' (in a more pronounced form where there was male emigration). In the servant-rich farming economy of the Eastern Alps, the gendered allocation of labour was, by contrast, less flexible. The hired farmhands and maids sometimes had very specialized areas of work. An almost symbolic expression of this is the figure of the 'beautiful milkmaid', which only existed in this form in the Eastern Alps. Peasant farmers were happy to leave their Alpine pastures to the maids in summer. They recruited them from all age groups, but the Romanticism of the nineteenth century only took note of the young among them, and endowed them with their own liberal and erotic ideals.[10]

The gap in authority between the older and younger generation was pronounced everywhere, but also variable. In the case of age-related incapacity or widowhood, it could shift in favour of the young. Here it is worth mentioning the institution of the 'Altenteil', a share of property reserved by a peasant farmer upon retirement, which acted as an early pension system and developed particularly on the large farms in the Eastern Alps. In these areas, there was initially a strong obligation to remarry. In the leadership of the farm, both the male and the female positions had to be occupied. If the peasant or his wife died, then within a short time they would generally be replaced through remarriage. Later, there was a rise in the number of cases where the widower or widow retired from farm management and left the leadership to the next generation by contractual agreement. In the eighteenth and especially the nineteenth centuries, it also became increasingly common for a complete married couple – older, but not widowed – to retire to a particular house or building on the farm.[11]

5.3 Territorialization of Power

The development towards statehood was a long, collective process driven by competition between rulers. Following steep demographic and economic growth in the period around 1200, personal power relations were increasingly supplemented and overlaid by institutional relationships. In the process, strictly demarcated and spatially continuous territories gradually emerged. At the same time, interactions between territories became systematic, with permanent embassies and extensive peace treaties. The Italian Wars, which broke out shortly before 1500, gave a strong push in the direction of such a state system with formal relations. At that time, the kings of France and Spain, the German Emperor and other rulers considered wealthy Italy – also the heart of the Roman tradition and the church – as the key to dominance in Europe. A particular role was played here by the great city states Milan and Venice. At the threshold of modernity, the Alpine region thus found itself in the middle of a tense set of power relations. It was a military deployment zone and lay near to the hotspots of European politics.[12]

The first known map commissioned by the French monarchy owed its creation to precisely this situation: the king wanted to know which passes to use to reach the Italian territories with his army. On the 'Carte d'Italie' printed in 1515, the Alps appeared from the 'Mons de Gaule' to 'S. Godard', and the accompanying text pointed out that Montgenèvre was preferable for crossing with guns (see section 3.1). On the other side, the German king and later Emperor Maximilian I did not tire of forging plans for his Italian policy and canvassing them in the Empire. Italy also had a special significance for his own Habsburg power base. Several Austrian hereditary lands which he had united under his rule bordered directly onto Venice. Moreover, a short time after his death in 1519, Milan fell to Spain, where the 'Casa d'Austria' reigned thanks to a marriage which Maximilian had initiated. Maximilian had no fixed residence, but moved from place to place with his court. In the last decades of his life, he very often stayed in a castle near Innsbruck. He loved hunting, and styled himself as a chamois hunter and the supreme huntsman of the Empire. He was buried in the church where he was baptised in the Vienna Neustadt, but a grave monument which he had helped to plan was later erected in Innsbruck. To this day, it remains one of the most impressive and artistically significant imperial graves on the continent.[13]

The struggle for power in Italy played out against a backdrop of important military and tax innovations and brought large parts of Europe together into a close community of conflict. In these circumstances, the process of state formation entered a new phase: in the sixteenth century, and especially from 1550, there was a rapid consolidation of territorial state institutions in the Alpine region, whose main features survived until the French Revolution – and, in part, beyond. Aside from this chronology, however, the Alpine territories had few similarities. It was precisely their differences that were striking, even simply geographically speaking: some two-thirds of the political units had possessed a residence or meeting place beyond the mountains since the onset of state formation; a third, however, were located entirely in the Alps. Some territories were transalpine and linked areas on either side of pass crossings; others, in contrast, lay only on one side of the Alpine ridge, and thus in a more particular sphere of influence.[14]

5.4 Communes, Nobles, Princes

The differences in internal constitution that evolved between the Alpine territories from the late Middle Ages are particularly interesting. Here, we can distinguish communal, noble and princely forms of regional constitutional development. In contemporary commentary and later historiography, the communal form attracted a great deal of attention. In his major work of 1576, Jean Bodin, the French constitutional theorist and defender of the divine right of kings, described the Three Leagues (later Grisons) as 'the most popularly governed of any Commonweale that is', on account of its widespread voting rights.[15] This high-altitude territory was indeed a relatively independent communal republic at the transition to modernity, with very localized power division and no clear centre. In the 1520s, the Grisons fought and won their peasants' war, and in the following decades largely abolished tithes and taxes. Until the introduction of cantonal taxation in the middle of the nineteenth century, the population paid no direct taxes to the federal state of some 200 communities. Communalization and small-scale decentralization formed the prevailing trend in the early modern period. The nobility had little formal support and depended on strong local backing.[16]

For Bodin and many of his contemporaries, democracy had a negative connotation. It meant inefficient and unjust mob rule. 'The lords of the three Cantons of the Grisons being more popular are the more subject unto seditions and sturres [sic]', he observed. Bodin classified confederate rural districts in a similar category: Uri, Schwyz, Unterwalden, Zug, Glarus, Appenzell, all found in the Alps or their foothills. Their adult citizens, according to Bodin's account, elected their authorities at public meetings by a show of hands, and sometimes forced their neighbours with raised fists to lift their hands. The constitutional theorist could reasonably have included the territory of the Valais, too. It became a communal republic like the Three Leagues, but retained the bishop as its formal head of state. Farther to the west, there was also the 'Grand Escarton' of Briançon. This transalpine communal association, long formed of five parts, was, however, required to pay an annual tax to the French king as the legal successor of a regional feudal lord.[17]

Whether all of these areas count as the communal type or not, in terms of the whole Alpine region its spread was limited. Noble and princely constitutional developments were considerably more significant in spatial terms. There, too, communes had great local importance, but within a different context and with less external prominence. In large parts of the Eastern Alps, the local community only formally emerged after the 1848 Revolution and the resulting constitution. The nobility here played a leading role in the early modern period. For example, the Carinthian estates, in which lords and knights dominated and peasants were not represented, were granted the town of Klagenfurt in 1518 by the Emperor. In Klagenfurt the estates found a permanent venue for their assemblies and soon created an efficient administration. The basic unit of the country was the noble manorial system, which was subjected to novel controls with the construction of state institutions and increased taxation. In a first phase, the regional nobility won considerable power through this, until central interventions from Vienna increased from around 1750.[18]

The Duchy of Savoy was exemplary of the princely constitutional development. It was part of the Savoyard–Piedmontese state formation which extended over the Alps into the northern Italian plain. In 1561, the last assembly of the three estates took place in Chambéry. After this, the Duke no longer engaged in negotiations with this traditional representative institution. Taxes were now unilaterally decreed and raised regularly. The princely centralism which made itself ever more strongly felt in the Duchy also affected the communes. They served as units of taxation and their financial situation became a public matter. Princely influence peaked in the communal regulation of 1738, an additional decree simultaneous to the tax edict. The regulation transferred formal power in the communes to a small council, which would co-opt members from among the most prosperous and capable, while general assemblies, insofar as they had met at all, were banned. 'Our authority is despotic', Duke Viktor Amadeus II had declared shortly beforehand. He meant that his authority in Savoy was not limited by any corporation, but was understood in a more general sense, not without reason.[19]

5.5 Trajectories of Regional Development

Power relations as they existed before the consolidation of territorial state institutions in the sixteenth century were a starting point for the respective paths of constitutional development. At that time there were influences from communes, nobles and princes in practically every region, but with very different forms and emphases. Where one power held particular importance, it stood a good chance of gaining further importance and dominating the remaining powers when it came to state formation. This political dynamic produced a regional and interregional process of differentiation. At the same time, these actors had interests of unequal extent and so of different potential for development. The most limited was the communal, and the greatest the princely potential. In the long run, however, communal organizations proved essential, whereas the nobility, which had possibly strengthened in the early modern period, receded. By around 1900, the development towards large nation states had brought about a separation between status-related and economic rights practically everywhere. There was no place for personal subservience in a national society of citizens.[20]

The French Revolution of 1789, and the period of the Napoleonic Wars which followed it, exerted a great influence on this process. There had been unrest and uprisings for a long while, but not on this scale. The Revolution brought a sudden enlargement and intensification of the political sphere. It also exemplified the coherence of the French kingdom as it had emerged during the early modern period. At that time, the king consistently referred to the regions as the 'provinces', and passed over their former rights in order to bind them more closely to the court. This also happened in the Dauphiné, most of which lay in the Alps. From the 1760s, new resistance arose there towards the tax policies and centralization efforts of the monarchy. In summer 1788, there was violent unrest in Grenoble, which temporarily forced the governor to flee. Without royal permission, an assembly of the Dauphiné general estates gathered in the nearby town of Vizille, opposing fiscal reform and demanding more rights, especially for the third estate. The assembly is considered one of the harbingers of the great upheavals of the following year. When, on 14 July 1789, the Bastille prison in Paris was stormed and the country was seized by general panic, the Alpine regions were involved in turn. Everywhere the alarm bells were rung, women and children were taken to safety, and men called to armed militias. This formed the start of an unusually deep and long-lasting politicization of society.[21]

The rapid expansion of the French revolutionary armies from 1792 initially contributed to this process. In the following twenty years, Napoleon Bonaparte and his entourage brought the greater part of the Alpine region under one more or less strong and constant rule. His crossing of the Great St Bernard Pass in May 1800 with an army of around 40,000 men and much heavy military equipment became famous. The official oil painting of this event shows the 30-year-old 'First Consul' on a fiery horse before an imposing mountain scene. At his feet, stone inscriptions name the few commanders in European history who succeeded in this heroic act: Hannibal – Charlemagne – Bonaparte (see section 3.1). Napoleon apparently shared the Enlightenment enthusiasm for mountains, which, especially in the case of the Alps, were identified with freedom and democracy. A few years after the crossing of the Pass, he said to a Helvetic delegation: 'It is the mountainous part of Switzerland which interests me. The small cantons are the only thing that I respect, the only thing that hinders me and the other powers from annihilating Switzerland; they alone make it interesting in the eyes of Europe.'[22] In contrast to Bodin, the monarchy was now caught in the crossfire of criticism. This gave a boost to democracy and made the relatively unchanged mountain region concerned into a political example.

While, in the years around 1800, there were well-organized, loyal revolutionaries in large parts of the Western Alps, in some other Alpine regions it was quite the reverse: resistance formed against French ideas and weapons. The uprising in Tyrol in 1809 became a kind of beacon for the emerging anti-Napoleonic war of liberation. The princely county had, as of late, been subordinate not to the house of Habsburg in Vienna, but to the French ally Bavaria. The new regime was not perceived positively, and made itself even more unpopular through modernization and land appropriation. The Vienna-coordinated uprising began in April and ended after a long series of battles and skirmishes in November, in a Tyrolean defeat. Shortly afterwards, Andreas Hofer, who had led the uprising, was executed by order of Napoleon, which subsequently made him into a martyr and romantic national folk hero.[23]

5.6 Drawing Borders from the Seventeenth to the Nineteenth Century

The formation of territorial and then nation states showed itself in impressive and often drastic ways on the borders of the important political units. From the perspective of the centres, the outer limit of their spheres of power needed special protection, on which a great deal was spent. Since the Alpine region was on its way to becoming an area with a high density of borders in the political as well as the geographical sense, the interventions of rulers had unusual impact there. This was first seen clearly in the Western Alps, where two states met who had taken up the cause of centralization early on: France and Savoy–Piedmont. For at least three centuries, there were repeated military confrontations and cessions of territory between them. The first large-scale mountain war was ended in 1602 by a peace agreement which made some ground-breaking decisions for the future course of the border. But the peace would prove short-lived, and after further conflicts the hardest battles in this section of the Alps followed at the beginning of the eighteenth century. In the context of the Spanish War of Succession, the merce-nary troops of Ludwig XIV and Viktor Amadeus II confronted one another over ten years. The peace treaty of Utrecht in 1713 brought an exchange of regions and relocated the border in the central section of the Western Alps along the watersheds.[24]

Mountains had already served for demarcation on earlier occasions in Europe, but the Peace of Utrecht was the first large-scale treaty in which geographical conditions were mentioned without historical endorsements. Later, this became more and more common. For exam-ple, in 1760, a treaty between France and Savoy sought to fix the border between the two states definitively, 'which fixing, as far as the territory may permit, will be established according to riverbeds or watersheds, and assisted by a rectification or exchange of different enclaves'. The territorialization of the border by means of the elimination of enclaves was prepared by military fortification lines, which had been erected on both sides for some time and at great expense. The use of mountains as 'natural borders' was easier, however, if one had only the general situ-ation in mind, and did not examine the course of the border in detail. The extensive cession of territory from Savoy and Nice to France in 1860 (as remuneration for support in the Italian unification movement) fulfilled such geo-strategic goals as far as military circles were con-cerned. However, the border across Mont Blanc which this necessitated remains contested to this day.[25]

For the local population, the location of the border had many consequences. In cases of conflict, endangered communes sometimes paid taxes or protection money to both sides. The new borders, drawn according to abstract geographical criteria, often had no regard for com-munal territory – for example, cutting off the Alpine pastures from the villages. Instead of resolving conflicts, this created more of them. The location of the border opened up a wide field of activity for smuggling, both petty and large-scale. In the middle of the eighteenth century, one smuggler band became famous. It contained up to 300 men, and shifted all manner of goods between France and Savoy–Piedmont: furs, leather, grain, tobacco, lead, dyed cloth, salt and colonial goods. At strategic points, the building of great fortresses and the increasing presence of the military altered the economy and everyday life in dramatic ways. In the nineteenth century, Briançon was practically turned into a single fortress; in the end, army personnel made up a fifth of the population of the region. The militarization of the high mountains also began at this time, with fortifications high up in the peaks and new special and elite troops. Italy created the *alpini* in 1872; France followed shortly after with the *chasseurs alpins*.[26]

5.7 'La Grande Guerra' (1915–1918)

By far the largest mountain war was fought not in the west, but in the east. The Kingdom of Italy – which emerged from the core state of Savoy–Piedmont – dissolved its alliance with Austria-Hungary in 1915 and declared war. It allied itself with the side of Great Britain, France and Russia, who had been at war with the German Empire and Austria-Hungary since the previous year. The Italian-Austrian front ran for 600 kilometres through the Eastern Alps, partly in very high mountains. As on other fronts of the First World War, unrelenting and deadly trench warfare now set in. With almost no regard for human life or topographical conditions, soldiers had to fight for the smallest territorial victories. The military leadership stationed them at altitudes of up to 3,500 metres, where they were exposed to extreme weather conditions. There was also tunnel warfare: miners dug long tunnels under enemy lines and blew up the mountains. The central section of the front lay in the valley of the river Isonzo/Soča in the Julian Alps of modern-day Slovenia. The Italian High Command wanted to force a breakthrough to the east and north here, and eleven times gave orders for large-scale but practically futile attacks. In the twelfth battle of Isonzo from October 1917, their own troops were then pushed back heavily. One year later, in new international circumstances, the tide turned, and the Italian army occupied large areas under the Habsburg monarchy in the Tyrolean, Friulian and Slovenian Alps.[27]

It is not known exactly how many victims this war claimed. But it is certain that it was a tragedy of the greatest magnitude. The number of dead, wounded and physically or mentally impaired soldiers exceeded

Figure 6   Chasseurs alpins *on Mont Blanc, 1901*

a million. Then there were hundreds of thousands of civilians who lost their lives as a result of material hardship, hunger, forced labour and other effects of war. There were innumerable evacuees, interned persons and prisoners of war. In the armies, draconian discipline was enforced. The civilian population was helpless at the mercy of the military leadership, especially in areas close to the front. When the inhabitants of the Isonzo Valley returned after the war, they found their settlements largely destroyed and the fields devastated. The shape of the mountains had changed as a result of incessant artillery fire. For every corpse that the returnees collected, they received 10 lira, and 1 lira for 10 kilos of barbed wire. Steel parts, brass and copper were higher in price, but harder to find.[28]

Austria-Hungary was broken up in the peace treaties of 1919. The Austrian part, with its Alpine region, made up one-eighth of the Habsburg dual monarchy. The Kingdom of Italy turned into a fascist dictatorship after a few years. To crowd Austria out of northern Italy, it had had to cede Savoy to France in 1860. After the First World War, the kingdom expanded north and east, so that the borders in Tyrol and Slovenia now also ran through the Alpine ridge. The only significant exception from this political territorial pattern was Switzerland, which remained a transalpine and federally constituted state. In retrospect, it appears that the paths to the nation state in this region followed different and more or less painful trajectories. To build the 'imagined' communities of nation states, much blood was spilled on their borders. The most terrible mountain war took place from 1915 to 1918 between Italy and Austria-Hungary. In Italy, in particular, this shaped the populations' image of the mountains. 'Oh mountain, for us you are sacred', sang the soldiers after the desperate defence of Monte Grappa, where in 1917 the luck of the war turned once more. Some spoke of a holy blood offering on the altar of the mountains. In the opinion of the Prime Minister, Italy had received its 'natural borders' from God.[29] To understand this emotional way of speaking, we must engage with the cultural dimension of Alpine history. This is the subject of the next two chapters.

6

RELIGIOUS CULTURE, EARLY SCIENCE

As recent cultural history has shown, it can be useful to treat religion and science as part of the same phenomenon in the premodern period. Christianity was one of the religions of the book, grounded in the Holy Scriptures. The clergy engaged in scientific studies, while scholars and naturalists had long been involved in the interpretation of religious texts. Both fields belonged to elite culture as well as – to varying extents – to the culture of a wider population. Moreover, both fields were part of a large-scale European network of communication and discussion. Considering premodern religion and science in the Alpine region within this framework also gives us a yardstick for its specificities.

6.1 Scholars' Tales

In 1811 – while Germany lay under Napoleonic rule – the young linguist and archaeologist Jacob Grimm remarked: 'In the high mountains, in self-contained valleys, there still lives a timeless meaning at its purest; in narrow villages, with few paths and no roads, where no false enlightenment has arrived or carried out its work, there still resides a hidden store of national customs, legends and faith.' Grimm wanted to recover this treasure, by bringing together 'all oral tales of the whole German fatherland' with the help of informants.[1] The undertaking was not carried out as planned, but in the end it was a success – far beyond the fatherland. A new epoch began in this field with the brothers Grimm and their generation. 'Tales' and other 'folklore' were now diligently collected, selected, edited and published. Those from the 'high mountains' were particularly popular: in 1858, Theodor Vernaleken, teacher and seminar director, published a volume of *Alpensagen [Alpine Tales]*, which he had collected in Switzerland and Austria from oral and written sources. Jacob Grimm also allowed Vernaleken to include his own fragments in the *Alpensagen*. In 1889, the collection by the writer and teacher Maria Savi-Lopez, the *Leggende delle Alpi [Legends of the Alps]*, appeared in Turin. It was also a voluminous work, dedicated to Her Majesty the Queen of Italy.[2] These are only two examples among a multitude of small- and large-scale initiatives.

We should not assume that these publication activities in the Romantic period exactly reproduced what people told each other in the past or the present. Research has convincingly shown that, in various ways, the collections of tales fell short of their claim to render oral folklore accessible. The collectors were generally selective, preferring, for instance, the mythological and demonological over other narrative material. The results were then often presented as residues of ancient, pre-Christian forms of belief. The oral had long been associated with the literary tradition. The tales already circulated in manuscripts and printed works of all kinds and so changed their form over and over again. One speaks of the 'mixed communication' of oral and literary traditions.[3] It is also easy to be misled about literacy rates in the mountains. True, low population density may have been an inhibiting factor, but the south and west of the Alps were subject to urban influence from early on (see sections 4.1, 5.1). In the Hautes Alpes, the teaching profession even developed into a speciality for migrants, who taught students in different destinations. In the early modern period, the mountain region was therefore among those with the highest literacy rates in France.[4]

The example of dragons illustrates that the relationship between tales and reality could also change during the early modern period. In sixteenth-century Europe, a serious dragon lore emerged which was initially based primarily on ancient and Christian traditions. While Roman sources depicted dragons as a particular kind of snake, in Christian writings they were given wings and interpreted as a sign of evil. In the sixteenth and seventeenth centuries, educated elites in many universities and other institutions engaged with the topic. Sources were checked, new witness accounts and material evidence (strange bones and carcasses) were collected, and hypotheses were devised regarding the appearance, lifestyle and breeding of dragons. In the first phase, the field of knowledge was strongly influenced by demonology, after which zoology gained in importance. In 1699, Johann Jakob Scheuchzer (1672–1733), Zurich's city doctor, well known for his early research trips in the Alps, sent a survey on the 'natural wonders' of Switzerland to his correspondents, in which he also asked about dragons. In 1723, he then compiled earlier and newly collected documents in a meticulous summary publication.[5]

Scheuchzer himself was unsure of the status of dragons. Some reports he held to be fables, untrue and fabricated. On another occasion, however, he stated that a region was so mountainous and so rich in caves 'that it would be strange indeed if there were no dragons there'. Scepticism in the European scholarly world had been growing very generally for some time. When Scheuchzer's main work was re-published in 1746, the editor added a cautionary note to the chapter on dragons. Those who knew the nature of 'superstitious and credulous people, especially in times gone by', would not be surprised by these stories. And, in an edition of 1764, the dragon chapter was omitted altogether, citing earlier misbelief and superstition unworthy of the enlightened present as the justification.[6] Dragons only enjoyed a revival under the new sign of Romanticism, for example in the case of Jacob and Wilhelm Grimm, who held dragons to be a product of ancient folk literature and attributed a spiritual significance to them. In their *Deutsche Sagen* *[German Tales]* of 1816, they also included Scheuchzer's dragon reports and wrote in admiration that '[t]he Alpine people of Switzerland have preserved many legends of terrible dragons and mighty serpents that once lived in the mountains many years ago. They frequently descended into the valleys, where they wreaked havoc and destruction.'[7]

6.2 Witches' Sabbaths – an Alpine invention?

The affinity of the dragon discourse to the Alps, and especially to the Swiss Alps, was based on common assumptions about the habitat of the animal (lonely mountain caves) and the literary tradition (the above-average density of dragons in Swiss chronicles and natural science). The discourse on witches operated somewhat differently, and also concerned the Alpine region in a particular way. Modern research shows that the oldest fifteenth-century writings identifying a new devilish sect refer to the Western Alps. The suspected area stretched from the Dauphiné over the Savoyard territories into the Bernese Oberland. The Pope observed in 1440 that Savoy was crawling with witches, sorcerers and Waldensians. They had caused the Duke of Savoy – recently appointed antipope at the Council of Basel – to set himself up against the authority of the church. The Western Alps and their surrounding areas had in fact been unsettled for some time. After a series of trials against suspects of all sorts, the idea of a new kind of conspiracy against Christendom established itself among several observers and participants. This 'witches' Sabbath' seemed to them far more dangerous than traditional forms of heresy and black magic (or *maleficium*). They imagined nightly orgies at which a hidden sect met with Satan, worshipped him obscenely and wished to annihilate the Christian world in league with him.[8]

Up to the eighteenth century, this suggestive image of the enemy legitimated witch-hunts, which claimed the lives of tens of thousands in Europe, and especially in Germany. It is hard to say why the phenomenon emerged in this area in particular in the 1430s. During the Great Schism (1378–1417), there had always been two popes, one in Rome and one across the Western Alps in Avignon. Even at that time, the area seems to have had a certain strategic significance, which was borne out at the Council of Basel with the election of the Savoyard antipope. There were also internal developments which heightened political and religious tensions in society. But the witches' Sabbath was above all the result of a many-voiced demonological and theological discourse, and its protagonists were mostly from elsewhere. 'In the first years it seemed necessary to situate the Sabbath in an Alpine and isolated scenery', writes one expert. The mountain world apparently offered a suitable background for horror stories, as it was seen as a refuge for the demonic spirit world at the edges of Christendom, as well as for the apostates who had turned their backs on the official church.[9]

It has also been suggested that the witch hunt in the mountains might

have particular climatic causes. The high points of the European persecution in the 1580s and 1620s coincided with an increase in climatically
determined harvest failures, which made the accusation of organized
weather magic and black magic plausible. This may also have been the
case in the Alpine region, but not necessarily to a greater degree than
usual: so far, neither a particular magnitude of harvest failures nor a
particular intensity of persecution has been empirically documented
(see section 4.5).[10] There are many indications that the question of
witches was handled very differently by different courts and authorities. When, in 1485, the Dominican monk Heinrich Kramer returned
from Italy, where he had obtained a bull from the Pope authorizing the
inquisition of witches in Germany, he tried to initiate an exemplary
prosecution in Innsbruck. But his procedure seemed so unjustified to
the local elites that he was expelled. This failed prosecution prompted
Kramer to write the *Hexenhammer* [*Hammer of Witches*], which became
the most important handbook of demonological repression and was
republished many times. The Tyrolean administration, on the other
hand, subsequently steered a careful and restrained course regarding
witchcraft accusations.[11]

In the sixteenth century, the Roman Inquisition became responsible for many Italian Alpine areas. In general, the Inquisition also
favoured a controlled approach, and restrained local zealots. Some
famous micro-historical studies by Carlo Ginzburg investigate special
inquisition processes in Friuli. For example, Paolo Gaspurotto from
the region of Cividale attracted the interest of the clerical authorities from 1575, because he knew remedies for sicknesses caused by
black magic. Furthermore, he called himself a *benandante*, a 'good
walker', and on certain nights held battles with evil sorcerers and
witches for the good of the community. In the course of the inter-
rogation, the 'night walker' was himself labelled as a witch by the
Inquisitors. He and other *benandanti* got away with their lives. Things
went less well for the miller Domenico Scandella, called Menocchio,
from Montereale Valcellina. He was denounced in 1583 by the Holy
Office, because he had expressed heretical ideas. He believed that in
the beginning the world was a chaos of earth, air, water and fire. Just
like cheese from milk, a mass was formed from the chaos, and in it
worms appeared: they were the angels and the Lord God! These and

other beliefs eventually cost the miller his head. He was executed by papal order.[12]

Much later, Anna Göldin shared a similar fate in the Protestant part of Glarus. According to the report of the *Zürcher Zeitung* [*Zurich News*] on 9 February 1782, she stood accused of a 'monstrous act'. She was supposed to have used pins to bewitch the daughter of a magistrate, whom she served as a maid. Anna Göldin entered history as the 'last witch'. Her short trial avoided the term 'witchcraft', which had always been contested and had become disreputable in the eighteenth century. Her execution caused outrage, and was described as a judicial murder even at the time.[13] For those who necessarily connect belief in witchcraft with backwardness, the context is irritating. For Glarus was by no means an isolated mountain valley, and, with its cottage industry, belonged to those regions already producing for a global market.

6.3 Confessional Tensions

The invention of the witches' Sabbath in the fifteenth century seems to have been an expression of rising religious concern. Such a trend made itself felt in several domains in the late Middle Ages, and was one of the factors that led in the early sixteenth century to the Reformation and division of the Western church. In the second half of the century, this led to the formation of confessional churches primarily supported by territorial states, according to the principle *cuius regio, eius religio* ('whose realm, his religion'). The Roman Catholic and reformed Protestant confessions developed in conflictual but not dissimilar ways. External demarcation and internal moral discipline played an important role here; the word and the Scriptures gained in importance in religious practice. In our area, the conflicts may have been of particular importance. In the sixteenth century, the Alps became a border zone between the Roman church to the south and the Protestant territories to the north. In the Alpine region itself, nearly all areas remained Catholic or were re-Catholicized after a multi-confessional period. Only in the Bernese Oberland and in eastern Switzerland (parts of the Grisons, Glarus, St Gallen and Appenzell) did the Reformation win the upper hand in the long term (see section 1.6).[14] In view of the overall situation, the mixed position of confessions is of primary interest.

We will outline this with the help of the history of the Grisons and Carinthia.

The Reformation in the Grisons was both a factor in and an indicator of the pronounced localism which dominated this territory and increased from the sixteenth century. Power was so little centralized that decisions about faith fell to individual communes and courts. A colourful patchwork of confessions therefore emerged. The majority of the diocese of the bishop of Chur converted to the new faith and so dispensed with his authority. By voting for or against the Reformation, they could also emancipate dependent neighbourhoods and acquire communal status. As a result of demarcations between and within confessions, the number of parishes increased in the early modern period from around 100 to a good 200. Most were confessionally uniform. In only a dozen parishes did Protestants and Catholics live together in the same place on the basis of an accord. Both local events and the integration of the Grisons into European politics caused conflict. A recent study distinguished different phases of confessional conflict between 1580 and 1740. These led once again to crucial tests for the federal state and cost several hundred lives.[15]

Nevertheless, there is a question of how far the formative power of religion reached. Interconfessional marriages seem to have occurred repeatedly up to the early seventeenth century; afterwards, they were exceptional for a long while. There are many reports of conversions. These were exploited for propaganda purposes, especially in the case of prominent people. When Catholics and Protestants met each other in everyday life, however, religious issues did not have to play a part. At the annual fair, for example, teasing between neighbouring communes with different confessions did not necessarily exceed the usual levels when dealing with others. Religion was indeed ubiquitous in the public sphere and official moral politics. But this does not mean that all people were constantly inspired by religious zeal. In 1709, an Engadin pastor published a detailed document against sleeping in church, in which he also named common justifications. Sleeping during the sermon was only a little sin, it was said in the village. It was a widespread issue which was little regarded and harmed no one. Yes, it was better to sleep than to stay awake and have one's heart filled with greed, fornication and vengeance.[16]

In the sixteenth century, the Reformation won many adherents in the Eastern Alps. Carinthia with its landed nobility and large farms was thus for the most part Protestant, when in 1600 and 1628 the Habsburg prince decreed the old faith for the Duchy. The nobility too now faced an alternative: conversion or emigration. Soon the country was officially re-Catholicized. However, under the surface of baroque Catholicism, there were also groups oriented towards Lutheranism through family prayers and a pronounced culture of the book. This was a little-institutionalized, illegal lay Christianity. Externally, one was a Catholic; internally, one remained a Protestant. In some regions, the existence of this 'clandestine Protestantism' was an open secret. At the beginning of the eighteenth century, the Carinthian authorities estimated the number of adherents at 20,000, almost a tenth of the population. At that time, they increasingly felt the need to confess their faith in public, too. After the mass expulsion of Salzburg Protestants in 1731 (see section 1.6), tensions heightened in Carinthia and other Habsburg hereditary lands, and sanctions ensued. Non-Catholics were to be brought to reason through mission stations and conversion houses. Where this failed, the authorities also resorted to deportation.[17]

On close examination, however, it is apparent in this case too that there were different forms of confessional coexistence, tolerance or indifference. Religious identities remained multidimensional and changeable. When the Enlightenment Emperor Joseph II, who had long set himself against the deportation of Protestants, became sole Regent, he issued a patent of toleration in 1781. However, he wanted it to apply only to Lutherans and Calvinists, and not to elusive 'enthusiasts'. Moreover, Catholicism should adopt a sober, 'reasonable' character. This also held for church furnishings, whose baroque splendour was now unpopular. But the population often thought otherwise. So, for instance, in the Carinthian village Eisenkappel, where the statue of Mary was to be 'stripped' of her festive skirts, a long-lasting feud with Vienna ensued which almost culminated in actual military action.[18]

6.4 The Sacred Theory of the Earth

An important aspect of the older cultural history of the Alpine region is its depiction in the form of travel reports, landscape descriptions, works of cartography, and scientific and theological speculation. From the late Middle Ages, such writings can be found in increasing numbers; growth was particularly strong in the sixteenth century and even more so in the eighteenth. They formed the foundation of the later tourist development of the area.[19] Some well-known examples are noteworthy from the broad spectrum of these texts.

- *De alpibus commentarius* by Josias Simler, 1574: the *Commentary on the Alps* is thought to be the oldest specialized tract on the topic. It is based on ancient and contemporary texts. Simler, a Zurich clergyman and scholar, had never seen the mountains. He planned a detailed description of the whole Swiss confederation and her allied territories. But in his eyes 'all Helvetia [was] an Alpine region and in this way rich in natural wonders'. So he compiled a general Alpine description and appended it straight onto the first regional monograph on the Valais.[20]

- *Journal du voyage de Michel de Montaigne en Italie par la Suisse & l'Allemagne en 1580 & 1581* [*Journal of the Voyage of Michel de Montaigne by Way of Italy through Switzerland & Germany in 1580 & 1581*]: the journal of an Italian voyage by this French humanist and essayist was partially edited by his secretary and first published in 1774. Montaigne had little time for clichés, and trusted to his own powers of judgement. He had always distrusted negative travel reports, he stated after crossing the Brenner, but now he was fully persuaded of their stupidity. Contrary to such reports, his own journey over the Alps was without difficulty and left pleasant impressions.[21]

- *Die Ehre des Herzogthums Crain. Das ist, wahre, gründliche, und recht eigendliche Belegen- und Beschaffenheit dieses [. . .] bishero nie annoch recht beschriebenen Römisch-Keyserlichen herrlichen Erblandes* [*The Glory of the Duchy of Carniola. That is the True, Thorough and Correct Site and Condition of this . . . Hitherto Never Rightly Described Wonderful Roman-Imperial Hereditary Land*] by Johann Weichard von Valvasor, 1689: this aristocratic universal scholar described the area of modern-day Slovenia from all perspectives in this multi-volume work. Valvasor was a member of the Royal Society in England and a critical observer. On the dragon question, for example, he took a sceptical position early on.[22]

Parallel to the increase in travel reports and landscape descriptions from the late fifteenth century, the number of cartographical works which mapped smaller or larger parts of the Alps also increased. The up-turn in the decades around 1600 was striking. One example of this is the 1591 *Provenciae descriptio* (*Description of Provence*), published by a royal judge. While up to that point only a few Provençal place names had been captured on maps, this work recorded several hundred. They were primarily settlements and pass routes; only exceptionally were mountains named. Cartographic coverage was closely connected to the stabilization of territorial states. The Alps, therefore, generally appeared only as a function of the political units concerned. Overall, however, cartographical works brought about a multiplication of printed geographical knowledge by as early as the eighteenth century.[23]

At the close of the seventeenth century, the mountains awakened particular interest in natural history and theology. The trigger was the work *The Sacred Theory of the Earth* by Thomas Burnet, the first volume of which appeared in 1681 and was soon available in several languages. In this work, the Cambridge-trained clergyman brought together the biblical story of creation with elements of the new science: God created the earth with a flat surface in a perfect oval form; only the Flood, brought about through the sinfulness of man, burst the shell of the earth asunder and left behind chaotically shaped and scattered mountains. Burnet's theory triggered an international controversy involving many of rank and reputation in the republic of letters.[24] The debate over 'natural theology' or 'physical theology' initiated the first opening of anthropocentric Christianity to the environment. Through this, the wonders of creation obtained a new religious value (see section 7.5). Mountains also gained in interest, because they offered a key to geological history. How, for instance, should the 'figured stones' (fossils) which were repeatedly found there be interpreted? Did they provide a glimpse back to the young, newly created world before the Flood? These were the questions that motivated the Zurich naturalist Johann Jakob Scheuchzer when he undertook annual Alpine trips with his students from 1700 and shared the results at great speed with his colleagues throughout Europe.

This and other research created the preconditions for the organized admiration of nature, which from the eighteenth century changed the perception of the Alps forever. As the following chapter shows, there were also other forerunners.

7

THE PERCEPTION OF THE ALPS

Writing the history of the perception of the Alps entails tracing and categorizing changes in the conceptions of the mountains as precisely as possible. These conceptions were articulated, in the modern period especially, at an individual as well as a collective, stereotypical level. Stereotypes are better than their reputation. On first orientation, everyone is dependent on cultural patterns before they can create their own differentiated, and where possible superior, picture of particular points. With our academic intentions, however, we rely on differentiation from the outset, and should avoid doubling historical stereotypes through stereotypical interpretations. As a check, we must always ask: how characteristic and widespread were particular ideas? Were there alternative concepts at the same time? How did social and ideal positions relate to one another?

7.1 Mont Inaccessible (1492)

In the year of our Lord 1492, on 26 July, the Lord Antoine de Ville, Lord of Domjulien, Beaupré, Montélimar and Saou, chamberlain and adviser to the King, in the name and at the order of the King and Dauphin Charles VIII, climbed the mountain which the local people usually call *Aiguille* [Needle] or *Mont Inaccessible* [Inaccessible Mountain], and which lies in our Dauphiné.

So begins the record of the notary who described and certified the undertaking. With the help of ladders as in a military siege, Antoine de Ville and two dozen people – among them priests, servants and local notables – managed to climb the steep faces. Up above, the mountain was solemnly taken possession of for the French king. The priests baptized it in honour of the holy Charlemagne, read masses and erected three crosses. The company remained for several days on the flat, flower-filled mountain pasture. The lord even ordered a house to be built, and locals brought up rabbits, which immediately made themselves at home. But the text also refers to the courage which the seizure of the mountain required: 'It is terrible to look at and even more terrible in the ascent and descent.'[1]

The expedition was announced by letter to the speakers of the Parliament of Grenoble, and the 'inaccessible mountain' ranked among the kingdom's most-noted natural monuments up to the eighteenth century. Its special form – an imposing tooth of rock, flat and green on top – had already given rise to legends. It is thought that the mountain was related to medieval conceptions of earthly paradise as a high, enclosed garden. Charles VIII (1470–98) knew the area from earlier hunting parties and a pilgrimage. The exact motive for his order is not known, but the political and military context is unmistakeable. Later, the relationship to the monarchy also remained important. For instance, in 1701, Mont Inaccessible was used in a tract to portray Ludwig XIV in the appropriate light ('No mortal can ever reach it . . .'). After the July Revolution in 1830, it became entangled in the battle between royalists and republicans. First, a team staged a re-enactment of the royal occupation of 1492, again with priests. Two weeks later, another group made fun of this act, playing a game of boules on top of the mountain and singing the Marseillaise, among other things.[2]

At almost 2,100 metres, this Western Alpine mountain is not very high. More generally, height was not an important, precisely measured or measurable criterion for the evaluation of mountains at the transition to modernity. But with the scientific, cultural and technical developments of the early modern period, this criterion was brought more and more to the fore. Initially, the highest Alpine peaks were taken variously to be St Gotthard, because it is the source of several large rivers, and the Rocciamelone and the Monte Viso, which are visible from the Piedmontese plain. The Gotthard is not a mountain at all, but a pass, and none of the three reaches 4,000 metres, as a good eighty mountains in the Alpine region are now known to do. This mountain region gained increasing attention from the eighteenth century. In the years before 1780, naturalists from Geneva and England proved, using barometric and trigonometric measurements, that Mont Blanc is the highest mountain in the Alps (some even speculated in the whole Old World). At the same time, and as part of the same process, the glaciers and peaks of this region became points of interest for early tourists.[3]

7.2 From the Grand Tour to Tourism

Many forms of mobility were practised in premodern society. A prominent and well-documented one was the educational trips of the elites, often called the Grand Tour. This led young nobles and other members of the upper classes to the courts and cities of Europe, usually for long periods. From the end of the Middle Ages, a large-scale travel system emerged with customary routes and its own advice literature. Italy, in particular, had a great deal to offer: ancient heritage, famous cities, great art. To reach this attractive country, travellers from the north generally had to cross the Alps. For a long while, this crossing was treated more as a necessary evil. But, in the eighteenth century, the mountain landscape obtained an intrinsic value which was socially recognized. An example of this change is William Windham's expedition to the foot of Mont Blanc. The well-off Englishman and his tutor set out on a European tour in 1737. After many stages, the two arrived at Geneva, where in 1740/1 they established a cultural coterie together with compatriots. When a British Oriental traveller joined the group, they decided to explore the relatively close glacier in Chamonix. From a mountaintop, the visitors looked out over the main glacier, which seemed to them like a windswept, then suddenly frozen, sea. They also descended onto this 'sea of ice' and there drank to the victory of British arms in the current naval war with Spain.[4]

A good fifty years later, a simple stone construction described as a 'temple of nature' already stood on the peak above the Mer de Glace,

Figure 7   *Illustration of the Windham report on Chamonix, 1742*

from which the famous and now popular natural wonder could be admired. This rapid expansion of the cultural repertoire was noted and discussed by many contemporaries. Thus, one Enlightenment newspaper stated in 1782 that, until ten or twelve years before, well-off and educated travellers were only interested in cultural heritage like ruins, sculptures and paintings, which were primarily found in Italy. Since then, however, they had discovered the love of nature. Researchers in their quest for new observations and philosophers hoping to rediscover the unspoiled customs of early times led the way. The Swiss confederation with its many mountains therefore became an interesting place, and one could 'with great likelihood assume that in future Switzerland will not be among the least visited lands of Europe'.[5]

In fact, travel in Switzerland, which primarily consisted of mountain scenery, grew ever more popular and soon became the fashion. Such trips increased more than eightfold between 1750 and 1790, as estimated from the number of published travel reports. The area most frequently visited was between Central Switzerland and Chamonix in Savoy, which was often counted as part of Switzerland. For example, once Alexander von Humboldt had crossed St Gotthard from Italy on his second Alpine journey at the end of August 1795, he went first to Lucerne and into the Bernese Oberland to Grindelwald (visiting glaciers) and Lauterbrunnen (a famous waterfall). After visiting a few towns, he then left Geneva in other company for the valley of Chamonix (glaciers, Mont Blanc), passed from there to the Great St Bernard, then via the Swiss plateau back to Lauterbrunnen and Grindelwald, up St Gotthard and to Lucerne. His two-month journey was determined by personal purposes, but in many ways kept to the conventional sights: particular glaciers, waterfalls, mountain panoramas and viewpoints. As far as the latter were concerned, Rigi by Lucerne soon established itself as the most important travel destination. An expert declared it 'one of the most beautiful mountains in Switzerland, and a wonderful observation point, whose outlook is with good reason so famous and frequented'. It was here in 1871 that the much-admired first rack railway in Europe was laid.[6]

In the meantime, the industrialization of the travel business set in, and with it the birth of modern tourism. Decisive impulses came from England, where economic development produced middle classes who could rival aristocratic families and their international lifestyle earlier than in other parts of Europe. New transport technologies, broadened economic possibilities and opportunities, particular cultural ideas and the need for cachet in the British Empire combined, as Laurent Tissor says, to form a 'socio-technical system', and generated unprecedented momentum. The pioneer of travel providers, Thomas Cook, also organized trips in the Alps after the mid-century. At this point, prices which had already been lowered through the construction of the railway network were once more considerably reduced. From the 1830s, publishers launched a new generation of informative, up-to-date guidebooks. At first, some fifteen new English guidebooks on Switzerland appeared each year. By the 1890s, this number had risen to no fewer than eighty-five new editions and publications annually.[7]

Now it was not *travellers* who were en route, but *tourists*. The term emerged in English around 1800 and was later adopted into other languages. Shortly before the French Revolution, the term 'Switzerland' also began to be transferred to other regions as a description of landscape (as with Saxon and Franconian Switzerland). In the early phase of Alpine tourism, those who wanted to praise an area to strangers had to claim that it matched or surpassed Switzerland.[8] This selective, philhelvetic view of the Alps did not mean that there were no travellers elsewhere. For centuries, the most-used route had been the Brenner Pass, where relevant infrastructure also developed early on. And then in the nineteenth and twentieth centuries, modern landscape-related tourism spread here and there across the whole Alpine region (see sections 8.4, 9.2). As an industry which depended on fashion, tourism always thrived on the cultural models and inspirations offered above all by poets and painters.

7.3 Poets and Painters

Did the Italian humanist Francesco Petrarch really climb Mont Ventoux in Provence on 26 April 1336, or did he only climb the mountain in the artful letter he later composed? Although research has long considered this question, answers vary.[9] In contrast, it is generally known that Friedrich Schiller took local details from already available descriptions when writing his 1804 drama *Wilhelm Tell*, set in Central Switzerland. He had never set foot in the area himself. In the case of the English Romantic William Wordsworth, imagination seems to have suffered under reality: in the autobiographical poem the *Prelude*, first published in 1850, he complained that the peak's 'soulless' appearance had destroyed his earlier 'living' image of the highest Alpine peak. Thomas Mann had the idea of writing his novel *Der Zauberberg* [*The Magic Mountain*] during his wife's stay at a rest home in Davos in 1912. He knew the atmosphere in the strongholds of the Alpine sanatoria through her letters and one personal visit.

So poetry and experience blended in every possible way. But the Petrarchan letter from the fourteenth century reminds us that mountains and the Alps have been a subject of European literature since its early phases. There are examples of this from the Renaissance to the Romantic, realist and experimental genres of the modern period. For example, there were descriptions of mountains and mountain journeys in the Swiss confederation and Tyrol composed in Latin. The scholar Marc Lescarbot chose the French language when he published a *Tableau de la Suisse* [*Picture of Switzerland*] in 1618 in alexandrines. He portrayed the Alps as a beautiful and magnificent landscape whose heights were nevertheless terrifying. A similarly mixed picture was presented shortly after 1700 by the Hamburg writer Barthold Heinrich Brockes in his collection of poetry *Irdisches Vergnügen in Gott* [*Earthly Delight in God*]:

Let us bring GOD a sacrifice
And, to raise up His omnipotence,
Extol the creation of the mountains,
Which are so terribly beautiful,
That they delight us
Yet also bewilder us,
Their greatness excites our desire
Their sheerness daunts the heart.[10]

Two eighteenth-century literary works are traditionally strongly associated with the turn towards the Alps: the nearly 500-line didactic poem *Die Alpen* [*The Alps*] by Albrecht von Haller, first published in 1732; and the French novel *Julie ou la nouvelle Heloïse* [*Julie or the New Heloise*] by Jean-Jacques Rousseau, which on its first publication in 1761 still bore the full title *Lettres de deux amans, habitans d'une petite ville au pied des Alpes* [*Letters from Two Lovers, Living in a Little Town at the Feet of the Alps*]. Both works were critical of civilization and fed on the contrast between an immoral society and intact nature (see sections 4.8, 5.2). Both were issued many times. While the epistolary novel immediately became a bestseller of the first order, it was a good twenty years before the didactic poem became famous. Apparently, it took the trends of the pre-revolutionary period to make the material socially acceptable. Regarding sales and attention, however, the children's books *Heidis Lehr- und Wanderjahre* [*Heidi: Her Years of Wandering and Learning*] and *Heidi kann brauchen, was es gelernt hat* [*Heidi: How She Used What She Learned*] by Johanna Spyri, from the years 1880/1, eclipsed everything else. The Heidi books enjoyed a practically uninterrupted print run. Later, they were adapted into numerous films and became a global success from the United States to Japan. The Alps appeared in Spyri as a pure, almost timeless refuge, without serious problems and modernization crises. A similar view was held by many articles which appeared in the new general interest magazines. The German *Die Gartenlaube* [*Arbour*], founded in 1853, particularly excelled in this regard.[11]

From the middle of the eighteenth century, as mentioned above, there was a rapid increase in Alpine travel reports. Some of them emanated from famous authors like Johann Wolfgang Goethe or Heinrich Heine. Together with new poems, novels, stories and reportage, they made the Alps into a literary landscape. On the one hand, the mountains were freshly invoked again and again; on the other, certain parts of the mountains (and by no means all of them) received continuous attention.[12] In visual culture, a similar trend emerged from the Renaissance onwards. Here too, a long list of famous painters can be given who engaged with mountain themes, for a short while or a lifetime, from Albrecht Dürer and Pieter Bruegel the Elder in the fifteenth and sixteenth centuries to J. M. W. Turner, Ferdinand Hodler and Paul Cézanne at the beginning of the modern period. The period of great, dramatic Alpine paintings was the nineteenth century, when the leading art critic John Ruskin described the mountains as 'cathedrals of the earth'. For the public, however, the many images intended for mass distribution, such as the serially produced coloured graphic prints, may have been at least as important as high art. A striking example is the Alpine panoramic wallpaper which was produced industrially in the first half of the nineteenth century. In the flat Netherlands and elsewhere, there were families at that time who were surrounded in their parlours day in and day out by the artfully arranged mountains of the Bernese Oberland.[13]

7.4 Competition on the Peaks

In 1786, the Chamonix crystal seeker and chamois hunter Jacques Balmat, together with the doctor Michel-Gabriel Paccard, succeeded in climbing Mont Blanc for the first time. However, the Genevan naturalist Horace-Bénédict de Saussure was publicly credited as the first climber for a long while. A quarter of a century before, he had announced a reward for the climb, and made it to the summit himself with a large pack in 1787. As he later recalled, he finally saw his heart's

Figure 8   *Sunrise on Mount Rigi with tourists, 1810*

desire: the countless mountaintops whose order had occupied him for so long. He stayed for more than four hours on the summit and carried out experiments and measurements with the help of his attendants. Saussure had already attracted attention with the first volume of his scientific and literary *Voyages dans les Alpes* [*Travels in the Alps*] in 1779. By the time he completed the work in 1796, he was a celebrity. The same thing happened in the case of women: in 1838, Mont Blanc was climbed by a French noblewoman who knew how to exploit her success journalistically, although a local woman had reached the summit thirty years before (Henriette d'Angeville, Marie Paradis). This indicates that a 'first ascent' in the eighteenth and nineteenth centuries often meant a first publication, and that incipient Alpinism was driven not least by competition for social status.[14]

The word 'Alpinist' entered European languages in the 1870s. It replaced expressions like 'Alpine traveller', and also distinguished its adherents from regular 'tourists'. The creation of the word suggests that the conquest of the heights was entering a new phase at that time. In the second half of the eighteenth century, 86 first ascents entered the annals of Alpinism; in the first half of the nineteenth century, 210; and in its second half, 1,010. As mentioned, these were only the documented cases; some mountains may already have been climbed by local crystal seekers, chamois hunters or Alpine shepherds more or less incidentally. By around 1900, most of the main peaks in the Alpine region were classed as 'conquered', and elite mountaineers had begun to look around other continents for fresh targets.[15] In the second half of the nineteenth century, Alpinism also entered its organized phase. In 1857, the British founded their Alpine Club, and in the following years similar associations developed in all countries. The Schweizer Alpen-Club [Swiss Alpine Club] (1863), the Club Alpino di Torino or Italiano [Alpine Club of Turin or Italy] (1863/7) and the Club alpin français [French Alpine Club] (1874) were all established. In Austria and Germany, mountaineering associations had already been formed in 1862 and in 1869, respectively, which then established the Deutscher und Österreichischer Alpenverein [German and Austrian Alpine Club] in 1873.[16]

Although the trend towards organized mountaineering was trans-national, and the ambitions of the new middle classes had so clear an impact on it, individual clubs presented themselves differently. They were also characterized by the national contexts in which they emerged, and so did not pursue identical goals. The British Alpine Club formed in the context of a Mont Blanc fever which broke out in 1852 and kept London on tenterhooks for a year. An entertainer who had climbed the highest Alpine peak the previous year started a show in Piccadilly which inspired a mass audience with the high mountains, and, according to *The Times*, was soon as firm a local attraction as Westminster Abbey. However, the founders of the Alpine Club wanted to differentiate themselves from this. To be admitted and selected, a new member had to show either skill as a mountaineer or mountain-related literary or artistic merit. Not without reason, the association was soon dubbed 'a club for gentlemen who also climb'. The Deutscher und Österreichischer Alpenverein presented itself very differently. According to one founder, it should 'unite all admirers of the sublime Alpine world'. This included women, who were excluded by the British gentlemen for more than a hundred years. Size varied according to these different orientations: while, shortly after 1900, the

British club had nearly 700 members, the younger German–Austrian club already had nearly 80,000.[17]

In the course of the nineteenth century, mountaineering changed from an exploratory activity rooted in natural science to a competitive sport with its own constantly re-negotiated rules. The 1871 collection of articles on mountain trips, *The Playground of Europe* by Leslie Stephen, is typical of this change. The well-read and highly educated author, sensitive to aesthetic impressions, became president of the British Alpine Club without presenting himself as a naturalist. The book was partly a justification of his dangerous passion, which was claiming ever more victims. The most sensational case had taken place a few years before on the Matterhorn: the young British mountaineer Edward Whymper, originally sent to the Alps by a publisher as an illustrator, climbed the steep mountain peak for the first time together with companions, in direct competition with an Italian group. On the descent, however, four team members lost their lives. The incident was made into a moral question by the European public and widely discussed. Stephen had his own ideas on Alpinistic ability, courage and recklessness. He had also experienced difficult moments, which he depicted fictionally in his essay 'A Bad Five Minutes in the Alps': 'Grim and fierce, like some primeval giant, that peak looked to me, and for a time the whole doctrine preached by the modern worshippers of sublime scenery seemed inexpressibly absurd and out of place.'[18]

7.5 'Delightful Horror'

At this point, we should pause and look back over the different actors in the history of the perception of the Alps. This history can be arranged schematically into several phases. Initially, there was the everyday experience of the local population and the travellers who occasionally or routinely crossed the Alpine region. Afterwards, travellers strayed from the beaten track more and more often. At first came visitors who were interested in botany, cartography, geology and other branches of natural science, for personal, scientific or political and military reasons. On their heels followed travellers who were enthused by the Alps for touristic or Alpinistic reasons. They were also inspired by archetypes from poetry and painting, which had been early contributors to this cultural

Figure 9   *Early Alpinism – W. A. B. Coolidge and his team, 1874*

expansion. In the nineteenth century, some nature-oriented intellectuals began to reflect upon the change whose result they were. In doing so, they generally drew a sharp distinction between 'ancient' and 'modern' perceptions. Soon their view also found its way into mass media. Thus, the widely distributed illustrated family journal *Die Gartenlaube* claimed in 1889 that the historical perception of the Alps had been the exact opposite of the current one: 'Snowy mountains were found unattractive and frightening, they were not admired, they were not enjoyed either – they were only goggled at in dismay as something monstrous.' Those who had to cross the Alps made their wills beforehand.[19]

This dichotomous presentation of avoidance and affection flattered the self-esteem of the industrial and imperialist century of 'progress', and continues to be passed down to the present day in popular Alpine literature. In opposition to this, however, we must insist on the complexity of the history of perception. As specialist research shows, in the sources we find a diversity of:

1. *Voices* The discourse on the Alps never formed a homogene-
ous whole. Even at those times when enthusiasm ran high, there
were dissenting voices. A famous example is François-René de
Chateaubriand, who in 1805 found the Alps ugly – in an emphatic
and politically motivated dismissal of Rousseau and his adherents.[20]
2. *Genres* The different genres of text followed their own rules to
some extent, and created different views of the mountains. Between
1750 and 1815, for example, German journalism reported on the
Alps in a restrained, sober and critical way, while rapturous lyrics
abounded in poetry.[21]
3. *Readings* The reception of texts is harder to deduce, but here too
there is a variety to be reckoned with. This is illustrated by the early
onset of the near interminable reinterpretation of Petrarch's mountain letter. Today, the majority of readers from an Alpinistic milieu
believe that the Italian humanist did indeed climb Mont Ventoux in
the fourteenth century, while literary scholars perceive the text as an
artistic construct (see section 7.3).[22]

Either way, Mont Ventoux is represented in the letter in an ambiguous way, with positive as well as negative connotations and evaluations.
Such a mixed picture can be traced across the centuries, sometimes in
one and the same text, sometimes across a range of different texts. There
are reports in which the fear of travellers at pass crossings is credibly
portrayed, but there are not many of them. Fear was a perfectly real but
by no means general feeling, and it did not cease with the turn towards
the Alps after 1750. It is also found in later texts, not least in those by
Alpinists who consciously sought out danger. In certain phases, the
cultivated public actively sought after what the English called 'delightful horror'. There are some indications that post-revolutionary taste
tended in this direction.[23] I know of no more pertinent paintings than
those of J. M. W. Turner. In the decade after his first Alpine trip in
1802, he painted a dizzying devil's bridge (*Teufelsbrücke*) at Uri (without
railings, though Turner knew better from his trip); a terrible, earth-
shattering avalanche in the Grisons (which naturally he could never
have seen); and a Hannibal picture set in a violent storm (see section
3.1).
Nevertheless, in the long run we can assume an increasingly positive

image of the Alps, especially from an aesthetic point of view. While previously mountains were considered as beautiful on a case-by-case basis, this later mutated into a conventional, almost general admiration. However, the central aspect of change was the enormous gain in attention which the Alps underwent. As set out above, from the middle of the eighteenth century many more Alpine texts and images circulated than before, and some areas and places were visited much more often. This change should also be seen against the background of the altered relationship between religion and nature (and natural science). Under the influence of scientific debate, the trend of 'natural theology' emerged before 1700, which derived the existence of God from the wonders of his creation and, in doing so, gave nature a religious value. Johann Jakob Scheuchzer, who engaged in Alpine research for the whole of his life, published the four-volume, richly illustrated work *Physica Sacra, oder Geheiligte Natur-Wissenschafft derer in Heiliger Schrift vorkommenden Natürlichen Sachen* [*Physica sacra, or the Sacred Natural Science of the Natural Things Occurring in the Holy Scriptures*] (see section 6.4) between 1731 and 1735. The huge wave of Alpine literature which followed also sometimes had religious features. There were tourists who conceived of the mountains as holy scriptures, and Alpinists who saw themselves as standing close to the creator of the world. The mountains were officially incorporated into sacred space via Christian crosses on their summits. From Austria, we know that such crosses were erected with much effort and pathos on prominent mountains from 1799. Later, this kind of religious punctuation became ubiquitous.[24]

7.6 Republican or Monarchist Alps?

Alongside religious, scientific and cultural dimensions, political affairs were also important to the perception of the Alps. Such issues concerned internal constitutions as well as questions of national belonging. In the decades before the French Revolution, and especially in Germany and France, the Swiss Alps were promoted to a symbol of freedom and democracy and thus became a utopian site for the rising middle classes. Just as the communal constitutions of these areas had served the monarchically inclined state theorists as a bad example, so they now became a political ideal under the sign of the bourgeois critique of absolutism (see sections 5.4, 5.5). Some even thought that 'despotism' had never spread into the mountains for physical reasons, since on the steep slopes it was always possible for the ruled to trample on the heads of their oppressors. The man of the moment was William Tell, imagined as a middle-aged Alpine hero of freedom, whose blood still ran in the veins of the mountain people. Tell was present in many forms – in histories, paintings, plays, operas – and soon received honorary citizenship of the French Revolution. The Revolution paid homage to the mountains in other ways, too. At its high point in 1793/4, artificial 'holy mountains' were built in many places in the squares and churches of the Republic. They served as an official representation of nature, with which society had reconciled itself. In ritual acts, 'the supreme being' – generally an attractive woman – revealed the laws of nature to the people on the *montagnes sacrées*.[25]

In the nineteenth century, monarchies also discovered the mountains – this time as a land of loyal people, immune to the turbulent times and their political upheavals. In 1822, Archduke Johann of Austria, a younger brother of Emperor Franz I, found 'strength, loyalty, simplicity, a still unspoiled people' in the mountains. His goal was to work with them to counter the giddiness of the times and, 'while everything moves convulsively, to stand quietly as a model of how things should be everywhere'. Through his life on a Styrian hill farm, his marriage to a postmaster's daughter and other unusual steps, the archduke became a perfect embodiment of the Romantic yearning for the Alps. The fact that he was able to lead many of his imperial relatives into the mountain world is also an indication of Alpine dispositions at the aristocratic pinnacle of state and society. Within the Habsburg monarchy, these dispositions particularly took shape in the Salzkammergut. From the 1820s, a sophisticated society life flourished there in summer around the great and the good of the Empire, who regularly came to take cures. It is hard to overestimate the significance of the preferences of Emperor Franz Josef, who, from 1857, relocated his summer residence from Vienna to Ischl, and apparently spent only three of the eighty-six summers of his life outside of the Salzkammergut. The monarch and keen hunter became a veritable Alpine icon.[26]

If, in 1800, it was said with Schiller: 'On the mountains is freedom! The breath of the tomb does not rise up into the pure air', by 1900 it was no longer clear which direction the mountain winds blew in. According to one observer, some still pointed towards the relationship between free Alpine air and republicanism. In view of the presence of monarchical forms of government in the mountains, however, it is better to speak of 'impartiality'. In any case, the Alps had proven themselves once more to be a European echo chamber: if the legitimacy of political power in the centres was challenged, its meaning could be outsourced in one way or another into the parallel universe of the mountains.[27]

7.7 National Mountains

However, there were also political forces that operated from within and used the mountain landscape for patriotic and national self-definition. In the Swiss confederation, this process began in the late fifteenth century when the country was first perceived as an independent entity in Europe. Humanists were already describing the confederation as an 'Alpine country' inhabited by an 'Alpine people' in 1550, particularly to differentiate themselves from the Holy Roman Empire to which they belonged. The mountain region generally attracted positive remarks in this proto-nationalist internal conception, sometimes qualified by the observation that at first sight it could appear rugged and wild. This perception, which was mainly created by urban scholars, was also fed by self-assertive voices from the mountain area itself. In the course of the nation building of the eighteenth and nineteenth centuries, Alpine references developed into a central source of identity which could be used from different political positions. The Alps meant the entirety of the mountains, especially the high ones, and not a particular peak. With time, however, an informal hierarchy naturalized itself. The Matterhorn, whose striking silhouette was already displayed in guidebooks before 1850, was discovered at that time by British mountaineers and became one of their favourites. With the tragic end to the first ascent of 1865, its fame in Europe rose dramatically (see section 7.4). But it was the contested project for a high mountain railway which seems to have first made the mountain into a national symbol. In 1907, the Swiss Heritage Society and Alpine Club were particularly against the planned tourist attraction, seen as a desecration. The Matterhorn belonged to all Swiss people, it was said, and not just to rich foreigners who could afford the train journey.[28]

As comparative analysis suggests, internal representations of Alpine areas could have a negative tone, especially when it came to the negotiation of taxes and levies. In such cases, people were happy to characterize their own regions as unfruitful. Otherwise, positive evaluations dominated, as in Switzerland. For example, the Habsburg county of Tyrol was called the 'land in the mountains' in records from the late sixteenth century onwards, parallel to political consolidation. A hundred years later, this positive internal view was already known beyond the borders of Tyrol. The *Spiegel der Ehren des Erzhauses Österreich* [*Mirror of the Honour of the Royal House of Austria*], which appeared in Nuremberg in 1668, compared Tyrol with an eagle straining skywards, and praised its economy: 'Chamois, springs, salt, wine and silver-ore yields / Show that the mountains too beget and bear riches.'[29] According to the historical and geographical context, political references to mountains could also occur much later. Italy, with its large cities and urban culture, took little part in Alpine discourse into the nineteenth century. There were some impulses from the direction of natural science, but an enthusiasm for mountains like that produced in the north by the Enlightenment did not take root in the south. A comparable engagement was first brought about by the unification of Italy and the proclamation of the new monarchy in 1861. The Alps now formed a common, unified border, on which mountaineers soon staged a nationalist 'war of flags'.[30]

Slovenian history offers an especially structured and intense political reference to the Alps. The highest mountain in the country, three-headed Triglav (2,870m), was central from the outset. In the second half of the eighteenth century, Sigismund Zois of Edelstein, one of those nobles committed to natural science and the emerging patriotic movement, offered a prize for the first ascent of Triglav, as Saussure had done for Mont Blanc. A group of four local men succeeded in 1778. The mountain then stood for a time at the heart of an international geological discussion and was also extolled in early Slovenian poetry about the beauty of the mountains, as in the ode 'Vršac' [The Peak] by Valentin Vodnik. In the nineteenth century, the nationalist movement against the Habsburg monarchy strengthened, as did the cultural and Alpinistic relationship with Triglav. Its prominent position was

Figure 10   *Slovenia's national mountain – 'Triglav' by Markus Perhard, 1844*

demonstrated in the twentieth century, when the socialist Slovenia which emerged from the German–Italian occupation of the Second World War in alliance with Yugoslavia needed an emblem. It fell back on the three-pronged Triglav symbol, which had been used by the Liberation Front, and supplemented it with a wavy line to indicate its sea connection. Slovenia later became one of the two countries in Europe with a mountain on its national flag (along with Slovakia).[31]

Overall, the modern interest in the mountain world was an expression of an altered understanding of nature. This is connected to a whole range of economic, political and cultural factors: urbanization and the intensification of agriculture, a scarcity of uncultivated land, the improvement of communications and transport, the national search for identity through references to landscape, scientific and religious developments, social distinction through stylistic renovation. We have seen that natural science often preceded other movements and that the perception of the mountains varied according to political background and had different geographical ranges. From the eighteenth century, the Alps also had a European significance. They became a central model for 'beautiful landscape', which circulated in many places and produced several variants.[32] In his Mediterranean book, Fernand Braudel described the Alps as exceptional mountains. For Braudel, the resources, the collective responsibilities, the capacity of the people and the numerous roads were exceptional. This characterization forms the central question of the present book (see sections 1.8, 2.3). What stands out here is the fact that Braudel did not reference the almost cult-like perception of the Alps, where the claim of exceptionality would have been particularly plausible. Of course, he wrote a work about the sixteenth century, when the mountains still appeared in a different light. Nevertheless, there is reason to believe that his work was strongly characterized by the Enlightenment, without reflecting on this influence. This could have led him to underestimate this cultural dimension. We will return to this later on.

8

WHICH MODERNITY?

In a travel description of 1882, an English author contemplated transport connections and the acceleration of technical developments, using the example of the Gotthard Pass. For a long while, there had only been paths for shepherds and hunters over the Alps, later supplemented by helpful bridges. Afterwards, the Roman roads arrived. In the Middle Ages, these roads were increasingly provided with stone bridges, then under Napoleon roads were built for carriages, and now the age of tunnel construction and the railway had already arrived. The gaps between innovations had therefore become ever shorter. The next innovation was sure to come soon and 'will probably have something to do with electricity'. The author also concluded from this accelerated sequence that his own epoch was ultimately the only one worth living in: 'The past was too slow, and the future will be much too fast.'[1]

8.1 The Traffic Revolution

The transition to modernity was characterized in the Alps by the generalization and expansion of transport over the large passes. In the western and central parts, this meant replacing merchant traffic undertaken by mules and other pack animals. In the eastern part, where vehicular transport had already spread from the late Middle Ages, light carts were replaced with heavier ones. In winter, sleighs still remained the most efficient form of transport. A sustained interest in the improvement of transport connections set in during the second half of the eighteenth century. When Johann Wolfgang Goethe drove over the Brenner in 1786 in a post-chaise, it only took him 27 hours from Innsbruck to Trent; his speed of around 8 kilometres per hour was higher than that of a scheduled 'ordinari' stagecoach at 5 to 6½ kilometres per hour. Somewhat slower still were the heavy freight carriages with their two- to four-horse teams. With the expansion of revolutionary and Napoleonic France, political and military motives gained the upper hand. This led, between 1796 and 1810, to the construction of new 'chaussées' over the Simplon, Mont Cenis, Montgenèvre and Tenda passes, built entirely according to the plans of engineers.[2]

Shortly before the middle of the nineteenth century, the age of the railway dawned. Once again, in the mountains the efforts required were particularly great. Indeed, the railway was considerably harder to make mountain-ready than the coach, since it could not climb steep stretches. Often a functional line could not be built without tunnels and bridges. Between 1854 and 1882, the first large tunnels at Semmering, Mont Cenis and the Gotthard were put into operation (see section 1.2). Altogether, eight transalpine railway lines were built by the early twentieth century. Thus, the increase in speed and transport capacity was accompanied by concentration on a smaller number of traffic routes. In the years before 1900, the first automobile appeared on the roads of the Alpine region. It caused a great stir and polarized public opinion. While some complained of the danger of traffic and the ruination of the roads, others were exhilarated by the speed. The regulation of new modes of transport varied greatly at first. In the Grisons, the government enacted a general ban on cars in 1900. It was first lifted in 1925, after no fewer than ten referenda, the last of which fell in favour of cars.[3]

The expansion of the internal transport network in the Alpine regions and communes took place at different speeds. Where touristic or military interests were involved, connections were generally rapidly modernized. At the beginning of the nineteenth century, a traveller from London to Zermatt needed around three weeks. Thanks to the railway, a journey to the Valais had shortened to 26 hours by 1874. The last stretch of road from the base of the Valais valley up to the

Figure 11 *The car takes off – advertisement for the new*
Grossglockner road, 1935

high-altitude site at the foot of the Matterhorn still consisted of a simple mule track. Because of the rising numbers of visitors, in 1860 a narrow road was partially built, and in 1891 a narrow-gauge railway was put into operation, which made this journey too, much shorter and more comfortable.[4]

Where isolated places were dominated by peasants, however, developments could be a long time coming. Thus, in the canton of Ticino, the transalpine connection on the Gotthard road was massively upgraded in the nineteenth century, while the side valleys remained hard to access. According to one historian, as a result, the region developed a partially new geography: 'Along the longitudinal axis the canton was shortened, but along the offshoots on the other hand it was extended, as if its body were supported by a great spine without vertebrae.'[5] This lag generally applied even more to the road networks that were strongly connected to agriculture and therefore depended on traditional transport technologies. In Ticino and other Southern Alpine regions, for example, many loads were carried in baskets on people's backs, without the help of animals, well into the twentieth century. Later, the motorization of agriculture and the better development of the Alpine pastures was also particularly difficult here.[6]

From mule tracks to roads and railway lines – there is reason to think that the topography of the Alpine region increasingly became a handicap over the course of these transport innovations. Even in the early modern period, the topographical complications were significant – in the case of navigable waterways, among other things. But the costly infrastructure of modern transport exacerbated the difference between the mountains and the flat areas surrounding the Alps. Even after the complete development of the railway network in the early twentieth century, the Alpine region was only loosely connected internally in spite of above-average investment, while at its edges many small branch lines led into the mountains, continuing the tightly knit network of the lowlands. Moreover, development of transport was associated at practically every stage with a loss of regional employment opportunities, and therefore encountered repeated resistance (chaussées made drovers superfluous, the railway replaced post and freight coachmen, and so on).[7] A parallel to this delayed and difficult modernization was the development of towns. True, Alpine towns grew at unprecedented rates in the late nineteenth century. But in the lowlands, the surge of urbanization was much greater, such that the gap between the two areas widened (see section 4.1).

8.2 Industrial Areas

Literary history knows him as *Der Arme Mann im Toggenburg* [*The Poor Man of Toggenburg*]. In this autobiography, Ulrich Bräker tells of how he escaped from Prussian military service at the battle of Lobositz in 1756 and was shortly afterwards set to boiling saltpetre by his father. His real desire, however, was not this dirty work, but to marry, and his chosen one also seemed to have economic acumen. 'She therefore advised me to set up a small business in cotton-yarn, as her brother-in-law W. had done; apparently he'd done quite well at it.' With a loan, the smallholder then bought up the processed yarn from the home spinners in the area and sold it in the town of St Gallen, where he bought raw cotton to sell back to the spinners in the country. This intermediate trade had its 'ups and downs'. When his father died and Bräker had to look after his younger siblings, he also set up a weaving cellar where he and his brothers made cloth, while his sisters spun and sowed; alongside this, he sometimes kept goats or cows, and planted carrots and vegetables.[8]

This mixed, variable form of cottage industry was not unusual for the region. From the transition to modernity, this part of eastern Switzerland had formed a commercial and industrial landscape, which experienced a sharp up-turn in the eighteenth century and also incorporated neighbouring areas like Glarus and Vorarlberg. The textile industry increasingly processed raw materials from distant lands and sold finished goods on large-scale markets. Initially, however, decentralized modes of production were the norm: urban merchants and various middlemen were responsible for the commercial side, while production took place in the country in many peasant households. Under pressure from the competition of English manufacturers, who lowered costs massively through new technology and organization, from the turn of the nineteenth century there were also mechanical, centralized spinning mills, weaving mills and textile printing works here – in other words, factories in the modern sense, which, through their social visibility and dynamism soon appeared as the symbol of a new age. Retrospectively too, 'industrialization' is often considered as a core element of 'modernity'. In our region, it had a heterogeneous character, as is shown by two examples from the Eastern and Western Alps.

In Styria and Carinthia, there was a long tradition of mining and processing iron (see section 4.7). From the 1820s, production expanded rapidly, especially at the famous Styrian Erzberg mine, and more and more people were employed. Alongside technical innovations came organizational ones. In 1840, the Steiermärkisch-Ständische Montanlehranstalt [Styrian Corporate School of Mining] was founded, and soon received the privileges of a mining university. In 1881 the foundation of the Oesterreichisch-Alpinen Montangesellschaft [Austrian-Alpine Mining Society] took place. It brought together the many dispersed businesses of the region under the roof of a joint-stock company. It initially comprised twenty-four forest businesses and thirty-seven mines, steel mills and factories, with a total workforce of almost 20,000 people. The society then gradually created new business structures. Against the background of this development, the population of the middle section of the Murtal increased rapidly. The five sites of Bruck, Leoben, Donawitz, Knittelfeld and Fohnsdorf more than doubled their number of inhabitants between 1869 and 1900.[9]

At the western end of the Alps, it was the clothing industry, and especially the production of gloves, which helped regions to grow. This production was coordinated and run from Grenoble but also radiated deep into the countryside. It really took off around 1700 and was significant into the twentieth century. Grenoble, for a long while the largest city of the Alpine region, was able to increase its importance further through this trade (see section 4.1). In 1730, the glove industry employed some 1,500 cutters and seamstresses. By around 1790, this number had trebled, and, after a revolution- and war-related crisis, the number climbed in the 1860s to around 32,000 people. At that time, almost half of urban workers were employed in the *ganterie* (glove trade), which soon introduced technical innovations too. The sales markets were throughout Europe and overseas. For example, Grenoble manufacturers maintained branches in Paris, London and New York.[10]

Historians have tried to identify and theoretically classify the driving forces of the Industrial Revolution more than any other subject. These efforts reflect the significance that is attributed to this upheaval for the position of the affected areas, the general structure of society and the life chances of individuals. The discussion concerns a whole range of economic, political and cultural factors, as well as various chronological sequences (stages of growth, cases of deindustrialization, the path dependency of industrial history). Franz Mathis has emphasized three factors for Austria, and with it a large part of the Eastern Alps: the mass demand for manufactured goods, the necessary raw materials, and relative overpopulation for labour potential. Wherever these factors were not present to a sufficient degree, industry either failed to take root in the nineteenth century or did so only partially. According to this approach, mass demand and labour potential are associated once again with population density and the level of urbanization.[11] Industrial developments did occur much more often on the fringes of the Alps than in their interior. St Gallen, where Bräker began his 'small business in cotton-yarn', was for example located in the northern foothills of the Alps, and the town Biella, the centre of another famous textile region, lay at the feet of the Southern Alps.

8.3 From Logging to Hydropower

At the beginning of the nineteenth century, Milan needed more than 250,000 tonnes of timber and firewood each year. Like many other towns in the areas surrounding the Alps, the Lombardian metropole obtained a large part of this supply from the forests of the mountain areas, which had retreated less far than those of the lowlands in the wake of human activity. Wood was transported along the watercourses, initially usually by drift – that is, without binding the trunks; lower down, these were often bound together into rafts on which other goods could also be carried. With economic growth, demand rose steeply in the eighteenth century and reached a high point in the nineteenth, before wood lost importance as an energy source in the face of coal. At that time, the 'protection of the mountain forests' also became a subject of political anxiety and intervention in all countries. In addition to scarcity phenomena, the development and expansion of central forestry administrations and the national interest in territorial integration contributed to this. In the centre of the discussion, however, stood flooding in the valleys, which was blamed on the deforestation of mountain areas. The argument proved politically effective – it was only in retrospective studies that other factors like climate variability were shown to be considerably more important to flooding.[12]

In the second half of the nineteenth century, the upper reaches of Alpine waters were harnessed for energy generation in a new way. Instead of driving mills and other small commercial enterprises with simple waterwheels, metal pressure pipelines were built in the steep terrain to use the hydropower, increased by the drop, to turn turbines for industrial purposes. The expanding paper industry in the region of Grenoble became the technological avant-garde. In 1869, Aristide Bergès (1833–1904) had a pressure pipeline with a drop of 200 metres built for his plant, which was supplemented in 1882 by another pipe with a drop of 500 metres. The mechanical energy generated was used to produce wood pulp. Bergès, who like other pioneers of hydropower had attended the central French school of engineering, seems to have been the first to speak of 'white coal' (*houille blanche*). This stressed the significance of the newly exploited energy in two ways: valuable like coal – but clean, not soot-blackened.[13]

The experience gained by the paper industry was shortly afterwards used to produce electricity, which became a very important factor for the whole Alpine region and made the area interesting to its surrounding areas in an economic and technological light. In the late nineteenth century, newly developed generators enabled mechanical energy to be transformed into electricity on a large scale. One of the applications was illumination with light bulbs, which had attracted attention since the first International Exposition of Electricity in Paris in 1881. This initiated a competition between cities for electric lighting and the production centres required for this purpose. Of the main cities in the Austrian provinces, Salzburg won the race in 1887, followed by Innsbruck and Vienna in 1889, Bregenz in 1891, Graz in 1894, Linz in 1898 and Klagenfurt in 1902. While the large towns were already embarking on the early stages of the electrification of lighting and other areas of life, small rural settlements in the Alpine region sometimes had to wait until the second half of the twentieth century. However, the greatest potential was usually found at these higher altitudes with their steep drops. Damming was developed for the increased and more even exploitation of this potential. Over time, the dam walls grew up to 250 metres and more.[14]

In the early days of hydropower, electricity could only be transmitted over short distances. Suitable mountain areas therefore had a location advantage for emerging electrochemistry and electrometallurgy (sodium, calcium, aluminium and so on), and also to an extent for the capital goods industry (power plants among other things). From the end of the nineteenth century, such industries spread into the deeply cut valleys of the Western Alps in particular, and gave them a new face. As electricity transmission became increasingly possible, this advantage diminished. Now exports to the surrounding regions and the respective national energy supply came to the fore. Before the First World War, almost two-thirds of French electricity was produced in the Alps, which accounted for only 7 per cent of the area. In Germany, it was estimated in 1930 that Bavaria accounted for approximately half of usable hydropower potential. One historian recently described the Alps in this period as 'Europe's Battery'.[15]

The struggle over rights of use was correspondingly fierce. In Switzerland, the national law on hydropower in 1916 fixed an upper limit on the interest payments of power plant operators. The limit prevented the formation of market prices and remained constant long-term, so that the mountain cantons co-financed the development of the centres in the Swiss Plateau. In a genuinely colonial way, in Italy the state and economy laid hands on the mountain valleys. The tragic symbol of this policy was the disaster of Vajont at Belluno. Despite warnings from geologists and protests from residents, it was decided to build the highest dam in the world there. On 9 October 1963, when the lake was almost full, part of the mountain plunged into the water. The huge flood wave this caused claimed the lives of 2,000 people farther down the valley. The Società Adriatica di Elettricità [Adriatic Electricity Company], which bore a great deal of the responsibility, had taken control of almost all the power plants in North-east Italy under fascism. Only a Friulian valley co-operative and a few other small operators were able to remain independent during this time.[16]

8.4 Tourist Economies

The tourist industry was one of the first users of 'white coal'. St Moritz could boast that it had installed electric lighting as early as the summer of 1879. The Austrian imperial household had the hunting lodge in Gastein and the villa in Ischl connected shortly afterwards, and in Salzburg there was even an 'Electrohotel' that emerged in 1894. Contemporaries reported fascinatedly on the 'electric play of colours in radiant salons filled with well-dressed people' in the Grand Hotels, which were springing up at that time in the most varied places (see sections 1.5, 7.2). Their architecture was entirely based on image, and technical comfort was to be of the newest sort. The sophisticated hotels soon distinguished themselves with elevators, central heating and running water in the bedrooms. The 'view' of the Alpine landscape was very important, whether it was of a lake, a waterfall, a glacier or a mountain itself. Alongside visual charms, medical offerings beckoned: reinvigorated thermal baths and recently created 'climatic health resorts'. During the *belle époque*, as the period was later named, the hotel industry experienced an unbelievable up-turn. In Switzerland, the leading country for Alpine tourism, the number of lodgings tripled between 1880 and 1912. In places with a high density of hotels, this boom also unleashed important effects for other fields of regional economic life.[17]

The tourism of the *belle époque* had an unmistakeably luxurious character. The guests mostly came from the upper middle classes and the nobility of the European centres, from Great Britain to Russia. The fashionable elite culture and the newly developed conventions of the admiration of nature contrasted sharply with other groups, and especially with most local people. This soon gave rise to ironic commentary and criticism of 'Fremdenverkehr', or foreign traffic, as the sector was not unfairly called. In 1885, the writer Peter Rosegger published a proposal for a tourist tax, probably written by Rosegger himself, in his magazine *Heimgarten*: 'Just as you can buy an arms licence or a hunting licence each year, so the tourist should have to purchase an entrance ticket to the Alps, at something like 5 Gulden for an annual pass, which would then be deducted from the taxes of Alpine farmers.'[18] Partly, the criticism was directed not only against foreigners and their new demands, but more generally against the modernity that they represented. Clergymen feared for the customs and morals of their parishioners and castigated imported 'materialism', to which they attributed great virulence. Under other economic conditions, these cultural confrontations could lead to real problems. When war broke out and the food supply became critical in 1917, the Austrian authorities issued an official ban on tourism under pressure from the public. This ban was repeated in 1920. Several times, there were hunger protests and violent attacks on hotels.[19]

The First World War was a real shock for tourism. Switzerland was spared from the war, but not from the crisis. Economically and politically, a desperate search was made for alternative solutions and relief measures. From 1916, interned prisoners of war from either side could be accommodated in Swiss hotels for a fee. Even before this, the government had issued a ban on the building of hotels under martial law. New tourist propositions now required proof of demand, which was diametrically opposed to recent liberal policies. After the war, the economy did not permanently improve, and two decades later the next war was already looming. For tourism, which was generally dependant on fashion and the economy, this was a long period of difficulty. In Switzerland, the number of lodgings in 1912 was not reached again until 45 years later. However, under the constant pressure to enhance attractions, the interwar period also brought some innovations, like cable cars, ski lifts and swimming pools. On average, the clientele now stayed for a shorter time at resorts, and was changing socially. The trend moved away from the elites towards a broad, nationwide tourism. Fascist Italy created the Opera Nazionale Dopolavoro [National Recreational Club] in 1925, and Nazi Germany later established the leisure organization Kraft durch Freude [Strength through Joy].

Geographically, Alpine tourism had been expanding from as early as the late nineteenth century, and its focal points had been relocated. The winners included Italy and, above all, Austria. Measured by the number of tourists per head of population, the modern 'Alpine country' which emerged from the Danube monarchy developed from the 1960s into the most important tourist area in the Alpine region. The general image of the mountain range was now characterized just as much by Austria as by Switzerland. From Tyrol to Styria, new versions of tourism which differed from the Swiss model also emerged. Semmering, for example, a tourist resort founded in 1880 on the mountain railway between Vienna and Trieste, had two sectors from the first: big hotels, and expensive villas owned by the Viennese elite. An observer could not decide whether Semmering was 'a countryside of town houses or a town of country houses'. This can be taken as an early example of the later widespread occurrence of Alpine holiday homes for town-dwellers. The Viennese initially used the place as a 'summer resort', and later also for the pursuit of the winter sports which were soon to change the tourist season forever.[20]

8.5 *Sport alpin*

Emerging winter sports used the 'white coal' of the Alps in yet another physical state: as snow and ice. Many stories and legends circulate about the origins of these sports, often highlighting a particular pioneering achievement, but they are hard to verify. Generally speaking, winter sports emerged in the Alpine region from the last third of the nine-teenth century, in various ways. Some were imported from elsewhere, like figure and speed skating. Others developed through the transfor-mation of local equipment, as with tobogganing. In general, large- and small-scale influences interacted in a complex back and forth. At first, physical activity served more as a pleasant and healthy pastime for hotel and resort guests. At the turn of the twentieth century, some of these activities adopted the hallmarks of modern sport. They were organized into clubs and codified with rule books. At their heart was performance measured through competition.[21]

Winter sports were only able to establish themselves with difficulty in the international Olympic Movement, launched in 1894. There were reservations about its fashionable, touristic milieu, which was not peopled with 'real' sportsmen, and the Scandinavians defended themselves against any competition to their already institutionalized Nordic Games. As the supporters gained ground, the war broke out. The Olympic Games of 1916 were to have taken place in Berlin, and a week of winter sports had also been planned. At the end of the war, Germany, now suspended from the Olympic Committee, organ-ized their own national games or '*Kampfspiele*'. They began in 1922 with a week of winter sports in Garmisch-Partenkirchen, which was often given out as a 'Winter Olympics' in the German press coverage. Two years later, a similar event was held under international auspices. France incorporated a week of winter sports in Chamonix into its Paris Olympics in 1924, which was later recognized as the first Winter

Olympics. It initiated a long series of Winter Olympics in or near the Alps (St Moritz, Garmisch-Partenkirchen, Cortina d'Ampezzo, Innsbruck, Grenoble, Albertville, Turin). Sixteen contests were held in Chamonix in 1924. At that time, Alpine skiing was still unrepresented, whereas a medal of honour was conferred for Alpinism. Afterwards, the number of contests increased continuously.[22]

Skiing, which soon became the dominant form of winter sport, spread particularly quickly in Austria. From around 1880, individuals had been experimenting with skis in various places. Often, they were well-off and enthusiastic town-dwellers. They were inspired by reports about Norwegian skiing and by the sensational book by the polar explorer Fridtjof Nansen *The First Crossing of Greenland* (1891). Soon ski clubs were founded and the first competitions were organized, especially in the context of more or less commercial winter sports festivals. However, the military was of central importance to the spread of skiing. Special detachments were created as early as 1890, and standardized training and equipment were provided after an initial phase. In 1913, the Austro-Hungarian army even founded a ski corps, and during the world war additional soldiers were continuously trained. In the bloody mountain battles of 1915–18, they were deployed many times (see section 5.7). This created the preconditions for the broad distribution of skiing. Indeed, the sport experienced a real boom in the interwar years and penetrated into isolated valleys. Moreover, it became a reference point for the modern physical culture characterized by a new youth movement.[23]

The youth movement of the interwar years also gave Alpinism a new face. Unlike earlier Alpinism, which had the ascent of high peaks in mind and so focused primarily on the Western Alps (see section 7.4), the younger generation applied itself to climbing the steepest and most difficult faces. In the Eastern Alps, especially in the Dolomites, now famous from the mountain war, they found an ideal training ground. Their climbing technique required new tools (pitons and ice picks, carabiners and so on), and for competitive comparison they began to classify the routes according to the level of difficulty. Older Alpinists, who had also taken considerable risks, were appalled by the audacity with which the new climber-heroes and 'Bergkamaraden', or mountaineering comrades, put their lives at risk. Added to this was the nationalist charge of Alpinism. What had begun as the discovery and experience of nature became a war by other means, as many contemporaries noted. This came to a dramatic head in 1938 on the north face of the Eiger in the Bernese Oberland. After the dreaded face had already claimed several lives, young mountaineers from Germany and Austria braved the face once more before a large public. Adolf Hitler apparently received hourly updates on the progress of the climb and claimed their 'victory' for the Third Reich.[24]

8.6 New Media

Changes in media, especially the advent of photography and film, also played a part in transforming the perception and touristic use of the Alps. Photography, one of the first new media of the industrial period, was held to be particularly realistic and could reach a mass audience through magazines, postcards and other means. The proliferation of picture postcards and their addressees created unprecedented access to the Alps. Attracted by unusual subjects, some photographers lugged their heavy equipment into the really high mountains as early as the 1860s. Two dozen porters were engaged for the first photography expedition up Mont Blanc, and at the summit they had to erect a makeshift laboratory to develop the used wet plates immediately. Other photographers experimented with dry plates, and so could reduce their equipment to around 15 kilograms, but had to take into account longer exposure times. Towards the end of the nineteenth century, handheld small-format cameras with film rolls came onto the market, at which point Alpinistic documentation and self-documentation soared.[25]

The great age of the postcard also began at this time, and was of particular importance for the tourist areas of the Alps. The subjects of the photos became an important factor in the popularization of idealized landscapes and continued older forms of popular landscape representation (see section 7.3). In 1905, an Englishman thanked a Swiss correspondent for the postcards which he had received from him: 'Dear Sir, I am very pleased with the views you have sent me as they confirm the opinion I had of your country. It would be a luck if some day I am able to see by myself.'[26] The cards alone apparently transmitted a feeling of being present and could partially replace seeing with one's own eyes. The 'best wishes' which were written on the cards gave the communication a personal character, but were simultaneously embedded in the conventions which developed alongside the medium. In the first half of the twentieth century, postcards enjoyed extraordinary popularity and sometimes characterized perceptions down to the smallest details. As one study has shown, in the case of the Three Peaks, postcards not only helped to make this previously little regarded massif into a well-known symbol of the Dolomites – they also established the perspective from which the rocky crags were impressed into the visual memory of particular periods.[27]

The first film with Alpinistic sequences was shot shortly after 1900. In the interwar period and during the Second World War, an independent genre developed, which entered history as the 'Bergfilm' (mountain film). These sometimes extremely successful films had titles like *Im Kampf mit dem Berge* [*The Battle with the Mountain*] (1921), *Die weisse Hölle vom Piz Palü* [*The White Hell of Piz Palu*] (1929), *Stürme über dem Mont Blanc* [*Storm over Mont Blanc*] (1930), *Berge in Flammen* [*Mountains in Flames*] (1931) and *Das blaue Licht* [*The Blue Light*] (1932). The most famous was *Der Berg ruft* [*The Mountain Calls*] (1937) by the South Tyrolean Luis Trenker. It dealt in a highly fictionalized way with the first ascent of the Matterhorn by Edward Whymper's team, which ended in 1865 with the death of several participants (see section 7.4). The film used the mountain landscape and the danger of mountaineering to stage what was in contemporary terms a very spectacular and entertaining story. 'Bergfilms' were shot in all countries of the Alps, but they were especially popular in the German-speaking regions. New research refers to the correspondence between the ultra-nationalism of the time and the values and ideologies transmitted in the films. But their widespread popularity was also thanks to the modernity of film and to the particular combination of landscape, hazardous sports and melodrama.[28]

8.7 The Crisis of Agriculture

In spite of the development of industry and tourism, agriculture remained the most important sector of the Alpine economy into the first half of the twentieth century. The proportion of the economically active population employed in agriculture still totalled a good two-thirds in 1870, and in some regions (Aosta, Valais, Valtellina) it was more than 80 per cent. It is reasonable to assume that in absolute numbers there had never been so many farmers in the Alps as there were at this time. With the marked decline in the proportion of the labour force employed in agriculture over the following decades, absolute numbers then began to fall. This was the beginning of a profound structural change which led to the increasing contraction of the Alpine agricultural population. The immediate causes were altered market conditions for agricultural goods and the advent of the mechanization of agricultural production. From the 1870s, cheap grain from non-European regions had come onto the market as a result of improved transportation, which lowered the prices of plant products considerably. Development of prices for animal products took a more favourable course for farmers – but, as many farms in the lowlands now made more space for this, competitive pressure also rose in Alpine animal husbandry.[29]

The technical revolution in agriculture began in the same period. New tools for tillage, harvest and transport came onto the market at short intervals, at first on the basis of horse power, then steam power, and eventually with combustion engines. Initially, however, many machines were too big and too heavy for work on rough terrain. So the new horse-powered machines could only be used on fairly flat meadows, although the acceleration of the hay harvest in the Alps would have been of great consequence. Mechanization made the fastest progress in the French Alpine region; in contrast to other Alpine regions, it had been forced to reckon with a demographic decline from the late nineteenth century, and so had an additional motive for technical innovation. In general, however, the mechanization of agriculture in the Alps remained modest for some time. When agricultural tools were statistically surveyed in Switzerland in 1939, not even 300 tractors were counted in the mountain cantons, which contained more than a quarter of all farms. This made up less than 4 per cent of Swiss tractor stock.[30]

In the First World War, there were supply crises in many places, which heightened agriculture's political importance. The period that followed was generally characterized by a nationalist agricultural policy. This began in fascist Italy under Benito Mussolini, where in 1925 a 'battle for grain' was declared. Switzerland, too, supported the expansion of grain cultivation, along with the downgrading of animal husbandry. The new motto of agricultural policy, inspired not least by Italy, was 'national economy'. To guarantee land supply, tillage received state subsidies. According to the government, the grain system should 'reconnect the town and the country and show the people the commonality of their interests'. The discussion was especially influenced by general ideas about the 'peasant character' and its ethical and moral value. The idea of self-sufficiency should also apply to individual families, according to the precept that 'The best peasant clothes are home-grown and home-spun.' The 'Heimatwerk', or heritage work, initiated by the farmers' association aimed in a similar direction. Agricultural politicians wanted to promote self-sufficiency in consumer goods and the production of craft wares in mountain areas, to improve farming incomes. In the context of the global economic crisis from 1929, this seemed particularly urgent.[31]

The situation in the Austrian Alpine region may have been even more difficult than that in Switzerland. Between 1918 and 1932, 40,000 hill farmers had to leave their farms. Auctions and seizures of agricultural holdings were the order of the day. The government-sponsored privileging of the agricultural sector was more for the benefit of large farms and the food industry than the bulk of medium-sized and small farms. After the annexation to Nazi Germany in March 1938, Austria – later called the 'Ostmark' and then the 'Donau- und Alpenreichsgaue', or Danube and Alpine regions – was incorporated into the dirigiste agricultural policy of the Third Reich, and was to participate in its 'battle for production'. A special mountain department was created to this end in the relevant ministry. A whole arsenal of Nazi claims justified this special status: hill-farming families with their allegedly large numbers of children were particularly worthy of protection as the 'blood source of the nation'. They had 'the original peasant virtues in their comparatively purest form'. Hill farmers were 'born fighters'; the farther up the mountain they worked, the harder the selection, and so the higher the 'national racial value'. The 'Nordic tradition' was therefore more prominent in the hill farms than in the valley.[32]

8.8 Fascism, National Socialism

How far peasants actually espoused such ideas is hard to say. On the other hand, the extremely nationalist orientation of the Alpine clubs of Italy, Germany and Austria is certain. Their middle-class members were largely recruited from the cities of the lowlands, and fell under the spell of national ideologies – or were forced to by the emerging dictatorships. Mussolini had barely seized power in 1922 when he was welcomed as a new member of the Club Alpino Italiano (CAI) 'with warm and heartfelt congratulations'. Shortly afterwards, his picture was to be exhibited in many club huts, and the front page of the club magazine henceforth bore a quote from the Duce: that it filled him with pride to belong to this Alpinist 'school of daring and Italianness'. The president of the CAI even thought that no one was more fascist 'than the man of the mountains'. It was similar with the Deutscher und Österreichischer Alpenverein (DÖAV). In 1927, for example, the speaker of the mountaineering group announced to a general assembly in Vienna: 'Our love of the mountains is a German love, a love of the German fatherland, the spirit which unites all tribes as in the Alpine club with the great German fatherland!' Both in fascist Italy and in the Third Reich, the Alpine clubs were integrated into the state sport machine and made into monopoly institutions. All other Alpinistic clubs were banned, especially those on the political left.[33]

More so than the CAI, the DÖAV also demonstrated strongly anti-Semitic attitudes. Individual sections wanted to adopt an 'Arian paragraph' in their statutes even before 1900. In the post-war period, there was an unbelievable wave of ethnic resentment and hatred. In 1921, the Austrian section in Vienna expelled its Jewish members in the agitated atmosphere of a tumultuous sitting. Jews were also to be banned from entry to the mountain huts. In response, Jews and liberally minded members founded the 'Donauland', or Danube section. German nationalist agitation now strove persistently for the exclusion of the Jewish section from the DÖAV, which it achieved in 1924. So, almost ten years before the seizure of power by Hitler and his National Socialist Party, the Alpine Club adopted a racist strategy which culminated under the Third Reich in the mass extermination of the Jewish population. Similar modes of thinking and behaviour had also been adopted early on by the gymnastic movement. In the interwar period, such positions quickly came into their own. In Austria, for example, many smaller places declared themselves 'pure of Jews' by resolution of the local council. By 1929, there were already nearly sixty of them.[34]

In the South Tyrol, the two like-minded dictatorships south and north of the Alps clashed in a particular way. The majority of the area was German-speaking, but it had belonged to the Kingdom of Italy since the partition of Tyrol in 1919 (see sections 1.6, 5.7). Since then, there had been a fierce battle over belonging, provoked especially by the national fascist campaign of forced Italianization. In 1939, Hitler and Mussolini agreed to an accord for the resettlement of the German population groups of these Southern Alps. The scattered 'Cimbri' were also included (see section 4.6). The population was therefore offered a vote: to opt for German citizenship and emigrate to the Third Reich, or to stay at home and assimilate themselves linguistically and cultur- ally to Italy. They were only given a very short period of reflection to make their decision. As was to be expected, there were severe tensions and family disputes in regional society. Most respondents eventually chose the so-called 'option' of German nationality and resettlement. Tellingly, however, by 1943 many fewer had actually emigrated, only around 75,000 people, not even half of the original voters who opted for resettlement. Many of them later returned, with the stigma of having chosen the wrong homeland.[35]

Hitler also developed a personal relationship with the Alps through his 'Berghof', or mountain homestead, in Bavaria. From the early 1920s, he regularly stayed in the rural and touristic Obersalzberg near Berchtesgaden. In 1933, he bought his previously rented holi- day retreat and had it developed into a spacious residence. A huge 'Führersperrgebiet', or Führer's restricted zone, soon emerged around the Berghof with imposing buildings, villas for Hitler's entourage and accommodation for numerous staff. The former owners of the prop- erties were turned out, with or without compensation. Obersalzberg developed into a second seat of government alongside Berlin, where state guests were received and central political decisions were made. Overall, Hitler spent almost a third of his time in office in this place. The mountains also served as a propaganda backdrop against which he could portray himself as down to earth, in touch with nature and a lonely, preeminent genius. A few days before the end of the Second World War, in April 1945, the British air force destroyed the whole restricted zone in a major attack which was repeatedly announced.[36]

8.9 Liberation (1943–1945)

In the last years of the war, many believed that Nazi Germany was building an 'Alpine fortress', where it wanted to present a prolonged resistance to the Allied troops. The rumour was discussed both in public and in the intelligence services and the Allied leadership. It was encouraged by the Swiss defensive strategy, among other things. This was based from 1940 on a 'national redoubt' (defensive system) in the Central Alps. After the defeat of France, the country was surrounded by the German–Italian Axis. In this desperate position, the government decided to concentrate defences in a quarter of its territory in inaccessible high mountains. Critics pointed out that this strategy was primarily symbolic, because it did not include the densely populated regions of the Central Plateau. Later, it also became clear that Switzerland owed its survival during the war in large part to economic cooperation with the Axis powers. But the Alpine redoubt would become very important to the country's self-perception. It gave earlier images of the Alps a completely new emotional content and characterized Swiss behaviour in post-war Europe. It is true that there was a long tradition of military associations between mountains and the nation. However, they had never before been implemented and staged in such an organized and popular way.[37]

On the Italian side, the Alps now became a symbol of freedom for the first time. As indicated above, the Enlightenment connection of the Alps with freedom had gained little traction in Italy in the eighteenth and nineteenth centuries. An enthusiasm for the mountains began with the proclamation of the Kingdom of Italy in 1861, but had a primarily military character (see section 7.7). When, in 1943, the Allies put the fascist dictatorship into difficulties in Southern Italy, the situation changed. At the beginning of September, the Allies concluded a ceasefire with a new state leadership from which Mussolini had been removed. Thereafter, the country was occupied by the German Wehrmacht, previously allied to Italy. So the struggle against fascism also became the struggle against a foreign occupying force. Soon, an armed resistance movement was formed from various political positions. This *resistenza* initially consisted mainly of small groups with little to do with one another, who retreated to inaccessible areas and sought to operate from there. 'Andare in montagna' (to go into the mountains) now had a new ring to it, and meant to join the partisans. The partisans' most public successes were in the summer and autumn of 1944 with the foundation of a liberated 'Republic' in the Alps (Val d'Ossola, Carnia) and the Apennines. However, after a short time they were bloodily suppressed once more.[38]

In his autobiographical novel *I piccoli maestri* [*The Outlaws*], the Italian author Luigi Meneghello tells of his experiences of hard times in the resistance in the mountains of Belluno and Asiago as a young student and *alpini* officer cadet. After the ceasefire of September 1943, he disposed of his military equipment so as not to be taken prisoner by the Wehrmacht, and set off home. In his village, everyone yearned for the end of the war. As the popular movement subsided, Meneghello decided to go to the mountains together with other intellectuals. They operated in changing formations of one to three dozen men with little experience, no proper plans and insufficient weapons. 'The same confusion reigned as in small anthills after the rain. Often we were out on patrol, in groups, in pairs or alone; something would be announced, but the next moment it had already changed again.' The author felt all the better when the mixed group stepped into action for once – for instance, to take revenge on a fascist in the village. 'How nice: students and *popolani* march armed over the beautiful steep slopes; we teach them a grain of radicalism, they have their stores of pragmatic wisdom. The whole thing is called an action, and we are about to act. Bravely stepping out, I savoured these notions.'[39]

In political discourse, the *resistenza* emerged rather differently from its portrayal in Meneghello's self-deprecating and reflective account. In Italy, it was immediately ascribed a central role in the liberation of the country. With this foundation myth, the country, which abolished the monarchy in 1946 and reconstituted itself as a democratic republic, could also put to one side the two decades of violence and aggression under which many had suffered.[40] As a result of the political alliance with Nazi Germany, after the war Italy had to accept a small territorial concession in the Western Alps (in favour of France), and a slightly larger one to the east (in favour of Yugoslavia). In Austria too, many were eager to present themselves as mere victims and to deny any perpetrator role during the time of the Third Reich. The country remained occupied by the victorious powers until 1955. It retained its pre-war borders and in its own self-perception became more than ever an 'Alpine republic' independent of Germany.

8.10 Forms of Modernity

Politically, the transition to modernity was not least a battle between monarchy and republic, democracy and dictatorship, each of which claimed the future for its own. Economically, industrialization, development of transport and electrification were seen as unmistakeable signs of 'progress' and 'modernity' until the middle of the twentieth century. In this light, the Alpine region seemed a preserve of the traditional and archaic, characterized by a peculiar 'cultural retardation'. As presented in this chapter, agriculture did indeed remain the most important sector of the Alpine economy for a long while. Industrialization kept within limits. It occurred more often on the fringes of the mountains than in the interior. New achievements in energy and tourism also initially had a regional or local character. Low population and urban density in comparison to the lowlands can be considered the underlying factors behind this form of development. In the eighteenth and even more so the nineteenth centuries, growth rates diverged. Although the population and cities of the Alpine region also grew at an increasing pace, the rise was meagre compared to that of the surrounding regions (see section 4.1). Transport and exchange were particularly important to processes of innovation. Since modern transport infrastructure required a much greater outlay, the topography of the mountains became more of a hindrance than ever.[41]

On close inspection, however, the outer and inner Alpine areas were by no means sharply separated and there was scope for different interpretations. Electric light for example, which gave the night a new lustre from *circa* 1880, shone especially early in Alpine tourist resorts. In certain other fields, too, the 'Playground of Europe', as the Alpinists christened it, offered space for innovation and the avant-garde. In the interwar period, this came in the form of skiers with their new physical culture and the daring mountaineering comrades. The Alps played an important conceptual role as a utopian space for alternatives to European civilization in its current condition. In Germany and France, in particular, in the decades before and after 1800, this promise bore the names of 'freedom' (as opposed to general oppression) and 'nature' (as opposed to social artificiality and corruption). In Italy until shortly before the collapse of fascism, the Alps symbolized the 'nation' above all else, and from 1943, thanks to the resistance, 'liberation'. In such moments of change, it became particularly clear that modernity had no fixed shape, but was constantly re-negotiated through discourse and counter-discourse.[42]

Even the Alpine peasants were in reality not as archaic as they were often made out to be in contrast to modernity. Through temporary migration and other connections, most of them had been in contact with current affairs for some while, and their farming first became a problem in the context of general intensification and mechanization. Let us summarize these two processes once more. *1. Intensification:* Driven by population growth, peasants in the modern period increased labour inputs and so productivity per acre, primarily by means of increased harvest frequency. In the high altitudes of the Alps with their short growing season, however, this intensification strategy was only applicable up to a certain point (see section 4.2). *2. Mechanization:* From the second half of the nineteenth century, the rising demand for foodstuffs and labour, as well as the new supply of industrially produced machines, led to a technical revolution triggered by industry. But, as a result of the rough and precipitous terrain, the mechanization of agriculture in the Alps remained modest for a long while (see section 8.7). In this case too, development did not lead to the 'domination of nature' that was hoped for and proclaimed by many contemporaries, but to the increasing dependence of society on the environment.

9

EUROPEANIZATION AND
ENVIRONMENTALISM

In the first half of the twentieth century, more than 50 million people died in Europe as a result of war and state-sponsored killing. After 1945, better times came. True, the continent was now divided by an 'Iron Curtain' between the capitalist, democratic West and the communist East, and during the Cold War it faced the threat of a conflict between the dominant powers, the USA and the Soviet Union. But peace prevailed till the end of this war-born situation in 1990. New generations grew up with the idea that the world could be peaceful and that prosperity generally went up.[1] Two post-war developments were especially important for the Alpine region: the European unification movement beginning in the 1950s, and the rise of environmental awareness after 1970. Both changed the basic aspects of Alpine history.

9.1 The Wounds of the Second World War

At first, things were difficult. In areas directly affected by the war, many people were living in emergency accommodation. The years 1943–5 had left behind massive destruction in some places. More than half of the buildings in Innsbruck and Klagenfurt were damaged or completely uninhabitable. Then there was the inadequate supply of food. Austria was only able to prevent famine in 1946/7 thanks to the aid organization of the United Nations. Most of the survivors suffered heavily from the loss of family members and somehow had to come to terms with the past. The macro-political situation changed quickly. Soon East–West competition became the dominant conflict line, pushing other questions into the background and laying down new priorities. Like Germany, Austria was divided between the four victorious powers into occupation zones. The Alpine regions were mostly in the American, British and French zones; the Soviet Union primarily governed Lower Austria; and in Vienna the victorious powers had their own sectors. As the Iron Curtain sank over Europe, and Germany broke into two states, some feared a similar fate for Austria. But with the treaty and the establishment of neutrality, the country won its independence on the Western side in 1955.[2]

Also between East and West was Yugoslavia, from which the new 'Alpine republic' Slovenia would later emerge. As in several other parts of Europe, here the Second World War had not only been a battle between the Allies and the Axis powers, but simultaneously a civil war over ethnic and cultural affiliation and political conviction. In 1941, the country was occupied by Germany and Italy and subjected to a racist politics of violence. Various local groups then organized themselves militarily, whether in league with the occupiers, in resistance to them, or with shifting alliances. The partisans of the communist Josip Broz Tito operated most successfully, and soon grew into a 'National Liberation Army' which, after victory over its many opponents, in 1945 took power in the former kingdom. The Yugoslavian war was one of the most brutal in Europe. 'Occupation, exploitation and terrorism towards civilians, "ethnic cleansing", persecution and mass extermination made existential issues an everyday phenomenon', writes one historian. This devastating tragedy, which had called forth such suffering and human guilt, weighed like a nightmare on the country and could be recalled if required.[3]

The new Federal People's Republic of Yugoslavia saw itself as a socialist state. But as Tito broke with the Soviet Union soon after the war, the country had an intermediate position: socially and politically, it tended towards the East, but in foreign policy, towards the West. Slovenia, its northernmost constituent republic, was initially reliant on a strong Yugoslavia to survive the border conflicts with Austria and, especially, Italy. But in the course of the post-war period, priorities shifted. As the wealthiest part of Yugoslavia, Slovenia had to give up considerable resources to other parts of the country, and with growing economic problems and the easing of the Cold War, internal tensions rose. After the death of Tito, a political generation emerged who increasingly focused on the interests of their own constituent republics. The powerful constituent republic of Serbia tended towards the strengthening of the central state, whereas Slovenia conversely favoured decentralization. In 1987, an intellectual published a *Letter to a Serbian Friend*: 'A brother is a brother', it went; 'The question, however, is whether I want to live with my brother in the same house.' Following this, there was a 'Slovenian spring', and in 1989 politicians published a 'fundamental charter for Slovenia'. The conflict between the constituent republics escalated parallel to the disintegration of the Eastern Bloc and to German reunification. In summer 1990, there was a 'ten-day war', in which the Slovenian territorial defence held their ground against the Yugoslav–Serbian People's Army, and in the following year Slovenia became an independent state.[4]

Austria 1955, Slovenia 1991 – twice in the second half of the twentieth century new republics emerged which lay predominantly in the Alpine region and also demonstrated or activated many Alpine cultural references. The reorganization took place against the background of the European unification movement, which began in the 1950s in reaction to the war and its extension via the East–West conflict. The three most important countries were France, West Germany and Italy, which together also possessed a considerable part of the Alpine region. The main stages can be briefly identified: the European Coal and Steel Union in 1951, the European Economic Community in 1957, the European Community in 1967, the European Union in 1992, common currency in 2002, and periodic expansion up to twenty-eight member states (2013). Austria entered the Union in 1995, Slovenia in 2004. A major exception was Switzerland, which held fast to its special political position, although in fact it was very closely integrated with neighbouring countries. Nation states were not only diminished by European unification, but also by emerging regionalism, which – as we are about to see – was more important than usual in the Alpine region.

Figure 12   *The consequences of war – the new border through Gorizia station, 1947*

9.2 Economic Growth and the Transformation of the Landscape

Surprisingly, a strong economic up-turn in Europe followed on the heels of the hard post-war years and continued for a relatively long period. In the early 1950s, the media were already talking of an 'economic miracle'. It was based, among other things, on the fact that industrial plants in Germany itself had been less damaged than might be assumed. Especially in Bavaria and Austria, the influx of people and resources from the East also had a stimulating effect on the economy. In addition, an impact was made by the 'European Recovery Program', known as the Marshall Plan, with which the USA sought to strengthen the market economy relative to the Eastern planned economy from 1948 to 1952. The exposed position of Austria at the beginning of the Cold War led to the country receiving considerably more financial aid per capita than other countries. Strong industrial growth also reached a series of Alpine regions, especially those which had already set out on that path. This did not fundamentally change the general distribution of industry, with its concentration on the fringes of the Alps and in wide river valleys. But the proportion of labour in this sector now exceeded 50 per cent in several regions.[5]

After some delay, Alpine tourism also recovered from its war-related crises. In Switzerland, the number of lodgings in 1912 was surpassed for the first time in the 1950s, and shortly thereafter Austria developed into the most important holiday destination in the Alpine region. The hotel industry met with competition from the rapid rise in second homes, which holidaymakers from the surrounding towns bought or had built in the tourist areas. This benefitted the construction industry, but also generated buildings which remained empty for months and weighed down infrastructure. In France, the state, together with entrepreneurs, created so-called 'stations de ski' – that is, high-altitude, specialized ski resorts for a broad public. A famous example is the Station Courchevel in Savoy, opened in 1946, around which there was soon a whole network of such resorts, some with avant-garde architecture. Criticism of tourism set in once more, parallel to economic growth and rising prosperity. This time, fundamental questions were also asked: was the tourist industry the key sector upon which all other development depended? Were there realistic alternatives to it in the modern society of consumption and leisure? In 1990, tourism provided around 15 per cent of all jobs in the Alps, but in strongly concentrated areas. The relatively few places with high tourism intensity were counterbalanced by the relatively many with low intensity. Opinion differed on the evaluation of such information.[6]

Agriculture was able to profit from the up-turn. Nevertheless, more and more farms were abandoned, and in most regions the proportion of farmers who had a side-line increased. In 2000, this proportion was some 50 per cent across the Alps. The fast progress of mechanization was a major reason for the stark differentiation between the actual mountain region and the flat valley bottoms. The mountainous areas, with their harsher production conditions, comprised a good four-fifths of the land in the Alpine region; here, land use declined substantially in the second half of the twentieth century. In contrast, the valley bottoms – earlier often boggy and only used as pasture land – were much more intensively cultivated. There was, therefore, a marked polarization in land use. Interestingly, the number of farms in the mountain region did not decline faster than in the valley areas, and overall this decline did not differ substantially from developments outside of the Alps. In most countries, the state promotion of agriculture after the war was greatly expanded. Thomas Philipp Streifeneder, author of a 2010 study on change in Alpine agricultural structures, believes that, without this support, 'a large part of the Alps [would] probably no longer be used agriculturally'.[7]

The polarization of land use also had deeper roots. The era of large-scale organized river diversion and improvements, which enabled a more intensive use of the wide river valleys, had already begun at the turn of the nineteenth century. On the other hand, extensification in the mountain region led to the reforestation of the Alps. Such a 'forest transition' – that is, a historical transition from net deforestation to net reforestation – can be observed in the course of industrialization and urbanization in many countries. In the Alpine region, this trend reversal can be located in the middle of the nineteenth century. In recent decades, it has accelerated greatly. The reforestation of the south was particularly pronounced. In the Northern and Central Alpine regions of Switzerland, forest land increased between 1880 and 2000 by 27–50 per cent. In the Southern Alpine regions, however, the increase was a good 100 per cent. Overall, this change provided the context for the advance of wild animals in recent times (see section 9.5).[8]

A large part of this reforestation took place on abandoned Alpine pastures. But scrub encroachment or forestation also affected areas which had previously belonged to landscapes used for more particular cultivation. Once again, this change was particularly dramatic on the southern face of the Alps. An example is the Canale di Brenta, a narrow valley on the edge of the Venetian Alps, where intensive tobacco cultivation spread from the eighteenth century. To this end, the inhabitants built an impressive terraced landscape supported by high walls. In the second half of the twentieth century, tobacco was largely given up, and parts of the terraces fell into disrepair. Shortly after 2000, one observer remarked: 'If you consider the landscape of Canale di Brenta today and direct your gaze to the abandoned terraced slopes – a true monument to the labour of this valley people – you become aware of the complexity of heritage, which soon disintegrates before our eyes.' Many locals and foreigners reacted similarly. Others felt that the past should not be glorified, and that pleasure should be taken in the positive aspects of change.[9]

9.3 The Rise of Regions

In the valley bottoms of the Alpine region, the pressure of agricultural use was not the only thing that increased in the second half of the twentieth century. Many of these areas were now also integrated into processes of urbanization, which tended to spread rapidly from the old centres and transformed formerly rural areas. For the early 1990s, a study identified a total of 189 so-called 'urbanized zones' across the Alps. They differed greatly in their size and structure. Large 'metropolitan areas' only spread in the areas surrounding the Alps, namely in the vicinity of Vienna, Munich, Zurich, Geneva, Turin and Milan. But these urban spaces intruded more and more into the mountain region.[10]

Like the rural and urban landscapes, the political landscape also changed in the post-war period. If previous developments had been determined by the formation of nation states and, since Napoleonic times, by nationalism, a new regionalism now found its voice. It was also a correlate to European integration, which qualified the importance of nation states and temporarily valorized border regions in order to bring together the areas on either side of the customs barrier. In the centralist states of Italy and France, regionalism had a different aspect from that in the other states in the Alpine region, which were more or less federally constituted. The first phase, up to 1970, was characterized by regionally specific confrontations with the nation state. Afterwards, in contrast, cross-border connections between regions emerged.[11]

In 1948, the new republican constitution of Italy came into force. It contained a passage on the protection of minorities and granted three Alpine areas the status of autonomous regions: the Aosta Valley, Trentino – Alto Adige / South Tyrol and Friuli – Venezia Giulia. This special status was the result of difficult negotiations with the central

Figure 13   *Urbanization – Grenoble's sea of lights at dusk, 2010*

state in the context of aspirations which ranged from autonomy to separatism. These harked back to historical shifts in the border and to the language problem, which had become more explosive thanks to the fascist forced Italianization. The Aosta Valley with its Franco-Provençal dialect had become more of a border region through the cession of Savoy to France in 1860. Resistance to the central Italian state received a sharp boost with the liberation after the Second World War. Many now called for real autonomous rights, some even for affiliation to France, where there was in fact a desire for annexation. To keep the French troops who wanted to appear as 'liberators' in check, the Aosta Valley was occupied by American units on 5 May 1945. With its special status granted, policy clashes in the region later subsided.[12]

Not so in the mostly German-speaking South Tyrol, where the contrasts since the involuntary cession to Italy in 1919 were considerably stronger and where autonomy only applied to the region of Trentino – Alto Adige / South Tyrol as a whole, in which the Italian-speaking population formed a majority. Alongside the autonomist South Tyrolean People's Party, a 'South Tyrolean Liberation Committee' was formed there, which, from 1956, adopted terrorist means, in turn provoking massive reactions from the Italian state. 'Still no peace in South Tyrol. Terror bombing and police actions endanger the settlement', read the headline of a German weekly in September 1964: 'Bomb attacks, fire-fights between terrorists and Carabinieri, reprisals against the rural population and police searches are commonplace.' Nearly two dozen people died at this time in numerous violent acts, most of them Italian nationals. When Austria, the constitutionally recognized protector of South Tyrol, brought the problem to the UN and discussions were intensified at all levels, a compromise was eventually reached, which led in 1972 to a new favourable statute of autonomy. Subsequently, South Tyrol developed into a model economic region admired far and wide, especially in Italy.[13]

In the same year of 1972, the foundation of the Arbeitsgemeinschaft Alpenländer [Association of Alpine States] (ARGE ALP) took place in North Tyrol at the invitation of the state governor. It initially included the Austrian states of Tyrol, Vorarlberg and Salzburg, the German free state of Bavaria, the Swiss canton of the Grisons, the Italian autono-mous province of Bolzano (South Tyrol) and the region of Lombardy. Later, additional members joined. Through regular meetings of the district presidents and senior officials, an exchange on economic and cultural issues was to be institutionalized. Although there had been cross-border contacts before, this stabilization was fairly pioneering in the European context. At first, the focus was on transalpine trans-port connections, and specifically on a motorway project from Ulm to Milan, which was propagated by the three main players (Bavaria, Tyrol, Lombardy). This project was in competition with more advanced motorway schemes in the Eastern Alps. This seems to be the reason that Tyrol did not support the accession of Styria to the ARGE ALP. Afraid of falling behind in development, Styria then decided to set up their own regional association. It was founded in 1978 under the name Arbeitsgemeinschaft ALPEN-ADRIA [Alps–Adriatic Working Group]. In 1982, a Western Alpine association finally emerged, the Communauté de Travail des Alpes Occidentales [Western Alps Working Community] (COTRAO).[14]

9.4 The Alpine Convention

So, in the course of a single decade, the defensive regionalism of individual border regions gave way to a dynamic regionalism which included the whole Alpine region and its surrounding areas. In 1988, the presidents of the three working groups then met in Lugano at a conference which was conceived as the beginning of regular contact. However, this was not to be. In the interim, other actors with other motives took the initiative and launched the Alpine Convention. The idea that the Alpine region was endangered by modern development and needed overall protection was pivotal to this process. These ideas had not been articulated before in such a comprehensive way: previously, isolated sections of nature such as parks or plant species had been placed under protection. That a whole mountain range could now be worthy of protection must be seen in the context of the 'ecological turn', which altered the awareness of Western industrial countries from around 1970 (see section 9.5).

In January 1989, the German Minister for the Environment, Klaus Töpfer, announced to the press that he would invite his colleagues from all neighbouring states to an Alpine conference in Berchtesgaden that October, to discuss emerging problems and solutions. This set the agenda, and two years later the environment ministers attended a second Alpine conference in Salzburg. Meanwhile, a framework agreement for an international Übereinkommen zum Schutz der Alpen (Alpenkonvention) [Convention for the Protection of the Alps (Alpine Convention)] had been prepared, which they signed there on 7 November 1991. The preamble stated that the Alps were 'one of the largest continuous natural spaces in Europe' and a very diverse 'living, economic, cultural and recreational space' claimed by numerous peoples and countries. It was known, however, 'that ever growing human pressure increasingly endangers the Alpine region and its ecological functions, and that damages cannot be repaired at all, or only with great effort, at considerable expense, and usually only over long periods of time'. Economic interests must therefore 'be reconciled with ecological requirements'.[15]

With the framework agreement, the signatory states (Germany, France, Italy, Yugoslavia or Slovenia, Liechtenstein, Austria,

Switzerland and later Monaco) committed themselves to pursue a special environmental and development policy in the Alpine region, in
collaboration with the European Community. The territory to which
the policy would apply was delimited in detail and formed part of the
Convention. The general text was to be substantiated and rendered
usable for implementation through so-called implementation protocols
for twelve problem areas.

The impetus for the Alpine Convention came not from state bodies,
but from the International Commission for the Protection of the Alps,
CIPRA. It was founded in 1952 as the 'Commission Internationale
pour la Protection des Régions Alpines' and formed a branch of the
International Union for the Conservation of Nature (IUCN), which
had emerged shortly before as a UNESCO initiative. In the 1950s and
1960s, CIPRA engaged with issues of cross-border conservation, but
remained a small association characterized by individuals, and in the
end almost completely ceased operations. It was reinvigorated in 1974
on the occasion of an international symposium in Trent, which put
'the future of the Alps' up for discussion and spoke out for a broadened
engagement. Subsequently, the Commission adopted a new structure,
and became more fundamental and more professional. Under the influence of the heated environmental debates of the 1980s, when 'forest
dieback' and the disaster at the nuclear power station at Chernobyl
caused widespread concern, the Commission decided in February 1987
to prepare a programme to initiate a coordinated and mandatory environmental policy across the Alps.[16]

CIPRA exceeded expectations in how quickly it achieved this goal.
But it was not satisfied, because the ensuing institutionalization and
implementation processes proved protracted and the results were considerably less tangible and publicly impactful than had been hoped for
in the first flush of enthusiasm. The headlines of the CIPRA magazine
alone spoke volumes: for example, 'The Alpine Convention: Withdrawal
Would Be Possible' was the headline in 2004, and an anniversary edition in 2011 asked 'Who Will Kiss Her Awake? A Summary of 20 Years
of the Alpine Convention'. The development of the implementation
protocols was difficult, and, after the text had been agreed, ratification
by member states sometimes presented obstacles. An especially stub-
born reaction came from Switzerland, which had long been considered

the Alpine country *par excellence* and where the mountains loomed large for national identity. Here, the Alpine Convention was opposed by various overlapping forces: cantonal (because of a feared loss of influence), Eurosceptic (because of international integration) and neoliberal (because of environmental regulation). Even the Salzburg framework agreement had only been signed by Switzerland with a supplementary statement.[17]

Nevertheless, with time, things progressed. In 2003, the Alpine Convention obtained a permanent secretariat in Innsbruck with an outpost in Bolzano / South Tyrol. A Task Force Protected Areas, in French Chambéry, was later affiliated to this institution. It was the coordination entity for a European network of Alpine protected areas, which emerged in the 1990s under French initiative and was soon recognized as an instrument of the Alpine Convention. CIPRA, which now designed and successfully implemented numerous Alpine projects, proved itself to be creative. It followed a modern flexible strategy, because for some decades society and research had entered the 'age of the project', meaning that short-term engagements had generally become more important than long-term ones. But CIPRA and its media department also had sticking power, and projects like the community network Alliance in the Alps soon became permanent fixtures.

9.5 From Conservation to Environmental Protection

However, to understand properly the developments outlined, we must look further back in time and place these conservation efforts in a broader context. Under the influence of rapid modernization, a traditionalist movement began to form in the late nineteenth century, which in the German-speaking world was usually called 'Natur- und Heimatschutz', or 'nature and heritage conservation'. It took elements of the earlier Romantic and Alpinist conceptions of the mountains and added a practical, political dimension. Its most important forms of action were initially the creation of nature reserves and the battle against technical interventions in symbolically meaningful areas of nature. Thus, the Schweizerische Naturforschende Gesellschaft [Swiss Natural Science Society] initiated a commission for conservation in 1906. The moment it was established, a well-known professor of botany proposed the creation of a national park in Engadin, which he knew from his research. The peripheral location and sparse land use should give Alpine flora and fauna 'a magnificent haven', and perhaps also allow for the reintroduction of the eradicated ibex. With the help of the national government and a new conservation organization, they succeeded in developing this first Alpine national park by 1914. As Patrick Kupper has shown, the idea emerged against the background of an intense specialist debate in the Western world. The Swiss variant stood for 'total conservation' under the primacy of science. In contrast, other models were more touristically motivated. In the following hundred years, more than a dozen different national parks and many other protected areas emerged in the Alpine region, which together made up around a quarter of the total area.[18]

In the early days, the nature and heritage conservation movement stood up against railway projects on famous and popular mountain-tops. When, at the turn of the twentieth century, the more than 4,000-metre-high Jungfrau in the Bernese Oberland was to be opened to tourism through a technical masterstroke, Alpinists and the first heritage conservationists put up a fight. One politician raised his voice in Parliament 'against all attempts which seek to injure the beauty, purity and integrity of our high mountains'. In 1912, the inaugural year of the Jungfrau railway, an international heritage conservation congress in Germany spoke out against commercially oriented high mountain railways in general. The focus was now on the fight against a railway on the Zugspitze, which had become the highest mountain in the Empire upon German unification. At the high point of the conflict in 1925, there was a mass meeting in Munich, at which the main speaker cautioned the Bavarian government that mountains were 'sanctuaries not to be gawped at for money'.[19]

However, many mountain railway projects folded not because of political resistance, but thanks to funding problems. It was similar with projects for hydropower plants, which soon provoked a new form of conflict over use. They were only hindered when strong political and economic forces could be mobilized against the power of the electrical companies. A famous case occurred in the Urserental on the Gotthard, where, during the Second World War, the largest power station in the Alps was to have been built. The inhabitants of the valley would have been forced to resettle and held to the motto 'We won't negotiate, we won't sell, we won't go!' In 1946 an angry mob descended into violence, bringing the political end to the project in Switzerland.[20]

Around 1970, nature and heritage conservation was superseded and generalized almost overnight by the new environmental movement. The previously uncommon terms 'environment' and 'environmental protection' quickly rose to become important social issues. The movement was sustained via a public political style which challenged established forces. On the political spectrum, the movement tended to move from right to left. Internationally, it was embedded in a discourse on the 'limits of growth', later turning to sustainability, biodiversity and climate change. This ecological turn changed public perceptions, but in specific conflicts local conditions continued to play a significant role. An example of this is the emerging resistance to traffic on transalpine crossings. In Tyrol, the administration's slogan in the post-war period was 'traffic is life'. With the dramatic increase in transport over the Brenner, the tables turned, and several citizens' initiatives made clear from around 1985 that noise and air pollution suggested quite the opposite slogan. It came to a head with sensational street blockades and other campaigns, with publications bearing titles like 'Brenner Crime Scene' or 'Only Self-defence Can Help Us Now'. Parallel to this, the Austrian accession negotiations were under way with the European Community, where transport representatives set the tone and exerted corresponding pressure.[21]

In the long term, resistance to modern development became, in a sense, more urban. Beginning with famous mountain peaks at the end of the nineteenth century, by the late twentieth century it encompassed everyday road traffic. With the polarization of land use and the expansion of the forests, the setting for a new conflict had also emerged: for or against wilderness. A focal point for the new debates was the advance of widely eradicated predators such as wolves, lynxes and brown bears, which had been internationally protected for some time. The first wolves migrated from Liguria into the French Southern Alps in 1992 and immediately provoked a bitter *guerre du loup* (wolf war) there. Supporters of the wolf included park operators, environmentalists and large sections of the metropolitan public. Their opponents were mainly recruited from the sheep farmers who carried great weight in the region

Figure 14 *Anti-wolf demonstration in the French Maritime Alps, 2012*

(see section 4.4), and were supported by the chamber of agriculture and local politicians. Wolves killed many sheep, but were supposed to be harmless to humans, according to the ecological school of thought. It was a coincidence that, at the very same time, historians began to prove that wolves had killed several thousand people in France between the sixteenth and nineteenth century, often children and adolescents. What were you supposed to believe now?[22]

9.6 Small Mountains in a Big World

In a global context, the status of the Alps was heavily dependent on the historical status of the European powers. The reputation of the mountains participated in the early modern expansion of the continent, its imperialist phase in the nineteenth century and the loss of this dominant position during the twentieth century. Although the Alps only constituted a vanishingly small part of the mountainous area of the planet, and by no means belonged to the highest elevations of the earth, in European natural science they had long formed a yardstick for the investigation of mountains worldwide (see sections 2.1, 7.1). Exact altitude measurement began here, and, during the eighteenth and nine-teenth centuries, the name 'Alps' was transferred to many areas through research and mountaineering. Soon one spoke of the Japanese Alps, the Alps of Sichuan in China, the Australian Alps, the Southern Alps, the Canadian and other Alps. Parallel to this, the name 'Switzerland' spread across all continents as a description for touristic, attractive landscapes (see section 7.2). In the twentieth century, there were hundreds of such Switzerlands. Interestingly, some of them derived not from the origi-nal, but from the 'Saxon Switzerland' in particular, which was evidently regarded by many as an ideal landscape.[23]

As this transfer of names alone makes clear, the Alps were a model for the successful development of tourism far and wide. For example, when in the decades around 1900 railway companies, hoteliers and financiers in North America wanted to encourage tourism in the Rocky Mountains and other mountain landscapes, they often took their inspi-ration from Alpine models. They employed mountain guides from the Alps and built hotels and whole settlements in Swiss chalet style. The touristic dominance and broadcasting of the Alpine region was also demonstrated by the Winter Olympic Games, which officially began with the games of Chamonix in 1924 (see section 8.4). Initially, the Alps held a near-monopoly on hosting the games. Up to the games of Innsbruck in 1976, the Alps had hosted two-thirds of all Winter Olympics. Afterwards, the ratio fell considerably: from 1980 to 2015, the Alpine proportion was only one fifth. The altered status of Europe in the world, the tourist development of many non-European areas and growing scepticism towards such large projects may have been the main reasons for this decline. Tourist markets in the Alpine region also generally tended towards stagnation in the late twentieth century, while elsewhere they grew considerably.[24]

Similar developments can be observed on a cultural level. The two Heidi novels by Johanna Spyri from the years 1880/1 were a global success. They inspired a large audience with their harmonious Alpine idyll over the course of many editions and translations, and also from 1921 in several film versions (see section 7.3). The musical and film *The Sound of Music* can be considered as a historically updated successor, which from 1959/65 was all the rage in the Anglo-Saxon world and was regularly shown on television there in later years. The musical told a story of love and family in Salzburg against the backdrop of National Socialism. The protagonists decide against Hitler's Germany and flee to the USA, where they are met with great success as a family of musicians with songs like 'Edelweiss' and 'Climb Every Mountain'. The film was a great success too, breaking numerous box-office records and influencing the image of the Austrian Alps to the present day. While, in this case, the idea emanated from Europe and was later developed in the USA, cultural artists from other continents soon joined the fray. The most well-known are the Alpine films of India. The first of them was called *Sangam* (*Union*) and followed an Indian couple on their honeymoon to Paris, Venice and the Bernese Alps. The film set a trend, which, from the late 1980s, led to serial production. 'Bollywood' films used the Alps as a stage for romantic singing and dancing performances, and so as a landscape of love according to the standards of Indian culture.[25]

In recent times, the Alps also became a topic of discussion for development policy. In spite of implementation problems, the Alpine

Figure 15 *India discovers the Alps – dance scene in front of Bernase high mountains in* Tandoori Love, *2008*

Convention of 1991 proved a model for other mountain regions (see section 9.4). According to the prevailing opinion, it is not directly transferable. However, many of its principles, and especially the experiences of the Alpine process, are helpful for the sustainable development of non-Alpine mountain regions. In any case, the members of the Alpine Convention cooperate with central Asian and Caucasian mountain communities, and in 2003 a Carpathian Convention inspired by the Alps was signed. Concerned scientists with a focus on the Alps were also instrumental in bringing the global mountain world onto the agenda for the twenty-first century as a 'major ecosystem', as enshrined at the 1992 Rio de Janeiro Earth Summit. From then on, many actors in the Global South could appeal to this text on the 'sustainable development of mountain areas'.[26] As demonstrated in this chapter, Europeanization and environmentalism changed the Alpine order in the post-war period. Here, however, these processes were not connected with new boundaries, and instead opened the door to non-European regions.

With these findings, we have arrived at the history of our own present, in which writing history is subject to particular challenges. The developments mentioned were experienced personally by many, which heightens the awareness of the problem: weren't other topics of Alpine history as worthy of reference as those selected? Shouldn't the interpretations outlined be expanded or reformulated? I have tried hard to pick out the most relevant points and examples from a broad spectrum, but the choice is necessarily subjective. Nevertheless, it should be possible to trace the important connections between earlier and contemporary history. We will attempt this in the subsequent and concluding chapter.

·

10

CONCLUSION

10.1 From Hannibal to Today

In the year 218 BC, the Carthaginian general Hannibal Barca crossed over the Western Alps into Italy with a massive army to attack the emerging Roman Empire on its own territory. Although this spectacular Alpine crossing during the Second Punic War is sparsely evidenced, it is deeply inscribed into the historical tradition. From the Renaissance, and even more so the nineteenth century, the story was taken up by countless authors and retold in various forms. In the process, it developed into a kind of founding myth of Alpine history. In reality, however, this history began much earlier. The Alpine region was used sporadically and seasonally from the end of the middle Palaeolithic period, around 50,000 years ago. Continuous settlement began after the end of the last Ice Age around 13,000 BC. In what follows, we will review some of the significant developments described in this book. A division into four periods seems better suited to this than the general five-period division with which we began (see section 1.4).[1]

1. *Prehistory – antiquity – early Middle Ages (thirteenth millennium BC – eleventh century AD)* The first inhabitants of the Alpine region were small mobile groups of hunters and gatherers. From around 5500

BC, they began to practise crop cultivation and animal husbandry. In the Bronze Age (from *c.*2200 BC), settlements became denser, and during the Ice Age (from *c.*800 BC), contacts with advanced Mediterranean civilizations intensified. Integration into the Roman Empire progressed gradually over more than a hundred years. After the great Alpine campaigns (25–13 BC), Roman rulers incorporated the Alpine region into their provincial administration and had roads built over the mountains into the conquered areas to the north. 'Rome' remained significant after the dissolution of the Empire in the fifth century AD, in the form of Christianity, the episcopal power structure and the idea of empire. The Alpine landscape seems to have retained a mosaic appearance for a very long time: from prehistory into the early Middle Ages, there were many wooded and sparsely used areas alongside cultivated and grazed land. A real turning point only occurred with the great population growth of the twelfth and thirteenth centuries.

2. *High and late Middle Ages – early modern period (twelfth–eighteenth/ nineteenth centuries)* From this population surge onwards, the semi-open landscape was transformed into a cultural landscape. Centres of settlement and land use multiplied, grew, and forced the forest back. Agriculture and Alpine husbandry became more intensive. Some regions soon specialized in cattle-rearing for urban consumers. Indeed, a marked increase in town-dwelling began parallel to the population surge in Europe. Urban centres also grew in the Alpine region, but the level of urbanization remained far less than in the lowlands, and this difference increased significantly over the course of the trend. There were also many changes in the political and cultural spheres: in the sixteenth century, the various territorial state institutions solidified, and with the Reformation, the Alps became a confessional border zone between the Roman church and the Protestant north. The formation of nation states in the eighteenth and nineteenth centuries made the Alps into a political border zone, too. Transalpine states like Savoy–Piedmont were divided, and only Switzerland, which remained localist, extended right across the mountains.

3. *Modern history (eighteenth/nineteenth – mid twentieth century)* From the middle of the eighteenth century, the travel culture of the

European elites opened up to new experiences of nature. While the Alpine range had previously formed an obstacle on their way to the classically cultivated land of Italy, it now obtained an intrinsic value. Naturalists had laid the way for this change in perception. The term 'tourist' emerged around 1800 to describe the ever more numerous travellers, and from the 1870s mountaineering 'Alpinists' were also distinguished. The proliferation of related texts made the Alps into a literary landscape. Overall, they experienced a dramatic increase in attention. The change was supported by transport developments, first with the construction of the great pass crossings, then through the railway and mountain railway. Industry was less widespread in the Alps than in their surrounding areas, and agriculture remained dominant for a long time. Accordingly, the area now appeared to many as traditional and backward. On close inspection, however, it is clear that 'modernity' was ambiguous and not precisely localized, but rather the product of social attribution.

4. *Contemporary history (mid twentieth century – the present)* After the upheavals of the two world wars, explosive economic growth began in the middle of the twentieth century. Industry, but especially tourism and the service sector in general, experienced a long-lasting up-turn. In 1990, tourism provided some 15 per cent of all jobs across the Alps, although they were very unevenly distributed. More and more farmers gave up their farms, and the mechanization of agriculture meant that the mountain area with its harsher production conditions became more sparsely cultivated. This encouraged the reforestation of large mountainous areas. In contrast, intensity of usage increased in the comfortable valley bottoms. Much of this land was also involved in the process of urbanization, which emanated from existing centres and transformed rural areas. In other words, there was a marked polarization in land use. In the context of the East–West conflict, two new republics emerged in this period, located for the most part in the Alpine region and redolent of many Alpine ideas: Austria in 1955 and Slovenia in 1991. The European unification movement boosted a modern regionalism, which, with the advance of environmental protection, also took an ecological turn. An expression of this multifaceted change was the intergovernmental Alpine Convention of 1991. It was only partially

implemented, but gave the Alpine region political outlines for the first time.

10.2 The Alps and their Surrounding Areas

In comparison to many European and non-European mountain regions, the Alps were heavily settled mountains from the late Middle Ages. In his famous 1871 collection of Alpine mountain travels, the British scholar and Alpinist Leslie Stephen also included an essay on the Carpathians. He visited them not least in the hope of discovering a new playground for the Alpine Club. In his eyes, the Carpathians possessed a charm evoked by their distance from 'ordinary civilised life'. But nature there was too overwhelming for him; he missed the signs of a 'happy country life' which rendered a large part of the Alps so attractive. This above-average level of human presence and usage shows itself through many indicators. For instance, intensive animal husbandry with hay harvesting and indoor feeding as practised in the Alpine region – for the British, an expression of the happy country life – was comparatively unusual. In many mountain areas, itinerant animal husbandry based on year-round pasture farming dominated into the nineteenth and twentieth centuries. If feeding the herds became impracticable, it was more usual to descend into the valleys than to produce large amounts of fodder in the highlands.[2]

So Fernand Braudel seems to have been right when he described the Alps in the middle of the twentieth century as *montagne exception-nelle* – very exceptional mountains. For him, the focus was on resources, collective responsibilities, the capacity of the people and the numerous roads. The baroque church art of the Eastern Alps, which he happened to know from an essay, also served as evidence. Braudel's thesis has accompanied us throughout this book (see sections 1.8, 2.3, 3.7, 4.8, 7.7). At this point, we can qualify it from a number of angles. Firstly, it has become clear that this thesis is to be understood historically: before the changes of the High and late Middle Ages, the Alps were nothing out of the ordinary, especially in comparison to the mountains around the Mediterranean which Braudel had in mind. During the sixteenth century, in contrast – which was Braudel's particular interest – the Alps had for some time been on a trajectory to above-average population and economic growth. Secondly, however, the question arises whether the criteria mentioned are appropriate: were resources, collective responsibilities and the capacity of the population really so special, comparatively speaking, and how can this be established? Would it not be more plausible to consider the perception of the Alps – that is, the emerging 'Alpine cult' of the European elites? This would then indicate, thirdly, that the exceptionality of the Alps had much to do with the exceptionality of their surrounding areas: it was there that the demand for nature emerged, and there that the Alpine roads which struck Braudel led. They connected the early centres of northern Italy, southern Germany and southern France.

In reality, the Alps were deeply connected to the surrounding areas historically, and from a comparative perspective these regions can definitely be described as unusual. Venice, Lombardy, the area around Lyon, the Upper Rhine and other regions have long belonged to the economic avant-garde of European history. There was also a development gap in the south-east between the better-off Slovenia and its southern neighbours. In recent times, the privileged European position of the areas surrounding the Alps has strengthened further. Thus, Bavaria has become a veritable economic powerhouse since the Second World War.

How did the Alps develop in relation to these surrounding areas? During the modern period, population and urban growth in the Alps seemed at first to run in parallel to that of the lowlands. True, the density in the mountains was considerably lower, but the rates of growth in the sixteenth and seventeenth centuries did not diverge noticeably. This changed in the eighteenth and nineteenth centuries, when population and urban growth in the Alps fell significantly behind: further development of Alpine agriculture seems to have been difficult; the topography hindered increased transportation; the urban concentrations of the lowlands developed a strong momentum. From a demographic and economic perspective, this also exacerbated the peripheral position of the Alpine region, and the difference continued in the twentieth century – at least during the first half. For some time, geographers have been discovering indications of a trend reversal. As before, developments in the Alpine region remain very variable regionally, but, as a whole, the region has exhibited above-average population growth since the 1970s.

There are also indications of a change in the balance of migration. However, these facts pertain to the total area of the states in the Alpine region, and not only to the areas surrounding the Alps, which are our preferred object of study. In a direct comparison between the Alps and their surrounding areas, there is so far no trend reversal to speak of.[3] We should also think of the polarization of land use, which is increasingly shifting the periphery problem into the Alpine region itself.

10.3 What Next?

On 18 July 2013, the cyclists of the Tour de France battled up the 1,000-metre Alpe d'Huez twice. The Tour de France has passed through this location in the Isère department from 1952, at first very sporadically, and later ever more regularly. Victory on this extreme stage means a great deal. And to raise the bar even higher, the cyclists now first had to climb the Alp, then descend a dangerous road and climb up it again. More than a million fans waited along the route, transforming the area into a party zone according to newspaper reports. The event shines a light on the sporting trends of the Alpine region and on modern event culture.[4] A diverse new approach to verticality can be observed from the 1980s, with mountain biking, paragliding, base jumping, free and solo climbing, extreme skiing and snowboarding, to give some examples. Even the fact that English names for these sports are retained in non-English languages shows that these are international trends, which use the Alps because there are good conditions there. It is similar with events. They can take place anywhere, even if they include the name 'Hannibal' and stage his Alpine crossing in a very elaborate manner, as has become usual on one Ötztal glacier since 2000. This spectacle takes place under late-night illumination and involves hundreds of performers, supported by helicopters and numerous snow groomers disguised as elephants.[5] In contrast to this, the first Hannibal re-enactment of 1935 managed with a single elephant and took place in the Western Alps. With a bit of luck, they may even have chosen the right historical pass (see section 3.1).

Event culture divides opinion. However, the dramatic increase of trans- and inter-Alpine traffic in the late twentieth century is more problematic by far, provoking fierce political reactions and also leading to open resistance (see section 9.5). The first report on the state of the

Alps given by the Alpine Convention in 2007 concerned itself with the question of transport and mobility. It predicted a further increase and added that, without substantial measures, the adverse effects would be severe. Traffic problems are not Alps-specific, but in the mountains they are concentrated and more visible. Climate change, which probably relates to traffic and industrial development, is also particularly obvious in the mountains: the glaciers have retreated massively from their greatest extent in the nineteenth century (see section 4.5). Some show glaciers from the period of early tourism now cut a puny figure. Even the largest glacier in the Alps, the Aletsch glacier in the Valais, has retreated by 1 kilometre. In 1678, a neighbouring parish took a vow, with papal approval, to hold an annual procession against the advance of the glacier. In 2010, the Holy See allowed an alteration to the vow: since then, the parish has prayed against climate change and for glacier growth. Further climate change could have multifarious consequences, both inside and outside the Alps. It is said that the Alpine rivers supply 170 million people in Europe with water. Hydropower also provides important renewable energy.[6]

The ecological approach of recent decades naturally focused on problems and tended to dim the image of the Alps. Those who are concerned with the future should also look further back, and make use of a longer historical experience. As we have seen, in European history the Alps have been a border between north and south since the Middle Ages; in the nineteenth and especially the twentieth centuries, they were described increasingly as a space of transit; and from the 1970s – in the course of the new regionalism – as a living space too (see section 1.1). The border function strengthened with the formation of nation states and the emergence of militant nationalism. It led to the most tragic moment in the known history of the Alps: the 'Great War' on the mountain border between the Kingdom of Italy and the Austro-Hungarian dual monarchy in the years 1915–18. The number of dead, wounded and disabled which the war cost is beyond imagination. It was an equally pointless and avoidable massacre (see section 5.7). That, a hundred years later, we have moved so far away from this with the European unification movement is an invaluable step forwards. The Alps have perhaps never been as peaceful at a transnational and transregional level as they are today.

European unification also facilitates the articulation of particular interests in the context of new political associations, such as the Alpine working groups, the Alpine Convention, and also numerous other fora. This self-perception of the Alps as a living space led some to concepts of an 'Alpine consciousness', and formed a broader basis for the democratic consideration of goods and claims when it came to questions of future development. The Alpine region was also transformed from the twentieth century into a landscape of national parks and protected areas. Today, these already make up around one quarter of the total area (see section 9.5). Together with other tourist offerings, a large-scale recreational zone for the growing metropolises of the lowlands is emerging. As elsewhere, there are different positions on the parks movement in the Alps. How much wilderness do we need and in what form? Shouldn't we promote a traditional cultural landscape and pin our hopes on regional economies? Or would this necessitate isolation from European development, which would be neither possible nor desirable, especially in a mountain region which has always been open like the Alps?[7] In my opinion, the key issue is political decision-making authority. As long as the metropolises and the states that represent them do not have a political monopoly – as long as the wider population in the Alpine region can introduce and negotiate their own ideas – there is little to oppose the parks movement. It can be seen as modern appreciation, and indicates that in future the Alps will remain a varied, living and fascinating space in comparison to the lowlands. In spite of all the historical scars, more than eighty 4,000-metre-high mountains still stand there, smiling at us from afar.

Notes

Selected studies on the history of the Alps are identified in the bibliography and are cited here using only the name of the author and the date of publication.

Preface

1 Daniel Anker (ed.), *Matterhorn. Berg der Berge*, Zurich, 2015, 278–91.
2 Jean-Jacques Rousseau, *Julie, or the New Heloise*, trans. Philip Stewart and Jean Vaché, Hanover, 1997.
3 Philippe Frei, *Transferprozesse der Moderne: Die Nachbenennung 'Alpen' und 'Schweiz' im 18. bis 20. Jahrhundert*, Berne, 2017, 83–5; Alexander von Humboldt, *Ansichten der Natur*, Stuttgart, 1969 (based on the 1849 edition), 118, 122 (see also the English translation: Alexander von Humboldt, *Aspects of Nature, in Different Lands and Different Climates: with Scientific Elucidations*, trans. Elizabeth Juliana Leeves Sabine, London, 1849).
4 Braudel 1995 (first edition 1949/66), vol. I, 33.
5 John R. McNeill, Observations on the Nature and Culture of Environmental History, *History and Theory*, 42/4 (2003), 5–43; J. Donald Hughes, *What is Environmental History?* Cambridge, 2006.

6 Elinor Ostrom, *Governing the Commons: The Evolution of Institutions for Collective Action*, Cambridge, 1990; Netting 1981.

7 William Cronon, The Trouble with Wilderness; or, Getting Back to the Wrong Nature, in Cronon (ed.), *Uncommon Ground: Towards Reinventing Nature*, New York, 1995, 69–90; Kupper 2014.

1 The Alps in European History

1 [Own translation.] Johann Heinrich Zedler (ed.), *Grosses vollständiges Universal-Lexicon aller Wissenschaften und Künste*, vol. I, Halle and Leipzig, 1732, 1334; *Martin Luthers Werke: kritische Gesammtausgabe*, Weimar, 1883–2009, *Abteilung Schriften*, vol. XIV, 546; Denis Diderot (ed.), *Encyclopédie ou dictionnaire raisonné des sciences, des arts et des métiers*, vol. I, Paris, 1751, 295; Cuaz 2005, 11; Bourdon 2011, 25; for ancient precursors: Heinz H. Herzig, Alpes muri vice tuebantur Italiam: Das Bild der Alpen und ihrer Pässe in den römischen Quellen, in Ulrich Fellmeth, Peter Guyot and Holger Sonnabend (eds.), *Historische Geographie der Alten Welt. Grundlagen, Erträge, Perspektiven*, Hildesheim, 2007, 183–98.

2 [Own translation.] Jean-François Bergier, Le trafic à travers les Alpes et les liaisons transalpines du haut Moyen Age au XVII siècle, in Bergier 1997, 1–2 (first published 1975).

3 Stephen 1871.

4 [Own translation.] Walter Danz (ed.), *Die Zukunft der Alpen. Dokumentation ausgewählter Beiträge des Internationalen Symposiums 'Die Zukunft der Alpen' vom 31. 8 bis 6. 9. 74 in Trento-Trient*, Munich, 1975, vol. I, 149.

5 Population 1500–2000: Jon Mathieu, Überdurchschnittliches Wachstum? Zur Bevölkerungsentwicklung des Alpenraums seit 1950, *Schweizerische Zeitschrift für Geschichte*, 65/2 (2015), 151–63.

6 Coppola and Schiera 1991, 49–94; Bätzing 1993, 24, 31, 75; Reto Furter, Hintergrund des Alpendiskurses: Indikatoren und Karten, in Mathieu and Boscani Leoni 2005, 73–96, here 96 (Alpine peaks).

7 Albert Heim, Eduard Spelterini and Julius Maurer, *Die Fahrt der 'Wega' über Alpen und Jura am 3. Oktober 1898*, Basel, 1899; Thomas Kramer and Hilar Stadler, *Eduard Spelterini – Fotografien des Ballonpioniers*, Zurich, 2007.

8 Georges Tscherrig, *Geo Chavez – 100 Jahre Flug über die Alpen*, 1910–2010, Visp, 2010.

9 *Dictionnaire encyclopédique* 2006, vol. I, 426, 706–7; vol. II, 214–15 (there were short tunnels as early as Roman times).

10 [Own translation.] Brunner 1935; Elisabeth Joris, Katrin Rieder and Béatrice Ziegler (eds.), *Tiefenbohrungen. Frauen und Männer auf den grossen Tunnelbaustellen der Schweiz 1870–2005*, Baden, 2006; Kilian T. Elsasser and ViaStoria (eds.), *Der direkte Weg in den Süden. Die Geschichte der Gotthardbahn*, Zurich, 2007, 26–9, blurb.

11 Guichonnet 1980, vol. II, 288–90.

12 Ernst Eichler, Gerold Hilty, Heinrich Löffler, Hugo Steger and Ladislav Zgusta (eds.), *Name Studies: An International Handbook of Onomastics*, Berlin, 1995–6, vol. I, 463–71, and vol. II, 1521–4.

13 Joutard 1986, 21–2, 25–6, 67, 99; Roger Devos and Bernard Grosperrin, *La Savoie de la Réforme à la Révolution française*, Rennes, 1985, 537.

14 No source: Hugo Müller, *Obwaldner Namenbuch*, Sarnen, 1952, 58; and Nathalie Henseler, *Gipfelgeschichten. Wie die Schweizer Berge zu ihrem Namen kamen*, Lenzburg, 2010, 129; it has been impossible hitherto to identify the 'Jungfrauberg' among the Alps of the region, see *Jahrbuch des Schweizerischen Alpenclubs 1921*, 102–34, and Hans Michel, *Buch der Talschaft Lauterbrunnen 1240–1949*, Interlaken, 1950.

15 Eichler et al. (eds.), *Name Studies*, vol. II, 1523.

16 Heinz Dieter Pohl, Bergnamen in Österreich: http://members. chello.at/heinz.pohl/Bergnamen.htm.

17 Bozo Otorepec, Triglav – ein Symbolberg, *Geschichte der Alpen*, 2 (1997), 137–42.

18 Paul Zinsli, *Grund und Grat. Die Bergwelt im Spiegel der schweizerischen Alpenmundarten*, Berne, 1945; Andrea Schorta, *Wie der Berg zu seinem Namen kam. Kleines Rätisches Namenbuch mit zweieinhalbtausend geographischen Namen Graubündens*, Chur, 1988.

19 Jon Mathieu, The Sacralization of Mountains in Europe during the Modern Age, *Mountain Research and Development* 26/4 (2006), 343–9.

20 The evidence for the following periods is found below in chapters 3–9.

21 Braudel 1995, vol. 1, 34; the passage also occurs in a slightly differ-
    ent form in the first edition of 1949. Critics have often related it to
    the Alps, but, shortly before, Braudel describes them as 'exceptional
    mountains' and considers them to be an atypical case at the very
    least – see below section 2.3.

22 For the discussion on retardation, see, for example, Niederer 1993,
    117–18, and Pier Paolo Viazzo, Transizioni alla modernità in area
    alpina. Dicotomie, paradossi, questioni aperte, *Geschichte der Alpen*,
    12 (2007), 13–28.

23 On this in general: *Dictionnaire encyclopédique* 2006, vol. II, 195–227,
    255–7; Bosi and Cavallero 2002.

24 [Own translation.] Claudine Remacle: Transmission des modèles
    architecturaux en Vallée d'Aoste du bas Moyen Âge au XIX siècle,
    Geschichte der Alpen, 16 (2011), 49–69, quoted 49; cf. also Remacle,
    Maison et paysages ruraux en Vallée d'Aoste. La pratique de la
    recherche, *Geschichte der Alpen*, 4 (1999), 121–35.

25 Bruno Orlandoni, *Architettura in Valle d'Aosta*, 3 vols., Turin,
    1995–6, here esp. vol. I, 193–202, 337–41, 357–8.

26 Rucki 2012, esp. 55–8, 128–33; Robert Obrist, Silva Semadeni
    and Diego Giovanoli, *Bauen. Oberengadin (Construir. Val Müstair,
    Engiadina bassa; Costruire. Val Bregaglia, Valle di Poschiavo) 1830–
    1980*, Zurich, 1986.

27 [Own translation.] Pastore 2011, 11–28, quoted 17; Edwin Huwyler,
    Verkaufsschlager Schweizer Chalet, 18.–20. Jahrhundert, *Geschichte
    der Alpen*, 16 (2011), 91–110; Anne-Marie Granet-Abisset: Le
    'chalet alpin'. La patrimonialisation d'un modèle architectural dans
    les stations d'altitude françaises depuis le XIXe siècle, *Geschichte der
    Alpen*, 16 (2011), 111–31.

28 Matthias Schirren, *Bruno Taut, Alpine Architektur. Eine Utopie – A
    Utopia*, Munich, 2004.

29 Jochen Martin (ed.), *Atlas zur Kirchengeschichte. Die christlichen
    Kirchen in Geschichte und Gegenwart*, Freiburg im Breisgau, 1987,
    46, 71.

30 On this in general, Kaspar von Greyerz, *Religion and Culture in
    Early Modern Europe, 1500–1800*, Oxford, 2008.

31 Euan Cameron, *The Reformation of the Heretics: The Waldenses of the
    Alps, 1480–1580*, Oxford, 1984; Guichonnet 1980, vol. I, 273–6.

32 Andreas Wendland, *Der Nutzen der Pässe und die Gefährdung der Seelen. Spanien, Mailand und der Kampf ums Veltlin (1620–1641)*, Zurich, 1995; Verein für Bündner Kulturforschung (ed.), *Handbuch der Bündner Geschichte*, Chur, 2000, vol. II, 141–71.

33 Heinz Dopsch and Hans Spatzenegger (eds.), *Geschichte Salzburgs*, Salzburg, 1986, vol. II, part 1, 262–82; Rudolf Leeb, Martin Scheutz and Dietmar Weikl (eds.), *Geheimprotestantismus und evangelische Kirchen in der Habsburgermonarchie und im Erzstift Salzburg (17./18. Jahrhundert)*, Vienna, 2009, 63–92, 331–60.

34 Guichonnet 1980, vol. II, 137–68; Werlen 1998; *Dictionnaire encyclopédique* 2006, vol. II, 235–7.

35 Cuaz 2005, 47–78; Rolf Steininger, *Südtirol im 20. Jahrhundert. Vom Leben und Überleben einer Minderheit*, Innsbruck, 1997; Andreas Moritsch (ed.), *Die Kärntner Slovenen 1900–2000. Bilanz des 20. Jahrhunderts*, Klagenfurt, Vienna, 2000.

36 Zedler (ed.), *Grosses vollständiges Universal-Lexicon aller Wissenschaften und Künste*, vol. I, 1334 (Styria is missing from the list); *Meyers Konversationslexikon*, 4th edition, Leipzig, 1885–92, vol. I, 401–2; in general on the formation of political space: Mathieu 2009, 14–20; *Dictionnaire encyclopédique* 2006, vol. II, 179–83.

37 [Own translation.] Guichonnet 1980, vol. I, 280–2 (quoted 281), 296–308, 402–4.

38 Cuaz 2005, 79–96; Mark Thompson, *The White War: Life and Death on the Italian Front 1915–1919*, London, 2008.

39 Paul Guichonnet, *Histoire de l'annexion de la Savoie à la France*, Roanne, 1982; Hans Conrad Peyer, *Verfassungsgeschichte der alten Schweiz*, Zurich, 1978, 146–7.

40 CIPRA (ed.), *CIPRA 1952–1992. Dokumente, Initiativen, Perspektiven für eine bessere Zukunft der Alpen*, Vaduz, 1992; Ständiges Sekretariat der Alpenkonvention (ed.), *Alpenkonvention. Nachschlagewerk*, Innsbruck, 2010.

41 Braudel 1995, vol. I, 33; on the context, see section 2.3.

2 Modern Scholars on the Alps

1 [Own translation.] Jon Mathieu, Von den Alpen zu den Anden: Alexander von Humboldt und die Gebirgsforschung, in Boscani Leoni 2010, 293–308, quoted 295.

2 Rudolf Stichweh, *Zur Entstehung des modernen Systems wissenschaftlicher Disziplinen. Physik in Deutschland 1740–1890*, Frankfurt am Main, 1984, 45–6; see also Felsch 2007; for early standard works of mountain research, see Mathieu 2011, 35.

3 [Own translation.] René Favier, Raoul Blanchard et la découverte des Alpes, in Mathieu and Boscani Leoni 2005, 53–72; Raoul Blanchard, La vie humaine en montagne, *Revue de Géographie de Lyon* 27 (1952), 211–17 (quoted 216–17).

4 Jon Mathieu, Cento anni di vita di un classico: l'opera di Aloys Schulte sul traffico transalpino, *Archivio Storico Ticinese* 128 (2000), 207–16.

5 *Geschichte der Alpen in neuer Sicht* (*Schweizerische Zeitschrift für Geschichte* 29/1), Basel, 1979, esp. the contributions of Jean-François Bergier and Fritz Glauser.

6 Braudel 1995, vol. I, 21.

7 [Own translation.] Lutz Raphael, *Die Erben von Bloch und Febvre. 'Annales' – Geschichtsschreibung und 'nouvelle histoire' in Frankreich 1945–1980*, Stuttgart, 1994, 109–37 (quoted 113); see also Lutz Raphael, *Geschichtswissenschaft im Zeitalter der Extreme. Theorien, Methoden, Tendenzen von 1900 bis zur Gegenwart*, Munich, 2003, 96–116.

8 [Own translation.] Heinrich Decker, *Barock-Plastik in den Alpenländern*, Vienna, 1943, 7 (Foreword from May 1942).

9 Braudel 1995, vol. I, 32–4; he adapted German texts and ideas of the period, but was a political opponent of National Socialist Germany.

10 'Le Alpi e l'Europa 1974–1977'; Martinengo 1988.

11 Cf. the review of historical research by Pier Paolo Viazzo in *Comunità alpine. Ambiente, popolazione, struttura sociale nelle Alpi dal XVI secolo ad oggi*, Rome, 2001.

12 Jean-François Bergier, Des Alpes traversées aux Alpes vécues. Pour un projet de coopération internationale et interdisciplinaire en histoire des Alpes, *Geschichte der Alpen* 1 (1996), 11–21, and the subsequent numbers of the annual journal.

13 *Dictionnaire encyclopédique* 2006; Tappeiner et al. 2008.

14 William Cronon, The Trouble with Wilderness; or, Getting Back to the Wrong Nature, in Cronon (ed.), *Uncommon Ground. Towards Reinventing Nature*, New York, 1995, 69–90; J. Donald Hughes,

What is Environmental History? Cambridge, 2006; Winiwarter and Knoll 2007.

3 In the Beginning was Hannibal

1 Michel Tarpin, Hannibal, les sources antiques et la construction d'un mythe, in Jospin and Dalaine 2011, 41–56; research on the history of memory surrounding Hannibal is still in its infancy.

2 Signot, in *Dictionnaire encyclopédique* 2006, vol. I, 657–8; Jospin and Dalaine 2011, 121, 135.

3 Simler 1984, 69–90; in the Latin original: Simler 1574, 76–86.

4 A. Hyatt Mayor, Goya's 'Hannibal Crossing the Alps', *Burlington Magazine*, 97 (1955), 295–6; Andrew Wilton, *J. M. W. Turner. Leben und Werk*, Fribourg, 1979, 153–6, 267–8 (see also the English edition: Andrew Wilton, *The Life and Work of J. M. W. Turner*, London, 1979); Lynn R. Matteson, The Poetics and Politics of Alpine Passage: Turner's Snowstorm: Hannibal and His Army Crossing the Alps, *Art Bulletin*, 62/3 (1980), 385–98; Rainer Schoch, *Das Herrscherbild in der Malerei des 19. Jahrhunderts*, Munich, 1975, 54–6.

5 Jospin and Dalaine 2011, 10, 128; Jourdain-Annequin 2011, 72–6.

6 Laura Dalaine, Par quel col Hannibal est-il passé? Une littérature sans fin . . ., in Jospin and Dalaine 2011, 127–37; W. C. Mahaney, V. Kalm, B. Kapran and P. Somelar, The Traversette (Italia) Rockfall: Geomorphological Indicator of the Hannibalic Invasion Route, *Archaeometry*, 52/1 (2010), 156–72.

7 The exhibition publication edited by Angelika Fleckinger gives many pointers regarding this reception history: *Ötzi 2.0. Eine Mumie zwischen Wissenschaft, Kult und Mythos*, Stuttgart, 2011.

8 [Own translation.] Elisabeth Rastbichler Zissernig, *Der Mann im Eis. Die Fundgeschichte. Die Interpretation der Quellen als Grundlage für die Rekonstruktion des archäologischen Befunds*, Innsbruck, 2006 (quoted 264–5).

9 Lorelies Ortner, Von der Gletscherleiche zu unserem Urahnl Ötzi. Zur Benennungspraxis in der Presse, *Deutsche Sprache*, 2 (1993), 97–127.

10 [Own translation.} Burkhard Hickisch and Renate Spieckermann, *Ich war Ötzi. Die Botschaft aus dem Eis*, Munich, 1994, 256.

11 The Institute for Mummies and the Iceman has published the *Yearbook of Mummy Studies* since 2011.

12 UNESCO World Heritage candidate 'Prehistoric pile dwellings around the Alps', Berne, 2009; on the state of research, see Philippe Della Casa, La préhistoire des Alpes: enjeux scientifiques, méthodes et perspectives de la recherche, in *Alpes et préhistoire* (*Le Globe*, 149), Geneva, 2009, 7–28.

13 Curdy and Praz 2002, esp. 69–107; Louis Chaix, Terres hautes, terres basses: exploitation des ressources animales dans les Alpes, de la Préhistoire à l'Antiquité, *Geschichte der Alpen*, 17 (2012), 135–47; on the relation between population and exploitation systems, see Ester Boserup, *The Conditions of Agricultural Growth: The Economics of Agrarian Change under Population Pressure*, London, 1993 (first published 1965).

14 Archaeobotanical and archaeozoological evidence is found in Della Casa 1999, 231–44, and Jospin and Favrie 2008, 53–61; for discussion on Alpine husbandry and transhumance, see Pauli 1984, 240–1; Della Casa 1999, 1–10; Noël Coulet: Vom 13. bis 15. Jahrhundert: die Etablierung der provenzalischen Transhumanz, *Geschichte der Alpen*, 6 (2001), 147–58; Colette Jourdain-Annequin and Jean-Claude DuClos (eds.): *Aux origines de la transhumance: les Alpes et la vie pastorale d'hier à aujourd'hui*, Paris, 2006; Jospin and Favrie 2008; Segard 2009, 125–42; Mandl and Stadler 2010, 43–62, 219–38; Carrier and Mouthon 2010, 32–4, 260–75.

15 Segard 2009, esp. 233–44; the number of Alpine pastures according to trend data is in Alfred Ringler, *Almen und Alpen. Höhenkulturlandschaft der Alpen. Ökologie, Nutzung, Perspektiven*, Munich, 2009, 464–73.

16 Anton Kern, Kerstin Kowarik, Andreas W. Rausch and Hans Reschreiter (eds.), *Salz-Reich. 7000 Jahre Hallstatt*, Vienna, 2008, 124–35 (see also the English edition: Anton Kern et al. (eds.), *Kingdom of Salt: 7000 years of Hallstatt*, Vienna, 2009); see also Martin Trachsel, *Untersuchungen zur relativen und absoluten Chronologe der Hallstattzeit*, 2 parts, Bonn, 2004; in general, see Pauli 1984, esp. 23–8, 124–8, 250–60.

17 [Own translation.] Nils Müller-Scheeßel, *Die Hallstattkultur und ihre räumliche Differenzierung. Der West- und Osthallstattkreis aus*

forschungsgeschichtlich-methodologischer Sicht, Rahden, 2000, 19 (quoted from 1882), 71–88.

18 Peter S. Wells, *Beyond Celts, Germans and Scythians: Archaeology and Identity in Iron Age Europe*, London, 2001 – for example, 41, 83, 104, 112–13; on cultural units in post-Roman times: Winckler 2012, 12–16, 285–8.

19 Maria A. Borello, Elisabetta Mottes and Helmut Schlichtherle, Traverser les Alpes au Néolithique, in *Alpes et préhistoire* (*Le Globe*, 149), Geneva, 2009, 29–60; Amei Lang, Die Alpen – ein kommunikationsförderndes Hindernis in der jüngeren Eisenzeit: Beispiele aus Inn-, Eisack- und Etschtal, *Geschichte der Alpen*, 7 (2002), 85–95; Martin Peter Schindler, Bronzedepotfunde und Metallzirkulation im 6. und 5. Jh. v. Chr. in den Zentralalpen, in Della Casa 1999, 277–82.

20 Axel Posluschny, 'Fürstensitze', Zentralität und Hinterland. Erste Aspekte einer Synthese aus Sicht des Projektes 'Fürstensitze' & Umland, in Dirk Krausse (ed.), *'Fürstensitze' und Zentralorte der frühen Kelten*, Stuttgart, 2010, 359–74.

21 Dio Cassius, *Roman History, Books 51–55*, trans. Ernest Cary, Cambridge, 2000, vol. VI, 337–9, on the Roman conquest of the Alps; in general, and for Rhaetian examples, Denis van Berchem, Les Alpes sous la domination romaine, in Guichonnet 1980, vol. I, 98–106; Historisch-antiquarische Gesellschaft Graubünden (ed.), *Beiträge zur Raetia Romana. Voraussetzungen und Folgen der Eingliederung Rätiens ins römische Reich*, Chur, 1987, 1–44; Werner Zanier, Der römische Alpenfeldzug unter Tiberius und Drusus im Jahre 15 v. Chr. Übersicht zu den historischen und archäologischen Quellen, in Rudolf Asskamp and Tobias Esch (eds.), *Imperium – Varus und seine Zeit*, Munster, 2011, 73–96.

22 Jürg Rageth, Weitere frührömische Militaria und andere Funde aus dem Oberhalbstein GR – zusätzliche Belege für den Alpenfeldzug; *Jahrbuch der schweizerischen Gesellschaft für Ur- und Frühgeschichte*, 88 (2005), 302–12; according to personal communication with Werner E. Stöckli, these militaria belong typologically to the period before the campaign of 15 BC.

23 [Own translation.] Jourdain-Annequin 2004, 49–50; Philippe Casimir, *Le Trophée d'Auguste à la Turbie*, Marseille, 1932 (quoted 57).

24 Harald Koschik (ed.), '*Alle Wege führen nach Rom . . .*': *Internationales Römerstrassenkolloquium Bonn*, Pulheim, 2004, esp. 101–30; Armon Planta, *Verkehrswege im alten Rätien*, vol. III, Chur, 1987, 13–79.

25 Heinz E. Herzig, Die antiken Grundlagen des europäischen Strassensystems, in Thomas Szabó (ed.), *Die Welt der europäischen Strassen. Von der Antike bis in die Frühe Neuzeit*, Cologne, 2009, 5–18; Herzig, Ohne Furcht reisen, wohin man will. Römerlob und Reisewirklichkeit bei den Griechen des 1. und 2. Jahrhunderts n. Chr., in Hans-Ulrich Schiedt Laurent Tissot, Christoph Maria Merki and Rainer C. Schwinges (eds.), *Verkehrsgeschichte – Histoire des transports*, Zurich, 2010, 53–8; Sabine Bolliger, Die Römerstrassen als Vorbild für den neuzeitlichen Chausseenbau. Mythos und Realität, in Schiedt et al. (eds.), *Verkehrsgeschichte*, 59–70.

26 Nowadays, a majority think that most towns comprised only a few thousand people, see Walter Scheidel, Roman Population Size: The Logic of the Debate, in L. de Ligt and Simon Northwood (eds.), *People, Land, and Politics: Demographic Developments and the Transformation of Roman Italy, 300 BC – AD 14*, Leiden, 2008, 17–70, here 33.

27 Segard 2009, 75, 246–7; the difference between the Alps and their foothills, based on their population lists, is evaluated following the schema used in Mathieu 2009, 90; see also Leveau and Rémy 2008, 385–8; Jourdain-Annequin 2004, 91.

28 Jean-Robert Pitte, *Terres de Castanide. Hommes et paysages du châtaignier de l'Antiquité à nos jours*, Paris, 1986, 54, 64.

29 Allgemein Norbert Brox and Jean-Marie Mayeur (eds.), *Die Geschichte des Christentums. Religion, Politik, Kultur*, esp. vols. II–IV, Fribourg, 1994–2001.

30 Jourdain-Annequin 2004, 117–18, 128; Winckler 2012, 172–235.

31 [Own translation.] Winckler 2012, 265–8 (quoted 296), and for similar findings on the Western Alps, see Segard 2009, esp. 233–44; the population figures for the Alpine region in the fifth and twelfth centuries published in *Dictionnaire encyclopédique* 2006, vol. II, 105, are speculative estimates but not indicated as such.

32 Hans Conrad Peyer, Der Einfluss der Alpen auf die Strategie im Früh- und Hochmittelalter (8.–13. Jahrhundert), *Revue internationale d'histoire militaire*, 65 (1988), 57–75; Ernst Oehlmann, Die

Alpenpässe im Mittelalter, *Jahrbuch für schweizerische Geschichte*, 3 (1878), 165–289, and 4 (1879), 163–324; Manfred Hollegger, *Maximilian I., 1459–1519. Herrscher und Mensch einer Zeitenwende*, Stuttgart, 2005, 186–90, 226.

33 John R. McNeill, *The Mountains of the Mediterranean World: An Environmental History*, Cambridge, 1992, 68–86; Peregrine Horden and Nicholas Purcell, *The Corrupting Sea: A Study of Mediterranean History*, Oxford, 2000, 80–2, 549.

4 Coping with Life – High and Low

1 [Own translation.] Jon Mathieu, Zur alpinen Diskursforschung. Ein Manifest für die 'Wildnis' von 1742 und drei Fragen, in *Geschichte und Region*, 11/1 (2002), 103–25, esp. 112–13.

2 Giorgio Chittolini, Stadt in den Bergen, Stadt in der Ebene. Die Beziehungen zum Territorium zwischen spätem Mittelalter und früher Neuzeit, *Geschichte der Alpen*, 5 (2000), 101–8, here 104. The lower limit of 5,000 inhabitants has been promoted by the data collection of Paul Bairoch (*The Population of European Cities from 800 to 1850*, Geneva, 1988). The statements here are based particularly on Mathieu 2009, 83–106, and two issues of *Geschichte der Alpen* (5 (2000) and 8 (2003)). The contribution of towns to economic growth is emphasized by Franz Mathis, Handel und Städtewachstum. Das Beispiel der österreichischen Alpen, *Geschichte der Alpen*, 8 (2003), 195–205.

3 Town continuity in Aosta, Gap, Grenoble, Sisteron and Susa, the last town without a see; alongside this evidence of continuity, there are also indications of discontinuity, see Alain Ferdière (ed.), *Capitales éphémères. Des capitales des cités perdent leur statut dans l'Antiquité tardive*, Tours, 2004, esp. 27–35.

4 Mathieu 2009, 85–92.

5 [Own translation.] René Favier, *Les villes du Dauphiné aux XVIIe et XVIIIe siècles*, Grenoble, 1993 (quoted 301).

6 The transalpine traffic which older literature was fond of emphasizing was not, however, of particular importance to any of the largest Alpine towns.

7 Mathieu 2009, 97–101, 112.

8 On population in the High and late Middle Ages: Carrier

and Mouthon 2010, esp. 85–7, 258–60; for the period 1500–
1900: Jon Mathieu, Überdurchschnittliches Wachstum? Zur
Bevölkerungsentwicklung des Alpenraums seit 1950, *Schweizerische
Zeitschrift für Geschichte*, 65/2 (2015), 151–63; the following is based
heavily on Mathieu 2009.

9 Work per hectare of land: Blanchard 1938–56, vol. VII, 344–5, and
Jean Miège, Inventaire des ressources agricoles de la Région Alpine,
in *Économie Alpine. Actes officiels du Congrès de l'Économie Alpine*, vol.
I, Grenoble, 1954, 119; the information on land use comes from
numerous studies, for example Fritz Schneiter, *Agrargeschichte der
Brandwirtschaft*, Graz, 1970; Pierre Dubuis, *Une économie alpine à
la fin du moyen âge. Orsières, l'Entremont et les régions voisines 1250–
1500*, 2 vols., Sion, 1990; on the theoretical foundations, see Ester
Boserup, *The Conditions of Agricultural Growth. The Economics of
Agrarian Change under Population Pressure*, London, 1993.

10 Mathieu 2009, 40–3, 55–7.

11 The classic overview of Alpine husbandry is Frödin 1940–1; see
now also Alfred Ringler, *Almen und Alpen. Höhenkulturlandschaft der
Alpen. Ökologie, Nutzung, Perspektiven*, Munich, 2009.

12 [Own translation.] Hermann Wopfner, *Bergbauernbuch. Von Arbeit
und Leben des Tiroler Bergbauern*, vol. III, Innsbruck, 1997, 3.

13 Jon Mathieu, *Eine Agrargeschichte der inneren Alpen. Graubünden,
Tessin, Wallis 1500–1800*, Zurich, 1992, 209–11; Raimund Rodewald,
*Ihr schwebt über dem Abgrund. Die Walliser Terrassenlandschaften.
Entstehung–Entwicklung–Wahrnehmung*, Visp, 2011, here esp. 26–7,
46–7.

14 [Own translation.] Martonne 1926, 164; the Valtellina example is
in Guglielmo Scaramellini, *Una valle alpina nell'età pre-industriale.
La Valtellina fra il XVIII e il XIX secolo. Ricerca di geografia storica*,
Turin, 1978, 36–45, 165–7, 178–9; in recent times, there has been
systematic but not very historically oriented research on terracing:
Scaramellini and Varotto 2008.

15 Mathieu 2009, 57–8.

16 There are two conference volumes on irrigation in the Valais in
Annales valaisannes, 1995 and 2010/11; on the Middle Ages generally: Carrier and Mouthon 2010, 252–6.

17 Mathieu 2009, 61–4; Carrier and Mouthon 2010, 224–8.

18 [Own translation.] Martonne 1926, 160; the regionally differentiated dating of these developments is difficult and also disputed.
19 [Own translations.] *Martin Luthers Werke: kritische Gesammtausgabe*, Weimar, 1883–2009, *Abteilung Tischreden*, vol. III, 3621; Thomas Maissen, Die Bedeutung der Alpen für die Schweizergeschichte von Albrecht von Bonstetten (ca. 1442/43–1504/05) bis Johann Jakob Scheuchzer (1672–1733), in Boscani Leoni 2010, 161–78, here 168; Claudius Sieber-Lehmann and Thomas Wilhelmi (eds.), *In Helvetios – Wider die Kuhschweizer. Fremd- und Feindbilder von Schweizern in antieidgenössischen Texten aus der Zeit von 1386 bis 1532*, Berne, 1998, 52–4; Mitterauer 1990, 301, 304.
20 Olaf Mörke, Kuh, Milch, Käse und der Stier. Das Rind in der politischen Symbolik der frühneuzeitlichen Eidgenossenschaft, in Thomas Stamm-Kuhlmann, Jürgen Elvert, Birgit Aschmann and Jens Holensee (eds.), *Geschichtsbilder. Festschrift Michael Salewski*, Stuttgart, 2003, 188–200; the most polemical traditional text emanated from a Zurich man (Felix Hemmerlin) and directed itself against those from Schwyz.
21 Doris Walser-Wilhelm and Peter Walser-Wilhelm (eds.), *Bonstettiana. Karl Viktor von Bonstetten, Schriften*, vol. I/1, Berne, 1997, 22–83; Mathieu 2009, 69–70.
22 For discussion on transhumance and its chronology, see section 3.3.
23 Heinz J. Zumbühl, Hanspeter Holzhauser: Alpengletscher in der Kleinen Eiszeit, *Die Alpen*, 64/3 (1988), 129–322; Samuel U. Nussbaumer, Heinz J. Zumbühl and D. Steiner, Fluctuations of the 'Mer de Glace' (Mont Blanc Area, France) AD 1500–2050: An Interdisciplinary Approach Using New Historical Data and Neural Network Simulations, *Zeitschrift für Gletscherkunde und Glazialgeologie*, 40 (2005/6), 1–182; Christian Pfister, Climatic Extremes, Recurrent Crises and Witch Hunts: Strategies of European Societies in Coping with Exogenous ShocksIn the Late Sixteenth and Early Seventeenth Centuries, *Medieval History Journal*, 10 (2007), 33–73, here 56–60.
24 For current research, see, for example, Heinz Wanner, Jörg Luterbacher, Carlo Casty, Reinhard Böhm and Elena Koplaki, Variabilität von Temperatur und Niederschlag in den europäischen Alpen seit 1500, in Urs Wiesmann, François Jeanneret,

Doris Wastl-Walter and Markus Scheryn (eds.), *Welt der Alpen – Gebirge der Welt*. *Ressourcen, Akteure, Perspektiven*, Berne, 2003, 61–76; Michele Brunetti, Ginaluca Lentini, Maurizio Maugeri, et al., Climate Variability and Change in the Greater Alpine Region over the Last Two Centuries Based on Multi-Variable Analysis, *International Journal of Climatology*, 29 (2009), 2197–225.

25 On crises, see, for example, Dubuis, *Une économie alpine à la fin du moyen âge*, vol. I, 44–8; Daniel Krämer, Der kartierte Hunger. Räumliche Kontraste der Verletzlichkeit in der Schweiz während der Hungerkrise 1816/17, *Jahrbuch der Schweizerischen Gesellschaft für Wirtschafts- und Sozialgeschichte* 27 (2012), 113–31; on climate impact generally: Jon Mathieu, Klimawandel und Wirtschaftsgeschichte der Vormoderne. Zur Methodendiskussion, *Jahrbuch der Schweizerischen Gesellschaft für Wirtschafts- und Sozialgeschichte*, 30 (2015), 21–33.

26 [Own translation.] Christian Pfister (ed.), *Am Tag danach. Zur Bewältigung von Naturkatastrophen in der Schweiz 1500–2000*, Berne, 2002, esp. 30–2.

27 Rizzi 2003–5; Peter Loretz and Jürg Simonett, Die dreimalige Entdeckung der Walser, in Kantonale Museen (ed.), *Auswanderungsland Wallis*, Sion, 1991, 255–61; Massimiliano Marangon:, 'Cimbri': mito etnogonico, identità di minoranza, situazione confinaria di lungo periodo, *Annali di San Michele*, 6 (1993), 279–96; generally also Carrier and Mouthon 2010, 288–97.

28 Braudel 1995, vol. I, 51; important migration studies are Viazzo 1989; Raffaello Ceschi, Nel labirinto delle valli. Uomini e terre di una regione alpina: la Svizzera italiana, Bellinzona, 1999; Fontaine 2003; Lorenzetti and Merzario 2005; on this, see also Arbeitsgemeinschaft Alpenländer 1991, and two special issues of *Geschichte der Alpen* (3 (1998) and 14 (2009)) on migration.

29 Giorgio Ferigo, 'La natura de cingari'. Il sistema migratorio dalla Carnia durante l'età moderna, *Geschichte der Alpen*, 3 (1998), 227–46; Mathieu 2009, 123–6; Lorenzetti and Merzario 2005, 3–14.

30 Leo Schelbert, *Einführung in die schweizerische Auswanderungsgeschichte der Neuzeit*, Zurich, 1976, 89–91; Luca Mocarelli, Milano: una 'città alpine'? Cambiamenti e trasformazioni tra Sette e Novecento, *Geschichte der Alpen*, 8 (2003), 225–44.

31 Philippe Braunstein (ed.), *La sidérurgie alpine en Italie (XIIe–XVIIe*

siècle), Rome, 2001, esp. 515–92; Luca Mocarelli, *Le 'industrie' bresciane nel Settecento*, Milan, 1996; for the social dimensions, see also Viazzo 1989, 153–77.

32 Sandgruber 1995, 69–76.

33 Sandgruber 1995, 113–17, 179, 184–8.

34 Jean-Jacques Rousseau, *Julie, or the New Heloise*, trans. Philip Stewart and Jean Vaché, Hanover, 1997, 65–6; Jon Mathieu, Integrationsprozesse in der alpinen Wirtschaftsentwicklung: Thesen und statistische Hinweise, 1500–1900, in Piola Caselli 2003, 93–103.

35 Case studies in Pfister 2002 and Piola Caselli 2003; Carrier and Mouthon 2010, 281–5; Andrea Bonoldi, Andrea Leonardi and Katia Occhi (eds.), *Interessi e regole. Operatori e istituzioni nel commercio transalpino in età moderna (secoli XVI–XIX)*, Bologna, 2012.

36 Reto Furter, Frühneuzeitlicher Transitverkehr über die Alpen, in Hans-Ulrich Schiedt, Laurent Tissot, Christoph Maria Merki and Rainer C. Schwinges (eds.), *Verkehrsgeschichte – Histoire des transports*, Zurich, 2010, 109–19; Stefan Brönnimann, Die schiff- und flössbaren Gewässer in den Alpen von 1500 bis 1800. Versuch eines Inventars, *Der Geschichtsfreund*, 150 (1997), 119–78; Bergier 1997, vol. I, 1–72; Bergier and Coppola 2007; Bruns 2010–12.

5 Paths to the Nation State

1 Albera 2011; see also Mathieu 2009, 162–3, 189–190, and Lorenzetti and Merzario 2005, viii; important local and regional studies are: Cole and Wolf 1974; Netting 1981; Viazzo 1989; Mitterauer 1990; Fontaine 2003; Derouet et al. 2010.

2 Albera 2011, esp. 152–5.

3 Mathieu 2009, 137–46; Mitterauer 1990, esp. 137–40; the author links the widespread keeping of servants in the Eastern Alpine region with the continuous work cycle of animal husbandry, but in a transalpine comparison this explanation is not convincing; the size of individual farms was the decisive factor.

4 Albera 2011, esp. 213–63, 477–82.

5 David W. Sabean, Simon Teuscher and Jon Matheiu (eds.), *Kinship in Europe: Approaches to Long-Term Development (1300–1900)*, New York, 2007; Lanzinger 2015.

6 Albera 2011 (quoted 494); the author also identifies connections between the lowlands and the Alps for the French Southern Alps. There the agnatic form of organization was increasingly superseded by unigeniture in the early modern period, following the example of the nobility (Albera 2011, 365–467).

7 [Own translation.] Albrecht von Haller, *Die Alpen und andere Gedichte*, Stuttgart, 1965 (quoted in the footnote to line 100); Albrecht von Haller, *Premier voyage dans les Alpes et autres textes 1728–1732*, ed. Aurélie Luther and Claire Jaquier, with Laure Chappuis Sandoz and Luc Lienhard, Geneva, 2008.

8 For the controversial discussions on stratification and hierarchy, see, for example, the positions of Randall McGuire and Robert McC. Netting, Levelling Peasants? The Maintenance of Equality in a Swiss Alpine Community, *American Ethnologist*, 9 (1982), 269–90, and Fontaine 2003.

9 Mathieu 2009, 161–94, and the studies cited in the following notes.

10 Maria Papathanassiou, Sennerinnen. Zur Geschichte ländlicher Frauenarbeit in den österreichischen Alpen vom späten 18. Jahrhundert bis in die Zwischenkriegszeit, *Geschichte der Alpen*, 16 (2011), 297–317; Jon Mathieu, *Eine Agrargeschichte der inneren Alpen. Graubünden, Tessin, Wallis 1500–1800*, Zurich, 1992, 283–8; Lorenzetti and Merzario 2005, esp. 3–14; Valsangiacomo and Lorenzetti 2010.

11 Thomas Held, Rural Retirement Arrangements in Seventeenth- to Nineteenth-century Austria: A Cross-community Analysis, *Journal of Family History*, 7 (1982), 227–54; P. Schmidtbauer, The Changing Household in Austria from the Seventeenth to the Early Twentieth Century, in Richard Wall, Jean Robin and Peter Laslett (eds.), *Family Forms in Historic Europe*, Cambridge, 1983, 347–78.

12 Charles Tilly, *Coercion, Capital, and European States, AD 990–1992*, Oxford, 1992, here esp. 44, 65, 162, 176, 185.

13 David Buisseret (ed.), *Monarchs, Minsters and Maps. The Emergence of Cartography as a Tool of Government in Early Modern Europe*, Chicago, 1992, 101–2; Manfred Hollegger, *Maximilian I., 1459–1519. Herrscher und Mensch einer Zeitenwende*, Stuttgart, 2005, esp. 237–8, 242–3, 246–7.

14 A short overview of the formation of political space is given in Mathieu 2009, 15–20.

15 Jean Bodin, *The six books of a Common-weale*, trans. Richard Knolles, London, 1606, 247 (first published 1576 in French as *Les six livres de la République*); in the Latin edition, the strongest characteristics of democracy are attributed to the rural Swiss districts, see Thomas Maissen, 'Die Gemeinden und das Volck als höchste Gewalt unsers freyen democratischen Stands'. Die Erneuerung der politischen Sprache in Graubünden um 1700, *Jahrbuch der Historischen Gesellschaft Graubündens* (2011), 37–84, here 40.

16 Verein für Bündner Kulturforschung (ed.), *Handbuch der Bündner Geschichte*, Chur, 2000, vol. II (early modern period).

17 Bodin, *The six books of a Common-weale*, 250; Mathieu 2009, ch. 7 (comparing Savoy, the Grisons and Carinthia); Hans Conrad Peyer, *Verfassungsgeschichte der alten Schweiz*, Zurich, 1978; Rosenberg 1988, 39–71 (Grand Escarton); see also the presentation by Carrier and Mouthon 2010, esp. 99–134, 299–374.

18 Claudia Fräss-Ehrfeld, *Geschichte Kärntens*, vols. I and II, Klagenfurt, 1984/1994.

19 [Own translation.] Roger Devos and Bernard Grosperrin, *La Savoie de la Réforme à la Révolution française*, Rennes, 1985 (quoted 418); Geoffrey Symcox, *Victor Amadeus II: Absolutism in the Savoyard State 1675–1730*, London, 1983.

20 For the divergence model inspired by the theory of path-dependent development, see Mathieu 2009, 205–9.

21 René Favier, Vom alpinen Fürstentum zum Königreich von Frankreich. Der Verlust der Freiheiten der Dauphiné im 16. und 17. Jahrhundert, *Geschichte der Alpen*, 10 (2005), 167–85; Jean Nicolas, *La Révolution Française dans les Alpes. Dauphiné et Savoie*, Toulouse, 1989.

22 [Own translation.] Wolfgang von Groote (ed.), *Napoleon I. und die Staatenwelt seiner Zeit*, Freiburg im Breisgau, 1969, 73.

23 Brigitte Mazohl-Wallnig and Bernhard Mertelseder (eds.), *Abschied vom Freiheitskampf? Tirol und '1809' zwischen politischer Realität und Verklärung*, Innsbruck, 2009.

24 Guichonnet 1980, vol. I, esp. 266–279; Wolfgang Kaiser, Penser la frontière – notions et approches, *Geschichte der Alpen*, 3 (1998),

63–74; Daniel Nordman, *Frontières de France. De l'espace au territoire XVIe–XIXe siècle*, Paris, 1998; Wolfgang Schmale and Reinhard Stauber (eds.), *Menschen und Grenzen in der Frühen Neuzeit*, Berlin, 1998.

25 Peter Sahlins, Natural Frontiers Revisited: France's Boundaries since the Seventeenth Century, *American Historical Review*, 95 (1990), 1423–51 (quoted 1440).

26 Rosenberg 1988, 47, 50–4; Nordman 1998, 350; Guichonnet 1980, vol. I, 301.

27 Brigitte Mazohl-Wallnig, Gunda Barth-Scalmani and Hermann J. W. Kuprian (eds.), *Ein Krieg, zwei Schützengräben. Österreich-Italien und der Erste Weltkrieg in den Dolomiten 1915–1918*, Bolzano, 2005; Hermann J. W. Kuprian and Oswald Überegger (eds.), *Der Erste Weltkrieg im Alpenraum. Erfahrung, Deutung, Erinnerung*, Innsbruck, 2006; Mark Thompson, *The White War: Life and Death on the Italian Front 1915–1919*, London, 2008; Jay Winter (ed.), *The Cambridge History of the First World War*, 3 vols., Cambridge, 2014, esp. vol. I, 266–96.

28 Thompson, *The White War*, esp. 381, 383; Petra Svoljšak: La Prima Guerra Mondiale e le sue ripercussioni sul margine occidentale dell'area alpina slovena, *Geschichte der Alpen*, 2 (1997), 115–35; Bruna Bianchi (ed.), *La violenza contro la popolazione civile nella Grande Guerra*, Milan, 2006.

29 Cuaz 2005 (quoted 83); Thompson, *The White War*, 182, 375.

6 Religious Culture, Early Science

1 [Own translation.] Reinhold Steig, Jacob Grimms Plan zu einem Altdeutschen Sammler, *Zeitschrift des Vereins für Volkskunde*, 12 (1902), 129–38 (quoted 133).

2 Theodor Vernaleken, *Alpensagen. Volksüberlieferungen aus der Schweiz, aus Vorarlberg, Kärnten, Steiermark, Salzburg, Ober- und Niederösterreich*, Vienna, 1858; Maria Savi-Lopez, *Leggende delle Alpi con 60 illustrazioni di Carlo Chessa*, Turin, 1889.

3 Rudolf Schenda and Hans ten Doornkaat (eds.), *Sagenerzähler und Sagensammler der Schweiz. Studien zur Produktion volkstümlicher Geschichte und Geschichten vom 16. bis zum frühen 20. Jahrhundert*, Berne, 1988; Ursula Brunold-Bigler, Die Überlieferung von Sagen,

in Verein für Bündner Kulturforschung (ed.), *Handbuch der Bünder Geschichte*, vol. III, Chur, 2000, 147–73; Nicolas Disch, *Hausen im wilden Tal. Alpine Lebenswelt am Beispiel der Herrschaft Engelberg (1600–1800)*, Vienna, 2012, 400–52.

4 Rosenberg 1988, 30–3; Xenio Toscani, *Scuole e alfabetismo nello Stato di Milano da Carlo Borromeo alla Rivoluzione*, Brescia, 1993.

5 Bernd Roling, *Drachen und Sirenen. Die Rationalisierung und Abwicklung der Mythologie an den europäischen Universitäten*, Leiden, 2010, 551–666; Michel Meurger, *Histoire naturelle des dragons*, Rennes, 2001; Claude Reichler, Draco Helveticus. Scheuchzer et Saussure: du merveilleux à l'étude ethnologique, in Patrick Coleman, Anne Hofmann and Simone Zurbuchen (eds.), *Reconceptualizing Nature, Science, and Aesthetics*, Geneva, 1998, 43–55.

6 [Own translation.] Johann Jakob Scheuchzer, *Natur-Geschichten des Schweitzerlandes*, ed. Johann Georg Sulzer, Zurich, 1746, vol. II, 221–2, 234; Urs B. Leu (ed.), *Natura Sacra. Der Frühaufklärer Johann Jakob Scheuchzer (1672–1733)*, Zug, 2012.

7 Jacob and Wilhelm Grimm, *The German Legends of the Brothers Grimm*, trans. and ed. Donald Ward, vol. I, Philadelphia, 1981, 188.

8 Martine Ostorero, Agostino Paravicini Bagliani and Kathrin Utz Tremp (eds.), with Catherine Chene, *L'imaginaire du sabbat. Edition critique des textes les plus anciens (1430 c. – 1440 c.)*, Lausanne, 1999; there is an overview in Wolfgang Behringer, *Hexen. Glaube, Verfolgung, Vermarktung*, Munich, 2000.

9 [Own translation.] Martine Ostorero, *Le diable au sabbat. Littérature démonologique et sorcellerie 1440–1460*, Florence, 2011 (quoted 47).

10 Pierette Paravy, La sorcellerie, une spécialité montagnarde? Le cas du mond alpin occidental. A propos d'un ouvrage récent, *Heresis*, 39 (2003), 19–33; Oscar di Simplicio, Mountains and the Origins of Witchcraft, in Richard M. Golden (ed.), *Encyclopaedia of Witchcraft: The Western Tradition*, Santa Barbara, 2006, vol. III, 790–2; Jon Mathieu, Klimawandel und Wirtschaftsgeschichte der Vormoderne. Zur Methodendiskussion, *Jahrbuch der Schweizerischen Gesellschaft für Wirtschafts- und Sozialgeschichte*, 30 (2015), 21–33.

11 Hansjörg Rabanser, Hexen- und Zaubereiverfolgungen in Tirol:

Neue Forschungsergebnisse, in Heide Dienst (ed.), *Hexenforschung aus österreichischen Ländern*, Vienna, 2009, 77–105.

12 Carlo Ginzburg, *The Night Battles: Witchdraft and Agrarian Cults in the Sixteenth and Seventeenth Centuries*, Baltimore, 1983 (first published 1966); Ginzburg, *The Cheese and the Worms: The Cosmos of a Sixteenth-century Miller*, Baltimore, 1980.

13 Golden (ed.), *Encyclopedia of Witchcraft: The Western Tradition*, vol. II, 450–1; Anna Göldin was officially rehabilitated by the Glarus cantonal Parliament in 2008.

14 Allgemein Bertrand Forclaz (ed.), *L'expérience de la différence religieuse dans l'Europe moderne (XVI–XVIIIe siècles)*, Neuchâtel, 2013; for the Alps: Simona Boscani Leoni and P. Ostinelli (eds.), *La Chiesa 'dal basso'. Organizzazioni, interazioni e pratiche nel contesto parrochiale alpino alla fine del medio evo*, Bologna, 2012; *Geschichte der Alpen*, 18 (2013) (special issue: 'Religion und Konfessionen').

15 Ulrich Pfister, *Konfessionskirchen, Glaubenspraxis und Konflikt in Graubünden, 16.–18. Jahrhundert*, Wurzburg, 2012; Georg Jäger and Ulrich Pfister (eds.), *Konfessionalisierung und Konfessionskonflikt in Graubünden, 16.–18. Jahrhundert*, Zurich, 2006.

16 Jon Mathieu, In der Kirche schlafen. Eine sozialgeschichtliche Lektüre von Conradin Riolas 'Geistlicher Trompete' (Strada im Engadin, 1709), *Schweizerisches Archiv für Volkskunde*, 87 (1991), 121–43.

17 Rudolf Leeb, Martin Scheutz and Dietmar Weikl (eds.), *Geheimprotestantismus und evangelische Kirchen in der Habsburgermonarchie und im Erzstift Salzburg (17./18. Jahrhundert)*, Vienna, 2009; contributions on Carinthia from Christine Tropper and Stephan Steiner in *Geschichte der Alpen*, 18 (2013), 91–103, 127–38.

18 Peter Hersche, *Musse und Verschwendung. Europäische Gesellschaft und Kultur im Barockzeitalter*, Freiburg im Breisgau, 2006, vol. II, 1021.

19 Reichler and Ruffieux 1998; Perret 2011; Peter J. Brenner, *Der Reisebericht in der deutschen Literatur. Ein Forschungsüberblick als Vorstudie zu einer Gattungsgeschichte*, Tubingen, 1990.

20 [Own translation.] Josias Simler, *Vallesiae descriptio, Libri Duo. De Alpibus commentarius*, Zurich, 1574 (quoted 6); older writings were

less detailed and/or framed differently – see, for example, Ivano Dal Prete, *Valerio Faenzi e l'origine dei monti nel Cinquecento veneto*, in Boscani Leoni 2010, 197–214.

21 Michel de Montaigne, *Tagebuch einer Reise nach Italien über die Schweiz und Deutschland*, trans. Ulrich Bossier, Wiesbaden, 2005, 92–3 (see also the English translation, Michel de Montaigne, *A diary of the journey of Michel de Montaigne into Italy, through Switzerland and Germany, in the years 1580 and 1581*, trans. William Hazlitt, Marlborough, 1865).

22 Aleksander Panjek, Valvasor e la montagna del ducato di Carniola (1689), in Mathieu and Simona Boscani 2005, 141–56.

23 Bourdon 2011; Aliprandi and Aliprandi 2005–7.

24 Michael Kempe, *Wissenschaft, Theologie, Aufklärung. Johann Jakob Scheuchzer (1672–1733) und die Sintfluttheorie*, Epfendorf, 2003, esp. 30–54, 194–213; Nicolson 1997, 184–270.

7 The Perception of the Alps

1 [Own translation.] Serge Briffaud, Visions de la montagne et imaginaire politique. L'ascension de 1492 au Mont-Aiguille et ses traces dans la mémoire collective (1492–1834), *Le monde alpin et rhodanien*, 16 (1988), 39–60 (quoted 60); Joutard 1986; Philippe Bourdeau, Erik DeCamp, Jean-Olivier Majastre and Oswald Vizioz, *Le mont Aiguille et son double*, Grenoble, 1992, esp. 115–16.

2 [Own translation.] Briffaud, Visions de la montagne et imaginaire politique (quoted 54).

3 Numa Broc, *Les montagnes vues par les géographes et les naturalistes de langue française au XVIIIe siècle. Contribution à l'histoire de la géographie*, Paris, 1969, 71–96; Martin Korenjak, Das Wasserschloss Europas. Glarean über die Schweizer Alpen, *Schweizerische Zeitschrift für Geschichte*, 62/3 (2012), 390–404; Mathieu 2011, 27–30; Bourdon 2011, 404, 414; William Coxe, *Lettres sur l'état politique, civil et naturel de la Suisse, traduites et augmentées par Mr Ramond*, vol. II, Paris, 1782, 71–8 (see also the English original, William Coxe, *Sketches of the natural, civil, and political state of Swisserland; in a series of letters to William Melmoth, Esq; from William Coxe*, London, 1779, although this differs in some important respects from the French).

4 Mathis Leibetseder, Kavalierstour – Bildungsreise – Grand Tour.

Reisen, Bildung und Wissenserwerb vom Ausgang der Renaissance bis zum Vorabend der französischen Revolution, Europäische Geschichte Online 2013; Joutard 1986, 91–106.

5 [Own translation.] Yasmine Marcil, Découvrir, comprendre, ressentir la montagne dans la presse périodique des années 1780, in Gilles Bertrand and Alain Guyot (eds.), *Discours sur la montagne (XVIIIe–XIXe siècles): rhétorique, science, esthétique*, Berne, 2003, 145–70 (quoted 169–70).

6 [Own translation.] Gavin R. de Beer, *Travellers in Switzerland*, London, 1949 (list of travelogues); Alexander von Humboldt, *Chronologische Übersicht über wichtige Daten seines Lebens*, ed. Kurt-R. Biermann, Ilse Jahn and Fritz G. Lange, Berlin, 1983; Johann Gottfried Ebel: *Anleitung, auf die nützlichste und genussvollste Art die Schweitz zu bereisen*, Zurich, from 1793 (quoted from the edition of 1810, part 4, 116); Adi Kälin, *Rigi – mehr als ein Berg*, Baden, 2012.

7 Laurent Tissot, *Naissance d'une industrie touristique. Les Anglais et la Suisse au XIX siècle*, Lausanne, 2000 (p. 20, quantification of travel guides); Laurent Tissot, From Alpine Tourism to the 'Alpinization' of Tourism, in Eric G. Zuelow (ed.), *Touring Beyond the Nation: A Transnational Approach to European Tourism History*, Farnham, 2011, 59–78; Cédric Humair and Laurent Tissot (eds.), *Le tourisme suisse et son rayonnement international (XIXe–XX siècles)*, Lausanne, 2011; Leonardi and Heiss 2003; *Geschichte der Alpen* 9 (2004) (special issue: 'Tourismus und kultureller Wandel').

8 See below section 9.6.

9 Heinz Hofmann, War er oben oder nicht? Retraktationen zu Petrarca, *Familiares* 4,1, in Wolfgang Kofler, Martin Korenjak and Florian Schaffenrath (eds.), *Gipfel der Zeit. Berge in Texten aus fünf Jahrtausenden*, Freiburg im Breisgau, 2010, 81–102.

10 [Own translation.] Hermann Wiegand, Die Alpen in der lateinischen Dichtung des 16. Jahrhunderts. Ein Ausblick, in Kofler, *Gipfel der Zeit*, 117–39; Karlheinz Töchterle, Zur Hölle in Schwaz, gen Himmel in Hall. Jacob Balde und Tirol, in Johann Holzner, Max Siller and Oskar Putzer (eds.), *Literatur und Sprachkultur in Tirol*, Innsbruck, 1997, 303–38; Martin Korenjak, Wie Tirol zum Land im Gebirge wurde. Eine Spurensuche in der Frühen Neuzeit, *Geschichte und Region*, 21 (2012), 140–62; Bourdon 2011, esp. 503–4

(Lescarbot); Richard Weiss (ed.), *Die Entdeckung der Alpen. Eine Sammlung schweizerischer und deutscher Alpenliteratur bis zum Jahr 1800*, Frauenfeld, 1934, esp. 28–9 (Brockes).

11 Walter Leimgruber, Heidiland. Vom literarischen Branding einer Landschaft, in Mathieu and Boscani Leoni 2005, 429–40; on Alpine literature generally, see also Nicolson 1997 (first published 1959); Loquai 1996; Stremlow 1998; Reichler and Ruffieux 1998; Reichler 2002; Lughofer 2014.

12 Barbara Piatti, *Die Geographie der Literatur. Schauplätze, Handlungsräume, Raumphantasien*, Gottingen, 2008 (on the example of Central Switzerland).

13 Philippe Joutard, La montagne dans la peinture et la gravure de la Renaissance: un signe de modernité, in Danielle Buyssens and Claude Reichler (eds.), *Voyages en détails: chemins, regards et autres traces dans la montagne*, Grenoble, 1999, 23–34; Stephan Kunz et al. (eds.), *Die Schwerkraft der Berge 1774–1997*, Aarau, 1997; Tobias Pfeifer-Helke, *Die Koloristen. Schweizer Landschaftsgraphik von 1766 bis 1848*, Berlin, 2011; Reichler 2013; Patricia Ducke, Die Alpen im Salon. Zur Entstehungsgeschichte der Schweizer Panoramatapeten, in Oehring 2011, 95–113.

14 Tanja Wirz, *Gipfelstürmerinnen. Eine Geschlechtergeschichte des Alpinismus in der Schweiz 1840–1940*, Baden, 2007, 30–87.

15 Mathieu and Boscani Leoni 2005, 90–6 (quantification of first ascents), 267–313.

16 Engel 1950; Pastore 2003; Scharfe 2007; Anneliese Gidl, *Alpenverein: Die Städter entdecken die Alpen. Der Deutsche und Österreichische Alpenverein von der Gründung bis zum Ende des Ersten Weltkrieges*, Vienna, 2007; Hoibian 2008; Hansen 2013.

17 Peter H. Hansen, Albert Smith, the Alpine Club and the Invention of Mountaineering in Mid-Victorian Britain, *Journal of British Studies*, 34 (1995), 300–24 (quoted 310); [own translation] Maike Trentin-Meyer, Die Anfänge des Alpinismus als urbanistisches Phänomen, *Geschichte der Alpen*, 5 (2000), 229–40 (quoted 230); Coolidge 1908, 244 (number of members in the Alpine clubs 1907); Ben M. Anderson, The Construction of an Alpine Landscape: Building, Representing and Affecting the Eastern Alps, c. 1885–1914, *Journal of Cultural Geography*, 29/2 (2012), 155–83.

18 Stephen 1871; Leslie Stephen, A Bad Five Minutes in the Alps, in Stephen, *Essays on Freethinking and Plainspeaking*, New York, 1877, 155–97 (quoted 172).

19 [Own translation.] Nicolson 1998, esp. 17–18; Stephen 1871, 1–68; *Die Gartenlaube. Illustriertes Familienblatt*, Leipzig 1889, quoted 611.

20 *Dictionnaire encyclopédique* 2006, vol. I, 177.

21 Holger Böning, 'Arme Teufel an Klippen und Felsen' oder 'Felsenburg der Freiheit'? Der deutsche Blick auf die Schweiz im 18. und frühen 19. Jahrhundert, in Mathieu and Boscani Leoni 2005, 175–90.

22 See also, in general, Jon Mathieu, Alpenwahrnehmung: Probleme der historischen Periodisierung, in Mathieu and Boscani Leoni 2005, 53–72; Keith Thomas, *Man and the Natural World: Changing Attitudes in England 1500–1800*, London, 2011 (first published 1983); and, for the Alps, Reichler and Ruffieux 1998; Christian Rohr, Zur Wahrnehmung von Grenzen im 15. Jahrhundert. Leonardo Brunis Bericht über seine Reise von Verona nach Konstanz 1414, in Ulrike Aichhorn and Alfred Rinnerthaler (eds.), *Scientia iuris et historia*, Munich, 2004, 869–901; Aurélie Luther: 'La grande peur dans la montagne?' Regards savants et viatiques sur l'espace alpin de la Conféderation entre la Renaissance et les Lumières, dissertation at the University of Neuchâtel, 2015.

23 In its scholarly version, the figure of delightful horror was part of a debate in art criticism and philosophy in the eighteenth and nineteenth centuries about the 'sublime'; an initial text is found in the letters that the Briton Thomas Gray wrote to his mother in 1739 from Grande Chartreuse at Grenoble – see, for example, Andrew Wilton, *Turner and the Sublime*, Chicago, 1980, esp. 26–7, 72, 98–102, 116–25.

24 Irmargd Müsch, *Geheiligte Naturwissenschaft. Die Kupfer-Bibel des Johann Jakob Scheuchzer*, Gottingen, 2000; Jon Mathieu, The Sacralization of Mountains in Europe during the Modern Age, *Mountain Research and Development*, 26/4 (2006), 343–9; Werner Oechslin (ed.), *Heilige Landschaft – Heilige Berge*, Zurich, 2013.

25 Guy P. Marchal, *Schweizer Gebrauchsgeschichte. Geschichtsbilder, Mythenbildung und nationale Identität*, Basel, 2006; Andreas Bürgi,

Relief der Urschweiz. Entstehung und Bedeutung des Landschaftsmodells von Franz Ludwig Pfyffer, Zurich, 2007, 143 (mechanistic idea of freedom); Hans-Christian and Elke Harten, *Die Versöhnung mit der Natur. Gärten, Freiheitsbäume, republikanische Wälder, heilige Berge und Tugendparks in der Französischen Revolution*, Hamburg, 1989, 10, 19, 127–40.

26 [Own translations.] Hans Magenschab, *Erzherzog Johann. Habsburgs grüner Rebell*, Munich, 2002 (first published 1981); Archduke Johann of Austria, *Der Brandhofer und seine Hausfrau*, ed. Walter Koschatzky, Graz, 1978 (quoted 21–2); Thomas Hellmuth, Die 'Erfindung' des Salzkammerguts. Imaginationen alpiner Räume und ihre gesellschaftlichen Funktionen, in Mathieu and Boscani Leoni 2005, 349–63; Roman Sandgruber, Die Entstehung der österreichischen Tourismusregionen, in Leonardi and Heiss 2003, 201–26, here 206.

27 [Own translation.] Coolidge 1908 (quoted 59); Jon Mathieu, Eva Bachmann and Ursula Butz, *Majestätische Berge. Die Monarchie auf dem Weg in die Alpen 1760–1910*, Baden, 2018.

28 Boscani Leoni 2010 (esp. the contributions of Thomas Maissen, Guy P. Marchal and Christian Sieber); Mathieu and Boscani Leoni 2005 (esp. the contributions of Simona Boscani Leoni and Jonas Römer); Oliver Zimmer, In Search of Natural Identity: Alpine Landscape and the Reconstruction of the Swiss Nation, *Comparative Studies in Society and History*, 40/4 (1998), 637–65; Stefan Bachmann, *Zwischen Patriotismus und Wissenschaft. Die schweizerischen Naturschutzpioniere (1900–1938)*, Zurich, 1999, 98–116 (Matterhorn).

29 [Own translation.] Cesare Mozzarelli and Giuseppe Olmi (eds.), *Il Trentino nel Settecento fra Sacro Romano Impero e antichi stati italiani*, Bologna, 1985, 708; Roger Devos and Bernard Grosperrin, *La Savoie de la Réforme à la Révolution française*, Rennes, 1985, 66; Martin Korenjak, Wie Tirol zum Land im Gebirge wurde. Eine Spurensuche in der Frühen Neuzeit, *Geschichte und Region*, 21 (2012), 140–62 (quoted 153).

30 Cuaz 2005 (quoted 52).

31 Matjia Zorn, Fremde und einheimische Naturforscher und Geistliche – die ersten Besucher der slowenischen Berge (Ende des 18. Jahrhunderts bis Anfang des 19. Jahrhunderts), in Mathieu

and Boscani Leoni 2005, 223–35; Bozo Otorepec, Triglav – ein Symbolberg, *Geschichte der Alpen*, 2 (1997), 137–42.

32 François Walter, La montagne alpine: un dispositif esthétique et idéologique à l'échelle de l'Europe, *Revue d'histoire moderne et contemporaine* 52 (2005), 64–87; and, generally, Walter, *Les figures paysagères de la nation. Territoire et paysage en Europe (16e–20e siècle)*, Paris, 2004.

8 Which Modernity?

1 Samuel Butler, *Alps and Sanctuaries of Piedmont and the Canton Ticino*, London, 1882, 56–7.

2 Brigitte Mazohl-Wallnig et al., *Der Weg in den Süden. Reisen durch Tirol von Dürer bis Heine*, Bolzano, 1998, 68–70.

3 Brunner 1935; Guichonnet 1980, vol. I, 290–6, vol. II, 252–64, 283–90; Verein für Bündner Kulturforschung (ed.), *Handbuch der Bündner Geschichte*, Chur, 2000, vol. III, 71–3; in general: *Wege und Geschichte. Zeitschrift des Inventars historischer Verkehrswege der Schweiz*, esp. 2002 (chaussées), 2005 (1) (historic roads and agriculture), 2007 (2) (Alpine transit).

4 Christoph M. Merki, Eine aussergewöhnliche Landschaft als Kapital. Destinationsmanagement im 19. Jahrhundert am Beispiel von Zermatt, *Geschichte der Alpen*, 9 (2004), 181–201.

5 [Own translation.] Raffaello Ceschi, *Le vie di communicazione della Svizzera italiana*, Milan, 1998 (quoted 19).

6 Jon Mathieu, *Eine Agrargeschichte der inneren Alpen. Graubünden, Tessin, Wallis 1500–1800*, Zurich, 1992, 132–43; Mathieu 2009, 70–4.

7 Stefan Brönnimann, Die schiff- und flössbaren Gewässer in den Alpen von 1500 bis 1800. Versuch eines Inventars, *Der Geschichtsfreund*, 150 (1997), 119–78; Hans-Ulrich Schiedt, Laurent Tissot, Christoph Maria Merki and Rainer C. Schwinges (eds.), *Verkehrsgeschichte – Histoire des transports*, Zurich, 2010, esp. 233–43; Jürg Simonett, *Verkehrserneuerung und Verkehrsverlagerung in Graubünden. Die 'Untere Strasse' im 19. Jahrhundert*, Chur, 1986.

8 Ulrich Bräker, *The Life Story and Real Adventures of the Poor Man of Toggenburg*, Edinburgh, 1970, 147–70 (quoted 151, 159); on this,

see Ulrich Pfister, *Die Zürcher Fabriques. Protoindustrielles Wachstum vom 16. zum 18. Jahrhundert*, Zurich, 1992.

9 Sandgruber 1995, 114–17, 184–8, 294; Piola Caselli 2003, 327; Mathieu 2009, 107–8, 238; Otto Hwaletz, *Die österreichische Montanindustrie im 19. und 20. Jahrhundert*, Vienna, 2001.

10 Vital Chomel (ed.), *Histoire de Grenoble*, Grenoble, 1976; Henri Morsel and Jean-François Parent, *Les industries de la région grenobloise. Itinéraire historique et géographique*, Grenoble, 1991, 21–48.

11 Franz Mathis, *Unter den Reichsten der Welt – Verdienst oder Zufall? Österreichs Wirtschaft vom Mittelalter bis heute*, Innsbruck, 2007, 15–22, 90–8; Mathis, Neun Wege – ein Ziel. Zur Wirtschaftsgeschichte der österreichischen Länder im 19. und 20. Jahrhundert, *Geschichte und Region*, 10 (2001), 13–41; for more on this debate, see: Sydney Pollard, *Marginal Europe: The Contribution of Marginal Lands since the Middle Ages*, Oxford, 1997; Leonardi 2001; Luca Mocarelli, Tra sviluppo e insuccesso: i diversi percorsi economici di alcune vallate manifatturiere delle Alpi italiane centro-occidentali tra età moderna e contemporanea, in Grange 2002, 79–90; Jean-Claude Daumas, Pierre Lamard and Laurent Tissot (eds.), *Les territoires de l'industrie en Europe (1750–2000). Entreprises, régulations et trajectoires*, Paris, 2007, esp. 9–34, 87–102, 323–39.

12 Andrea a Marca, *Acque che portarono. Il commercio del legname dal Moesano al lago Maggiore fra 1700 e 1850*, Prosito, 2001; Christian Pfister and Daniel Brändli, Rodungen im Gebirge – Überschwemmungen im Vorland: Ein Deutungsmuster macht Karriere, in Rolf Peter Sieferle and Helga Breuninger (eds.), *Natur-Bilder. Wahrnehmungen von Natur und Umwelt in der Geschichte*, Frankfurt am Main, 1999, 297–324; Mathieu 2009, 119–121; Tamara L. Whited, *Forests and Peasant Politics in Modern France*, New Haven, 2000; Mark Bertogliati, *Dai boschi protetti alle foreste di protezione. Comunità locali e risorse forestali nella Svizzera Italiana (1700–1950)*, Bellinzona, 2014.

13 Morsel and Parent, *Les industries de la région grenobloise*, 75–176

14 Bonoldi and Leonardi 2004, esp. 36, 169, 197, 297–308; Guichonnet 1980, vol. II, 264–74.

15 Landry forthcoming 2018.

16 David Gugerli, *Redeströme. Zur Elektrifizierung der Schweiz*

1880–1914, Zurich, 1996; Jon Mathieu, Zur vergleichenden Geschichte der Berge: Europa im 20. Jahrhundert, *Bohemia*, 54/1 (2014), 8–22, here 19–20; on Vajont: Armiero 2011, 8, 173–94 (incorrectly described as 'genocide').

17 [Own translation.] Bonoldi and Leonardi 2004, 120, 176–17; Roland Flückiger-Seiler, *Hotelträume zwischen Gletschern und Palmen. Schweizer Tourismus und Hotelbau 1830–1920*, Baden, 2001; Dal Negro 2007; Cédric Humair and Laurent Tissot (eds.), *Le tourisme suisse et son rayonnement international (XIXe–XX siècles)*, Lausanne, 2011.

18 [Own translation.] Wolfgang Kos (ed.), *Die Eroberung der Landschaft. Semmering, Rax, Schneeberg*, Vienna, 1992, 639.

19 Hackl 2004; Mathieu and Boscani 2005, 419–27; Roman Sandgruber, Die Entstehung der österreichischen Tourismusregionen, in Leonardi and Heiss 2003, 201–26.

20 [Own translation.] Kos (ed.), *Die Eroberung der Landschaft*; Andrea Leonardi, Dal 'Grand Hotel' alle stazioni di sport invernali: le trasformazioni del turismo alpino italiano, in Carlos Barciela, Carles Manera, Ramon Molina and Antonio di Vittorio (eds.), *La evolución de la industria turística en España e Italia*, Palma de Mallorca, 2011, 609–69; Jon Mathieu, Zwei Staaten, ein Gebirge: schweizerische und österreichische Alpenperzeption im Vergleich (18.–20. Jahrhundert), *Österreichische Zeitschrift für Geschichtswissenschaften*, 15/2 (2004), 91–105.

21 Thomas Busset and Marco Marcacci, Comment les sports d'hiver conquèrent les Alpes, in Busset and Marcacci 2006, 5–33.

22 Gerd Falkner, Kontinuitäten deutscher Skigeschichte: die Winterkampfspiele, in Busset and Marcacci 2006, 123–44; Pierre Arnaud and Thierry Terret, *Le rêve blanc. Olympisme et Sport d'hiver en France, Chamonix 1924 – Grenoble 1968*, Bordeaux, 1993; Yves Morale, La genèse des jeux olympiques d'hiver et l'idéologie universaliste: Chamonix 1924, in Paul Dietschy, Christian Viver, Jean-François Loudcher and Jean-Nicolas Renaud (eds.), *Sport et idéologie. Actes du VIIe Congrès International du Comité Européen de l'Histoire du Sport*, Besançon, 2002, 69–82.

23 Anneliese Gidl, Die Einführung und Verbreitung des Skilaufs in Österreich unter besonderer Berücksichtigung der Rolle

des Alpenvereins und des Militärs (1880–1925), in Busset and Marcacci 2006, 87–104; Bernhard Tschofen, Tourismus als Modernisierungsagentur und Identitätsressource. Das Fallbeispiel des Skilaufs in den österreichischen Alpen, *Geschichte der Alpen*, 9 (2004), 265–82; Andrew Denning, *Skiing into Modernity: A Cultural and Environmental History*, Oakland, CA, 2015.

24 Martin R. Gutmann, Solving the 'Final Problem of the Alps': Technology and Ideology in the Changing Culture of Interwar Mountaineering, forthcoming 2018; Amstädter 1996; Tanja Wirz, *Gipfelstürmerinnen. Eine Geschlechtergeschichte des Alpinismus in der Schweiz 1840–1940*, Baden, 2007, 363–8; Daniel Anker (ed.), *Eiger, the Vertical Arena*, Seattle, 2000.

25 Elisabeth Foch, *Berge der Photographen – Photographen der Berge*, Berne, 1990; Urs Kneubühl and Markus Schürpf (eds.), *Jules Beck. Der erste Schweizer Hochgebirgsfotograf*, Zurich, 2012.

26 Jens Jäger, Globalisierte Bilder – Postkarten und Fotografie. Überlegungen zur medialen Verklammerung von 'Ost' und 'West', *Zeitenblicke*, 10/2 (2011), 22.

27 Karin Walter, Die Ansichtskarte als visuelles Massenmedium, in Kaspar Maase and Wolfgang Kaschuba (eds.), *Schund und Schönheit. Populäre Kultur um 1900*, Cologne, 2001, 46–61; Anton Holzer, *Die Bewaffnung des Auges. Die Drei Zinnen oder Eine kleine Geschichte vom Blick auf das Gebirge*, Vienna, 1996.

28 Jan-Christopher Horak and Gisela Pichler (eds.), *Berge, Licht und Traum. Dr. Arnold Fanck und der deutsche Bergfilm*, Munich, 1997; Christian Rapp, *Höhenrausch. Der deutsche Bergfilm*, Vienna, 1997; Rémy Pithon, Image et imagerie, idylle et idéologie: le Bergfilm en Suisse et dans les pays de l'arc alpin: in Mathieu and Boscani Leoni 2005, 391–409; Dominik Schnetzer, *Bergbild und Geistige Landesverteidigung. Die visuelle Inszenierung der Alpen im massenmedialen Ensemble der modernen Schweiz*, Zurich, 2009.

29 Pedro Lains and Vicente Pinilla (eds.), *Agriculture and Economic Development in Europe since 1870*, London, 2009.

30 Cépède and Abensour 1960, 85–86; Blanchard 1938–56, for example vol. V, 138–40; Heiner Ritzmann-Blickenstorfer (ed.), *Historical Statistics of Switzerland*, Zurich, 1996, 568–9, 574–5 (cantons with an Alpine proportion of 100 per cent as in Mathieu 2009, 28).

31 [Own translation.] Werner Baumann, Mehr bäuerliche Selbstversorgung. Eine agrarpolitische Strategie der Zwischenkriegszeit, in Jakob Tanner, Hannes Siegrist and Béatrice Veyrassat (eds.), *Geschichte der Konsumgesellschaft. Märkte, Kultur und Identität (15.–20. Jahrhundert)*, Zurich, 1998, 49–61 (quoted 50, 54).

32 [Own translation.] Gerhard Siegl, Die nationalsozialistische Agrarpolitik im österreichischen Alpenraum: eine 'Tiefland-Agrarpolitik' im alpinen Hochland? *Geschichte der Alpen*, 17 (2012), 197–210 (quoted 201, 203–4).

33 [Own translations.] Pastore 2003 (quoted 130); Cuaz 2005 (quoted 106); Armiero 2011; Deutscher Alpenverein (ed.), *Berg Heil! Alpenverein und Bergsteigen 1918–1945*, Cologne, 2012 (quoted 216).

34 Amstädter 1996.

35 Klaus Eisterer and Rolf Steininger (eds.), *Die Option. Südtirol zwischen Faschismus und Nationalsozialismus*, Innsbruck, 1989; Günther Pallaver and Leopold Steurer (eds.), *Deutsche! Hitler verkauft euch! Das Erbe von Option und Weltkrieg in Südtirol*, Bolzano, 2011 (pp. 20–2 on the numbers problem).

36 Albert A Feiber, 'Filiale von Berlin'. Der Obersalzberg im Dritten Reich, in Volker Dahm (ed.), *Die tödliche Utopie. Bilder, Texte, Dokumente, Daten zum Dritten Reich*, Munich, 2008, 52–111; Wolfgang W. Weiss, Spurensuche am Obersalzberg. NS-Geschichte(n) zwischen Vermarktung und Verdrängung, in Bernd Ogan and Wolfgang W. Weiss (eds.), *Faszination und Gewalt. Zur politischen Ästhetik des Nationalsozialismus*, Nuremberg, 1992, 267–82.

37 Krüger and Schneider 2012, esp. 87–108; Guy P. Marchal and Aram Mattioli (eds.), *Erfundene Schweiz. Konstruktionen nationaler Identität*, Zurich, 1992, esp. 37–49, 191–216; Jean-François Bergier, Wladyslaw Bartoszewski, Saul Friedländer, et al., *Die Schweiz, der Nationalsozialismus und der Zweite Weltkrieg*, Zurich, 2002; Guy P. Marchal, *Schweizer Gebrauchsgeschichte. Geschichtsbilder, Mythenbildung und nationale Identität*, Basel, 2006, esp. 155–71.

38 Cuaz 2005, 137–48; Valsangiacomo 2007; Santo Peli, *Storia della Resistenza in Italia*, Turin, 2006.

39 [Own translation.] See also Luigi Meneghello, *The Outlaws*, London, 1967, 89–90 (first edition in Italian in 1964).

40 Aram Mattioli, *'Viva Mussolini!' Die Aufwertung des Faschismus im Italien Berlusconis*, Paderborn, 2010, 24–30.

41 On population and towns in the Alpine region and its surrounding areas up to 1900: Mathieu 2009, 25–46, 83–113, here esp. 34–5, 108–9; for the following period: Bätzing 2015, 304–22; Bartaletti 2011, 159–94.

42 On the historical treatment of 'modernity', see for example Peter Burke, *History and Social Theory*, Cambridge, 2005, esp. 141–89; on the critical discussion about the Alpine region: Tschofen 1999; Grange 2002; Lorenzetti 2010; *Geschichte der Alpen*, 7 (2012) (special issue on 'Tradition und Modernität').

9 Europeanization and Environmentalism

1 Generally: Tony Judt, *Postwar: A History of Europe since 1945*, New York, 2005; Tom Buchanan, *Europe's Troubled Peace, 1945–2000*, Malden, 2006.

2 Krüger and Schneider 2012; Keith Lowe, *Savage Continent: Europe in the Aftermath of World War II*, London, 2012; Ernst Hanisch, *Der lange Schatten des Staates. Österreichische Gesellschaftsgeschichte im 20. Jahrhundert*, Vienna, 1994.

3 [Own translation.] Tamara Griesser-Pečar, *Das zerrissene Volk. Slowenien 1941–1946. Okkupation, Kollaboration, Bürgerkrieg, Revolution*, Vienna, 2003; Marie-Janine Calic, *Geschichte Jugoslawiens im 20. Jahrhundert*, Munich, 2010 (quoted 154).

4 Holm Sundhaussen, *Jugoslawien und seine Nachfolgestaaten 1943–2011. Eine ungewöhnliche Geschichte des Gewöhnlichen*, Vienna, 2012 (quoted 267).

5 Andrea Bonoldi (ed.), *La rinascita economica dell'Europa: il piano Marshall e l'area alpina*, Milan, 2006; Gebhardt 1990; Bätzing 2015.

6 Hugues François and Emmanuelle George Marcel-Poil, Vallée de la Tarentaise: de l'invention du Plan neige à la constitution d'un milieu innovateur dans le domaine du tourisme d'hiver, *Geschichte der Alpen* 17 (2012), 227–42; Werner Bätzing, Der Stellenwert des Tourismus in den Alpen und seine Bedeutung für eine nachhaltige Entwicklung des Alpenraumes, in Luger and Rest 2002,

175–96, here 180 ('maximum 10–12 percent' touristic job opportunities, later rising to 'around 15 percent': see Werner Bätzing,
Lebensraum im Herzen Europas. Zwei Jahrzehnte Alpenkonvention
und Perspektiven für die nächsten zwanzig Jahre, *werk, bauen +
wohnen*, 9 (2011), 9); Ute Hasenöhrl, *Zivilgesellschaft und Protest.
Eine Geschichte der Naturschutz- und Umweltbewegung in Bayern
1945–1980*, Gottingen, 2011 (variations on the critique of tourism).

7 [Own translation.] Europäische Akademie Bozen 1996; Tappeiner
et al. 2008; Streifeneder 2010 (quoted 136).

8 Christian Ginzler, U.-B. Brändli and M. Hägeli,
Waldflächenentwicklung der letzten 120 Jahre in der Schweiz,
Zeitschrift für Forstwesen, 162 (2011), 337–43; Mark Bertogliati, *Dai
boschi protetti alle foreste di protezione. Comunità locali e risorse forestali
nella Svizzera Italiana (1700–1950)*, Bellinzona, 2014.

9 [Own translation.] Daniela Perco and Mauro Varotto (eds.), *Uomini
e paesaggi del Canale die Brenta*, Caselle di Sommacampagna, 2004
(quoted 215).

10 Perlik 2001.

11 Malcolm Anderson (ed.), *Frontier Regions in Western Europe*, London,
1983, esp. 1–17, 109–22.

12 Stuart J. Woolf (ed.), *Storia d'Italia. Le regioni dall'Unità a oggi. La
Valle d'Aosta*, Turin, 1995, esp. 721–42.

13 [Own translation.] Rolf Steininger, *Südtirol im 20. Jahrhundert. Vom
Leben und Überleben einer Minderheit*, Innsbruck, 1997, 361–527; *Die
Zeit*, 18 September 1964 (quoted); in Friuli – Venezia Giulia, the
constitutional principle of 1948 only led to a special statute in 1963.

14 Willy Erlwein, *Transnationale Kooperation im Alpenraum dargestellt
am Beispiel der Arbeitsgruppe der Alpenländer (Argealp)*, Munich,
1981; ARGE ALP (ed.), *Nachbarn im Herzen Europas. 20 Jahre
Arbeitsgemeinschaft Alpenländer*, Munich, 1992; Alfred Ableitinger,
Die Arge Alpen-Adria in der Zeit ihrer Gründung 1974–1978
(nach steirischen Quellen), *Geschichte der Alpen*, 10 (2005), 147–63;
Cotrao 1992.

15 [Own translation.] Ständiges Sekretariat der Alpenkonvention (ed.),
Alpenkonvention. Nachschlagewerk, Innsbruck, 2010 (quoted 58).

16 Walter Danz (ed.), *Die Zukunft der Alpen. Dokumentation ausgewählter Beiträge des Internationalen Symposiums 'Die Zukunft der*

Alpen' vom 31. 8 bis 6. 9. 74 in Trento-Trient, Munich, 1975; CIPRA (ed.), *CIPRA 1952–1992. Dokumente, Initiativen, Perspektiven für eine bessere Zukunft der Alpen*, Vaduz, 1992.

17 [Own translations.] The titles of the CIPRA magazine mentioned are from September 2004 ('CIPRA-info', No. 73) and February 2011 ('SzeneAlpen', No. 95); further documents can be found on the websites of the Alpine Convention and CIPRA; see also Stefan Brem and Stefano Bruno, *The Swiss Debate on the Alpine Convention: More than a Two-Level Game?* Zurich, 1997; Bätzing, Lebensraum im Herzen Europas, 6–13; Jon-Marco Church, La Convention Alpine, une organisation internationale: la pyramide à l'envers et le retour de l'Etat, dissertation at the University of Paris 1, 2011 (internet version).

18 Kupper 2014 (quoted 41); Kupper, Nationalparks transalpin: Natur und Nation in den Alpen, *Bohemia*, 54/1 (2014), 74–87.

19 [Own translations.] David Gugerli, Wie die Jungfrau zu ihrer Bahn gekommen ist. Technische Naturbeherrschung an einer anthropomorphisierten Landschaft, *Kunst + Architektur* 48/1 (1997), 42–55 (quoted 49); Wolfgang König, *Bahnen und Berge. Verkehrstechnik, Tourismus und Naturschutz in den Schweizer Alpen 1870–1939*, Frankfurt am Main, 2000; Thomas Ebert, *Gedächtnisgrate. Die Zugspitze als ökologischer Erinnerungsort*, Munich, 2013 (internet version) (quoted 56).

20 [Own translation.] Erich Haag, *Grenzen der Technik. Der Widerstand gegen das Kraftwerkprojekt Urseren*, Zurich, 2004 (quoted 112).

21 [Own translations.] Hasenöhrl, Zivilgesellschaft und Protest; Richard Hussl and Hubert Sickinger, *Transit-Saga. Bürgerwiderstand am 'Auspuff Europas'*, Innsbruck, 1993.

22 Frid Benhammmou, Une géopolitique du loup dans les Alpes-Maritimes. Du conflict à la coexistence, *Geschichte der Alpen*, 15 (2010), 261–79; Jean-Marc Moriceau, La dangerosité du loup sur l'Homme: une enquête à l'échelle de la France (XVIe–XXe s.), in Moriceau and Philippe Madelyne (eds.), *Repenser le sauvage grâce au retour du loup. Les sciences humaines interpellées*, Caen, 2010, 41–74.

23 Mathieu 2011, 6–10, 29–30; Philippe Frei, *Transferprozesse der Moderne: Die Nachbenennung 'Alpen' und 'Schweiz' im 18. bis 20. Jahrhundert*, Berne, 2017; Laurent Tissot, From Alpine Tourism

to the 'Alpinization' of Tourism, in Eric G. Zuelow (ed.), *Touring Beyond the Nation: A Transnational Approach to European Tourism History*, Farnham, 2011, 75–7.

24 Mathieu 2011, 147–50.

25 Ulrike Kammerhofer-Aggermann, Alexander G. Keul and Andrea Weiss (eds.), *The Sound of Music zwischen Mythos und Marketing*, Salzburg, 2000; Alexandra Schneider (ed.), *Bollywood. Das indische Kino und die Schweiz*, Zurich, 2002.

26 Lebensministerium der Republik Österreich et al. (eds.), *International Mountain Partnerships*, Vienna, 2006.

10 Conclusion

1 Evidence for the four periods can be found in chapter 3 (prehistory – antiquity – early Middle Ages), chapters 4–7 (High and late Middle Ages – early modern period), chapters 5–8 (modern history) and chapter 9 (contemporary history).

2 Stephen 1871, 228–62 (quoted 258, 261); Mathieu 2011, esp. 106–8; Michael Blatter, The Transformation of the Alpine Economy in the Fourteenth to Eighteenth Centuries: Harvesting 'Wild Hay' in the High Mountains, *Nomadic Peoples*, 13/2 (2009), 146–59; David Rodríguez-Rodríguez and Bastian Bornhard, Mapping Direct Human Influence on the World's Mountain Areas, *Mountain Research and Development*, 32/2 (2012), 197–202.

3 Bätzing 2015, 307–23; Bartaletti 2011, 162; Jon Mathieu, Überdurchschnittliches Wachstum? Zur Bevölkerungsentwicklung des Alpenraums seit 1950, *Schweizerische Zeitschrift für Geschichte*, 65/2 (2015), 151–63.

4 *Tiroler Tageszeitung*, Innsbruck, 18 July 2013; on the new leisure culture, see Stremlow 1998, 240–66.

5 Treated from a literary perspective in Elfriede Jelinek, *In den Alpen. Drei Dramen*, Berlin, 2002, 55–6.

6 [Own translation.] *Alpenzustandsbericht. Verkehr und Mobilität in den Alpen*, Innsbruck, 2007 (quoted 137); *Tages-Anzeiger*, Zurich, 27 July 2012 ('Walliser beten für den Gletscher'); CIPRA, Wasser im Klimawandel, *Compact*, 3 (2011) (internet version).

7 Mario F. Broggi, Wie viel Wildnis für die Schweiz? Ein Diskussionsbeitrag, *Schweizerische Zeitschrift für Forstwesen*, 166

(2015), 60–6; for the controversies on conservation in the Alps between Rudolf Erlacher and Werner Bätzing, see: *Jahrbuch des Vereins zum Schutz der Bergwelt*, vol. LXXX, Munich, 2015, 175–96; Werner Bätzing, *Zwischen Wildnis und Freizeitpark. Eine Streitschrift zur Zukunft der Alpen*, 2nd edition, Zurich, 2017.

BIBLIOGRAPHY

There are standard historical works on most Alpine regions and places. The following bibliography comprises some 100 titles and limits itself to books which cover the whole Alpine region or large parts thereof; some works of scholarly significance have also been included. Journalistic Alpine books have generally not been cited. Specialist literature on the topics of the present book is identified in the notes.

Albera, Dionigi: *Au fil des générations. Terre, pouvoir et parenté dans l'Europe alpine (XIVe–XXe siècles)*, Grenoble 2011.

Aliprandi, Laura, and Giorgio Aliprandi: *Le Grandi Alpi nella cartografia, 1482–1885*, 2 vols., Ivrea 2005–7 (second volume only on the Western Alps).

Amstädter, Rainer: *Der Alpinismus – Kultur, Organisation, Politik*, Vienna 1996 (Germany and Austria).

Arbeitsgemeinschaft Alpenländer (ed.): *Gewerbliche Migration im Alpenraum*, Bolzano 1991 (Central and Eastern Alps).

Armiero, Marco: *A Rugged Nation: Mountains and the Making of Modern Italy*, Cambridge 2011.

Bartaletti, Fabrizio: *Le Alpi. Geografia e cultura di una regione nel cuore dell'Europa*, Milan 2011.

Bätzing, Werner: *Der sozio-ökonomische Strukturwandel des Alpenraumes im 20. Jahrhundert. Eine Analyse von 'Entwicklungstypen' auf Gemeinde-Ebene im Kontext der europäischen Tertiarisierung*, Berne 1993.

Bätzing, Werner: *Die Alpen. Geschichte und Zukunft einer europäischen Kulturlandschaft*, Munich 2015 (from a geographical perspective, see section 2.1).

Bergier, Jean-François: *Pour une histoire des Alpes, Moyen Age et temps modernes*, Hampshire 1997 (collection of essays; first published 1975).

Bergier, Jean-François, and Gauro Coppola (eds.): *Vie di terra e d'acqua. Infrastrutture viarie e sistemi di relazioni in area alpina (secoli XIII–XVI)*, Bologna 2007.

Blanchard, Raoul: *Les Alpes Occidentales*, 7 vols., Grenoble 1938–56 (classic).

Bonoldi, Andrea, and Andrea Leonardi (eds.): *Energia e sviluppo in area alpina, secoli XIX–XX*, Milan 2004.

Boscani Leoni, Simona (ed.): *Wissenschaft – Berge – Ideologien. Johann Jakob Scheuchzer (1672–1733) und die frühneuzeitliche Naturforschung*, Basel 2010.

Bosi, Roberto, and Gianpaolo Cavallero: *I castelli delle Alpi*, Cavallermaggiore 2002 (primarily a volume of photography).

Bourdon, Étienne: *Le voyage et la découverte des Alpes. Histoire de la construction d'un savoir (1492–1713)*, Paris 2011 (Western Alps).

Braudel, Fernand: *The Mediterranean and the Mediterranean World in the Age of Philip II*, 2 vols., Berkeley 1995 (first French editions 1949/1966, see section 2.3).

Brunner, Pierre: *Les chemins de fer aux prises avec la nature alpestre*, Grenoble 1935.

Bruns, Steffan: *Alpenpässe. Geschichte der alpinen Passübergänge*, 4 vols., Munich 2010–12.

Busset, Thomas, and Marco Marcacci (eds.): *Pour une histoire des sports d'hiver / Zur Geschichte des Wintersports*, Neuchâtel 2006 (about the Alpine region especially).

Carrier, Nicolas, and Fabrice Mouthon: *Paysans des Alpes. Les communautés montagnardes au Moyen Âge*, Rennes 2010 (the French Alps especially).

Cépède, Michel, and Emmanuel S. Abensour: *La vie rurale dans l'arc alpin. Étude internationale*, Rome 1960.

Cole, John W., and Eric R. Wolf: *The Hidden Frontier. Ecology and Ethnicity in an Alpine Valley*, New York 1974 (exemplary case study of Trentino – Alto Adige / South Tyrol).

Coolidge, William Augustus Brevoort: *The Alps in Nature and History*, New York 1908 (classic, especially on Alpinism).

Coppola, Gauro, and Pierangelo Schiera (eds.): *Lo spazio alpino: area di civiltà, regione cerniera*, Naples 1991.

COTRAO (ed.): *L'homme et les Alpes*, Grenoble 1992.

Cuaz, Marco: *Le Alpi*, Bologna 2005 (the Italian Alps).

Curdy, Philippe, and Jean-Claude Praz (eds.): *Premiers hommes dans les Alpes de 50,000 à 5000 avant Jésus-Christ*, Lausanne 2002.

Dal Negro, Francesco: *Hotel des Alpes. Historische Gastlichkeit von Savoyen bis Tirol*, Baden 2007.

Della Casa, Philippe (ed.): *Prehistoric Alpine Environment, Society, and Economy*, Bonn 1999.

Derouet, Bernard, Luigi Lorenzetti and Jon Mathieu (eds.): *Pratiques familiales et sociétés de montagne, XVIe–XXe siècles*, Basel 2010.

Dictionnaire encyclopédique des Alpes, Vol. I: *Dictionnaire*, ed. Sylvain Jouty; Vol. II: *Encyclopédie*, ed. Pascal Kober and Dominique Vulliamy, Grenoble 2006.

Engel, Claire-Éliane: *A History of Mountaineering in the Alps*, London 1950 (classic; first published in French in 1950).

Europäische Akademie Bozen [European Academy Bolzano] (ed.): *Landwirtschaft im Alpenraum – unverzichtbar, aber zukunftslos? Eine alpenweite Bilanz der aktuellen Probleme und der möglichen Lösungen*, Berlin 1996.

Felsch, Philipp: *Laborlandschaften. Physiologische Alpenreisen im 19. Jahrhundert*, Gottingen 2007.

Fontaine, Laurence: *Pouvoir, identités et migrations dans les hautes vallées des Alpes occidentales (XVIIe–XVIIIe siècle)*, Grenoble 2003.

Frödin, John: *Zentraleuropas Alpwirtschaft*, 2 vols., Oslo 1940–1.

Gebhardt, Hans: *Industrie im Alpenraum. Alpine Wirtschaftsentwicklung zwischen Aussenorientierung und endogenem Potential*, Stuttgart 1990 (especially on the post-war period).

Grange, Daniel J. (ed.): *L'espace alpin et la modernité. Bilans et perspectives au tournant du siècle*, Grenoble 2002.

Guichonnet, Paul (ed.): *Histoire et civilisations des Alpes*, 2 vols., Toulouse 1980 (a standard work).

Hackl, Wolfgang: *Eingeborene im Paradies. Die literarische Wahrnehmung des alpinen Tourismus im 19. und 20. Jahrhundert*, Tubingen 2004 (the German-speaking areas).

Hansen, Peter H.: *The Summits of Modern Man: Mountaineering after the Enlightenment*, Cambridge MA 2013 (on the Alps especially).

Hoibian, Olivier (ed.): *L'invention de l'alpinisme. La montagne et l'affirmation de la bourgeoisie cultivée (1786–1914)*, Paris 2008.

Jospin, Jean-Pascal, and Laura Dalaine (eds.): *Hannibal et les Alpes. Une traversée, un mythe*, Gollion 2011.

Jospin, Jean-Pascal, and Tassadite Favrie (eds.): *Premiers bergers des Alpes: de la préhistoire à l'antiquité*, Gollion 2008.

Jourdain-Annequin, Colette (ed.): *Atlas culturel des Alpes occidentales. De la préhistoire à la fin du Moyen Âge*, Paris 2004.

Jourdain-Annequin, Colette: *'Les Alpes voisines du ciel'. Quand les Grecs et les Romains découvraient les Alpes*, Paris 2011 (the Western Alps).

Joutard, Philippe: *L'invention du mont Blanc*, Paris 1986 (collection of sources with commentary).

Krüger, Dieter, and Felix Schneider (eds.): *Die Alpen im Kalten Krieg. Historischer Raum, Strategie und Sicherheitspolitik*, Munich 2012 (with the exception of France).

Kupper, Patrick: *Creating Wilderness: A Transnational History of the Swiss National Park*, Oxford 2014 (first published in German in 2012).

Landry, Marc D.: *Europe's Battery. The Making of the Alpine Energy Landscape, 1870–1955*, forthcoming.

Lanzinger, Margareth: *Verwaltete Verwandtschaft. Eheverbote, kirchliche und staatliche Dispenspraxis im 18. und 19. Jahrhundert*, Vienna 2015 (North and South Tyrol, Salzburg, the Grisons).

Le Alpi e l'Europa. Atti del convegno di studi Milano 4–9 ottobre 1973, 5 vols., Bari 1974–7.

Leonardi, Andrea (ed.): *Aree forti e deboli nello sviluppo della montagna alpina*, Trent 2001 (the Italian and Austrian regions).

Leonardi, Andrea, and Hans Heiss (eds.): *Tourismus und Entwicklung im Alpenraum, 18.–20. Jahrhundert*, Innsbruck 2003.

Leveau, Philippe, and Bernard Rémy (eds.): *La ville des Alpes occidentales à l'époque romaine*, Grenoble 2008.

Loquai, Franz (ed.): *Die Alpen – eine Landschaft und ihre Menschen in Texten deutschsprachiger Autoren des 18. und 19. Jahrhunderts*, Munich 1996.

Lorenzetti, Luigi: *Destini periferici. Modernizazzione, risorse e mercati in Ticino, Valtellina e Vallese, 1850–1930*, Udine 2010.

Lorenzetti, Luigi, and Raul Merzario: *Il fuoco acceso. Famiglie e migrazioni alpine nell'Italia d'età moderna*, Rome 2005.

Luger, Kurt, and Franz Rest (eds.): *Der Alpentourismus. Entwicklungspotenziale im Spannungsfeld von Kultur, Ökonomie und Ökologie*, Innsbruck 2002.

Lughofer, Johann Georg (ed.): *Das Erschreiben der Berge. Die Alpen in der deutschsprachigen Literatur*, Innsbruck 2014.

Mandl, Franz, and Harald Stadler (eds.): *Archäologie in den Alpen. Alltag und Kult*, Innsbruck 2010.

Martinengo, Edoardo (ed.): *Le Alpi per l'Europa. Una proposta politica. Economia, territorio e società. Istituzioni, politica e società*, Milan 1988.

Martonne, Emmanuel de: *Les Alpes. Géographie générale*, Paris 1926 (classic).

Mathieu, Jon: *History of the Alps 1500–1900: Environment, Development, and Society*, Morgantown 2009 (first published in German in 1998).

Mathieu, Jon: *The Third Dimension: A Comparative History of Mountains in the Modern Era*, Cambridge 2011.

Mathieu, Jon, and Simona Boscani Leoni (eds.): *Die Alpen! Zur europäischen Wahrnehmungsgeschichte seit der Renaissance*, Berne 2005.

Mitterauer, Michael: *Historisch-anthropologische Familienforschung. Fragestellungen und Zugangsweisen*, Vienna 1990 (articles on the Eastern Alps).

Netting, Robert McC.: *Balancing on an Alp: Ecological Change and Continuity in a Swiss Mountain Community*, Cambridge 1981 (an exemplary case study; see Introduction and section 2.4).

Nicolson, Marjorie Hope: *Mountain Gloom and Mountain Glory: The Development of the Aesthetics of the Infinite*, Seattle 1997 (classic, first published in 1959).

Niederer, Arnold: *Alpine Alltagskultur zwischen Beharrung und Wandel.*

Ausgewählte Arbeiten aus den Jahren 1956 bis 1991, Berne 1993 (folklorist-historical essays).

Oehring, Erika (ed.): *Alpen. Sehnsuchtsort & Bühne (Ausstellungskatalog Residenzgalerie)*, Salzburg 2011.

Pastore, Alessandro: *Alpinismo e storia d'Italia. Dall'unità alla resistenza*, Bologna 2003.

Pastore, Alessandro (ed.): *I villagi alpini. Le identità nazionali alle grandi esposizioni*, Turin 2011.

Pauli, Ludwig: *The Alps: Archaeology and Early History*, London 1984 (popularizing synthesis; first published in German in 1980).

Perlik, Manfred: *Alpenstädte – Zwischen Metropolisation und neuer Eigenständigkeit*, Berne 2001.

Perret, Jacques: *Regards sur les Alpes. 100 livres d'exception, 1515–1908*, Paris 2011 (especially on the Western Alps and Switzerland).

Pfister, Ulrich (ed.): *Regional Development and Commercial Infrastructure in the Alps: Fifteenth to Eighteenth Century*, Basel 2002.

Piola Caselli, Fausto (ed.): *Regioni alpine e sviluppo economico. Dualismi e processi d'integrazione (secc. XVIII–XX)*, Milan 2003.

Reichler, Claude: *Le découverte des Alpes et la question du paysage*, Geneva 2002.

Reichler, Claude: *Les Alpes et leur imagiers. Voyage et histoire du regard*, Lausanne 2013 (on this, see the website www.unil.ch/viaticalpes).

Reichler, Claude, and Roland Ruffieux (eds.): *Le voyage en Suisse. Anthologie des voyageurs français et européens de la Renaissance au XXe siècle*, Paris 1998.

Rizzi, Enrico: *Atlante delle Alpi Walser*, 3 vols., Anzola d'Ossola 2003–5.

Rosenberg, Harriet G.: *A Negotiated World: Three Centuries of Change in a French Alpine Community*, Toronto 1988 (an exemplary case study).

Rucki, Isabelle: *Das Hotel in den Alpen. Die Geschichte der Oberengadiner Hotelarchitektur ab 1860*, Baden 2012 (also on other regions).

Sandgruber, Roman: *Ökonomie und Politik. Österreichische Wirtschaftsgeschichte vom Mittelalter bis zur Gegenwart*, Vienna 1995.

Scaramellini, Guglielmo, and Mauro Varotto (eds.): *Paesaggi terrazzati dell'arco alpino. Atlante*, Venice 2008.

Scharfe, Martin: *Berg-Sucht. Eine Kulturgeschichte des frühen Alpinismus*, Vienna 2007.

Segard, Maxence: *Les Alpes occidentales romaines. Développement urbain et exploitation des ressources des régions de montagnes (Gaule Narbonnaise, Italie, provinces alpines)*, Paris 2009 (partly beyond the Western Alps).

Simler, Josias: *Die Alpen – De Alpibus commentarius*, ed. Deutscher Alpenverein, Pforzheim 1984; originally an appendage to a description of the Valais: *Vallesiae descriptio, Libri Duo. De Alpibus commentarius*, Zurich 1574 (the first specialist tract about the Alps).

Stephen, Leslie: *The Playground of Europe*, London 1871 (classic essays on early Alpinism).

Streifeneder, Thomas: *Die Agrarstrukturen in den Alpen und ihre Entwicklung unter Berücksichtigung ihrer Bestimmungsgründe. Eine alpenweite Untersuchung anhand von Gemeindedaten*, Munich 2010.

Stremlow, Matthias: *Die Alpen aus der Untersicht. Von der Verheissung der nahen Fremde zur Sportarena. Kontinuität und Wandel von Alpenbildern seit 1700*, Berne 1998.

Tappeiner, Ulrike, Axel Borsdorf and Erich Tasser (eds.): *Mapping the Alps: Society – Economy – Environment*, Heidelberg 2008 (a systematic survey of many areas for *c*.1990–2005).

Tschofen, Bernhard: *Berg, Kultur, Moderne. Volkskundliches aus den Alpen*, Vienna 1999.

Valsangiacomo, Nelly (ed.): *Le Alpi e la guerra. Funzioni e immagini*, Lugano 2007 (Second World War, Central and Western Alps)

Valsangiacomo, Nelly, and Luigi Lorenzetti (eds.): *Donne e lavoro. Prospettive per una storia delle montagne europee, XVIII–XX secc.*, Milan 2010.

Viazzo, Pier Paolo: *Upland Communities: Environment, Population and Social Structure in the Alps since the Sixteenth Century*, Cambridge 1989 (pioneering historical–anthropological study).

Werlen, Iwar (ed.): *Mehrsprachigkeit im Alpenraum*, Aarau 1998 (with historical reflections).

Winckler, Katharina: *Die Alpen im Frühmittelalter. Die Geschichte eines Raumes in den Jahren 500 bis 800*, Vienna 2012.

Winiwarter, Verena, and Martin Knoll: *Umweltgeschichte. Eine Einführung*, Cologne 2007 (with Alpine examples).

Journals, Book Series and Websites
Histoire des Alpes – Storia delle Alpi – Geschichte der Alpen, Zurich from 1996 (trilingual annual journal; available after a waiting period on the website of the Laboratorio di Storia delle Alpi [Alpine History Workshop] of the Università della Svizzera italiana and on the journal repository http://retro.seals.ch).
Mountain Research and Development, from 1981 (global, particularly geographical, mountain research).
Revue de Géographie Alpine, Grenoble from 1913 (now particularly cultural-geographical, with English translations).

Many publications are now available as downloads. There is also an increasing number of internet databases, such as the collection of illustrations for Alpine travel literature; see Reichler 2013.

IMAGE CREDITS

Fig. 1:   Eidgenössisches Archiv für Denkmalpflege, Sammlung Eduard Spelterini / Wikimedia Commons.

Map 1:   © Reclam.

Fig. 2:   Bruno Taut: Alpine Architektur in 5 Teilen und 30 Zeichnungen, Hagen 1919.

Map 2:   © Reclam.

Fig. 3:   La Méditerranée et le monde méditerranéen à l'époque de Philippe II, Paris 1966.

Fig. 4:   © Raymond Schmid, Bourgeoisie de Sion, Médiathèque Valais - Martigny.

Fig. 5:   AIS Archiv, Foto Nr. 2065, Institut für Romanische Sprachen und Literaturen und Jaberg-Bibliothek, Universität Bern.

Fig. 6:   Le Petit Journal. Supplément Illustré, August 1901.

Fig. 7:   William Windham et al.: An Account of the Glacières or Ice Alps in Savoy, London 1744.

Fig. 8:   Aquarell, um 1810, Kunstmuseum Bern.

Fig. 9:   Alpine Club Photo Library, London.

Fig. 10: Wikimedia Commons.

Fig. 11: Leporello, around 1935.

Fig. 12: Musei provinciali di Gorizia.

Fig. 13: Claude Mansiot.

Fig. 14: Rémi Leconte.

INDEX